Migrating to DB2

Migrating to DB2

Lockwood Lyon

QED Technical Publishing Group
Boston • Toronto • London

P.O. Box 82-181
Wellesley, MA 02181

Library of Congress Catalog Number: 91-2799
International Standard Book Number: 0-89435-381-0

Printed in the United States of America
91 92 93 10 9 8 7 6 5 4 3 2 1

Library of Congress Cataloging in Publication Data

Lyon, Lockwood
Migrating to DB2 / Lockwood Lyon.
p. cm.
Includes bibliographical references and index.
ISBN 0-89435-381-0 :
1. Data base management. 2. IBM Database 2. I. Title
QA76.9.D3L97 1991
005.75'65--dc20 91-2799
CIP

Contents

Preface ix

Introduction 1

The Emergence of DB2 as a DBMS 1
DB2 Migration—What It Means 3
The Purpose of this Book 4

Section I — DB2 Considerations 7

Chapter 1. Impact on Technology 9

Impact on Existing Systems 9
Systems Development Tools 23
Third-Party Tools 27

Chapter 2. Impact on Practices 29

Current Systems Design Methodologies 29
Systems Development Tools 33
Referential Integrity 44
Maintenance Procedures 47
Testing 51

Chapter 3. Impact on Staffing 59

The IS Staff: Evolution, or Revolution? 59

Section II — DB2 Installation and Implementation 71

Chapter 4. Common Preimplementation Problems 73

Choosing a Relational DBMS for the Wrong Reasons 73
The Evolution of the Information Systems Staff 77
Training for the DB2 Environment 79
DASD Usage in the DB2 Environment 82
Systems Design in the Relational Environment 84
Taking Advantage of Microcomputers 85
Using Third-Party Products in a DB2 Environment 86
Planning Ahead for System Enhancements 89
Transaction Processing Using Ad Hoc Queries 92
Misusing the On-Line Environment 93

Chapter 5. Common Post-Implementation Problems 97

Worrying About Performance (Too Late!) 97
Not Acquiring or Using Third-Party Tools 99
Lack of DASD Space 101
Failure to Involve the Vendor 103
Lack of Outside Technical Specialists 104
Attempting to Fool the RDBMS 105
Bottom-Up Performance Tuning 105
Converting Hierarchical Systems to DB2 107

Chapter 6. Integrating DB2 into an IMS Environment 109

DB2 and IMS Coexistence 109
SQL Techniques in IMS Programs 119
IMS-to-DB2 Migration 126

Section III — Design and Construction of DB2 Application Systems 133

Chapter 7. Converting Applications Using Other DBMSs to DB2 135

Overview of the Conversion Project 135
Conversion Considerations 144
Source DBMS Inventory 145
Workload Analysis 147
Database Design 148
DBMS Coexistence Strategies 159
Special Features and Considerations 163
List of References 172

Chapter 8. Migrating DB2 Systems to Production 175

Test to Production 175
The Migration Effort 176
Summary: Migrating from Source to Target Subsystem 184

Appendix: Partial List of Third-Party Tools 187

Audit Reporting 188
Catalog Information 190
Database Editing 196
Data Compression 200
Data Reporting 202
Migration Aids 205
Performance Monitoring 212
Plan Analysis 216
Security Management 219

Bibliography and References 223

DB2-Related Books 223
Suggested Reading—Articles 226

Glossary 239

Index 251

Preface

For the past several years I have spent a lot of time doing DB2 database design, application design, and programming. During this time over thirty books have appeared on DB2. Most of these books seem to be organized around the syntax of Structured Query Language (SQL), along with a few programming tips and tricks. Few, if any, addressed the broader issues of database management system (DBMS) coexistence, distributed processing, and database conversion. In particular, none addressed the issue of converting applications from one DBMS to another.

The Purpose of This Book

This book addresses the related questions of coexistence and conversion with an emphasis on DB2 systems. How will these systems affect our technology? How will they affect current analysis and design practices? How will the information systems staff be affected? What problems have shops encountered implementing DB2 systems, and how have they integrated DB2 into current environments?

One industry group estimates that worldwide there are more than four thousand DB2 licenses. With these numbers growing almost daily, and with more and more distributed relational systems being designed with PCs, future systems practitioners should have an organized view of the new way things will be done:

- Future applications will be written in, or interface with, one or more database management systems.

- Company growth will spur the need for distributed systems.
- Microcomputers will be used by analysts and programmers to design, code, test, and implement complicated systems.

With all these changes transpiring, what will happen to DB2 applications? Managers and database administrators must plan to maintain these applications and interface them with older, non-relational systems.

The Audience

This book will be of interest to managers, analysts, and programmers. In addition, managers overseeing development projects that must interface with IMS or DB2 systems will also gain insight into the latest design and development techniques. Professionals who want to stretch their knowledge of DB2 will also find this book helpful.

The Products

The IBM program products mentioned throughout this book exist on several release levels in the industry. Most of the topics in this book refer to features common in the latest releases. For convenience these release levels are summarized below. When a characteristic of a different release is being highlighted it will be referred to using a specific version and release.

CICS/ESA	Version 3, Release 1
DATABASE 2	Version 2, Release 2
IMS/ESA	Version 3, Release 1

As always, those wishing a more thorough review of the material contained herein are directed to the appropriate IBM manuals.

In addition to these IBM products, the Appendix mentions several third-party vendor products that are commonly used in DB2 environments. Information about these products was gathered from vendors and is only as accurate as their marketing literature.

Organization

The Introduction reviews where we stand today in applications development, particularly in regard to DB2 environments. It also presents some ideas for the future, on how DB2 is evolving, and about migration and conversion. The first section concentrates on the impact of DB2 on current technology, practices, and staffing. The second section addresses common DB2 implementation problems encountered by many IS shops. The final section addresses specific conversion and migration issues.

This book is not meant to be a substitute for appropriate software reference manuals, nor should any facts presented herein be taken at their face value. To paraphrase an acquaintance of mine, "One manual is worth a thousand professional opinions." To get the actual truth, consult the relevant manual.

Acknowledgments

My thanks to Barbara, who inspired this book, and to the staff at QED, who put up with me throughout the entire process. A special note of thanks to Dave Seibert, who provided technical editing assistance. Anyone having questions or comments about this book may direct them to the author on CompuServe™ [71600,2673], or in writing in care of the publisher.

Introduction

THE EMERGENCE OF DB2 AS A DBMS

The DBMS "of Choice"?

More and more mainframe DP shops are installing DB2. In my role as a DB2 consultant and educator I started asking DP managers and CIOs how they justified the costs of DB2. (Of necessity these costs included not only the software, but also additional required hardware, staff training, third-party tools, and outside services.) The vast majority (over 90 percent) had not performed a formal cost/benefit analysis, or even a feasibility study. In most cases the reasons cited for justifying bringing in DB2 were one or more of these:

- DB2 is IBM's database management system of the future. IMS, for example, will not be supported as part of Systems Application Architecture (SAA).

- Our competitors, or other companies in industries where we compete, are developing new systems in DB2.

- Relational databases are state of the art.

- IBM recommended that we migrate to DB2.

Regardless of the stated reason(s), DB2 has risen to prominence as the "DBMS of choice" in the IBM mainframe world.

Common Problems

As I gathered statistics about DB2 usage, I also asked about any problems that DP shops encountered that they attributed to bringing DB2 "in." The list became long and varied, and ranged from the simple to the complex; however, most shops seemed to confront the same problems. Some of them were as follows:

- Implementing systems in DB2 required substantially more DASD space than those in (say) IMS.

- There were no heuristics (tricks of the trade) for designing DB2 systems. No one knew how long it would take, how many programmers would be required, or how much testing would be necessary.

- Few tools are included with the DB2 software product that assist with program development or environment management. These had to be purchased from third-party vendors.

- Learning elementary SQL was simple. Learning to write SQL well so that DB2 performed efficiently was difficult.

These problems are described in this book, along with some of the solutions that shops tried.

A Plethora of Publications

DB2's rise has been closely paralleled by a corresponding growth in the number of publications relating to it. At last count over 200 articles and 30 books are in print covering DB2 or SQL. This compares with approximately five books each for IMS, CICS, or VSAM. Why the big difference? IMS, CICS, and VSAM have been around for over 15 years. I suspect the huge difference here is due to an uneasiness in the industry about DB2, and about relational database management systems in general.

Many of the DB2 books cover much of the same material in approximately the same way: normalization and normal forms, basic SELECT statements, table creation, and tips on writing "efficient" SQL. It is puzzling to me that this material is repeated in so many books, yet people remain willing to buy them (sometimes several of them).

This book takes a different tack. No normalization techniques, no description of normal forms, and no SQL (very little, anyway). Instead, the book concentrates on a procedure that is becoming more and more popular: the problem of moving old systems to—or implementing new ones in—DB2. I call this process *migration.*

The term *migration* seems to be popping up everywhere – in articles, in books, and at shops I visited. It is used for a variety of different things, depending upon the environment. Many third-party products use *migrate* as part of the product name or that of a feature (as in "... assists in DB2 migration ..."). To get a better understanding of this subject, let us pause for a minute and digest what the term is used for.

DB2 MIGRATION—WHAT IT MEANS

An Extended Definition

According to Webster's New World Dictionary, the word *migration* means "to move from one place to another." In data processing, however, migration has come to acquire a set of additional meanings incorporating the following:

- *Test to Production.* When a newly developed system has passed the system test stage it is ready to be placed into production. This involves what may be a complicated procedure of moving programs, object modules, files, database definitions, database data, and other environmental definitions from one environment to another, possibly replacing an already existing system or systems. The actual movement of data and object definitions is called a migration.

  In the DB2 world this process is sometimes complicated by the addition of another environment between Test and Production. Called variously Quality Assurance, Education, or Production/Test, this intermediate environment acts as a pristine production environment into which a production system is placed as part of acceptance testing. Implementing a new system, then, consists of *two* migrations: Test to Intermediate, then Intermediate to Production.

- *Database management system conversion.* Strangely, many DP shops are converting some application systems from one DBMS to another (usually DB2). Why is this? The usual reason: "because." A common scenario is conversion from IMS/DB to DB2. In general, shops find that the new system doesn't perform as well as it should, despite using a state-of-the-art DBMS. Some of the reasons for this phenomenon are described this book.

  A major portion of the conversion effort revolves around moving data and data definitions from one database environment to another, rather than redesigning databases and systems. This process, then, becomes a migration.

- *Hybrid systems.* As the enterprise grows and expands it takes up more and more geographic space. The great majority of *Fortune* 1000 companies have divisions or branches in multiple states and countries. Managing such an enterprise requires strategic planning of information systems resources. In particular, it may involve integrating multiple dissimilar hardware platforms and database environments. As DP systems are enhanced to encompass distributed processing and distributed databases, the time comes when it is necessary to migrate from a single-DBMS, single-mainframe environment. DB2 is destined to play a role in this process.

THE PURPOSE OF THIS BOOK

Provide Insight into Common Problems

Many large companies are implementing DB2 for the first time. Predictably, they will repeat mistakes made by other companies that have already gone through this process. This book discusses many of the problems encountered in either bringing DB2 into a DP shop or implementing the first several DB2 application systems. In each case, problems are accompanied by a review of solutions, ones that succeeded and ones that misfired.

Provide Migration Guidance

This book reviews several migration scenarios, based on the definitions presented earlier. DP departments migrating to DB2 can use these as case studies, either to guide their efforts or to provide lists of migration concerns.

Book Outline

This book is divided into three sections.

Section I—DB2 Considerations. Section I attempts to answer three sets of questions:

- How much will the DP environment be affected by bringing in DB2 as a new DBMS?

- What changes will the appearance of DB2 require us to make? Will we design systems differently?

- What will happen to our staff? Will they require training? How much? How will we manage them?

Chapter 1 covers DB2's impact on our technology. This revolves around hardware and software issues and includes the impact on existing systems, the use of Computer-Assisted Software Engineering (CASE) tools, using microcomputers in the development environment, requirements for procuring third-party tools, and future hardware issues.

Chapter 2 focuses on DB2's impact on our information system practices. DB2 changes the way we design systems, not simply because it is relational, but because set-at-a-time thinking is different from traditional transaction processing. In addition, it illustrates the new Systems Development Life Cycle (SDLC) phases, referential integrity considerations, and changes to the ways we will do maintenance, testing, performance tuning, and backup and recovery.

Chapter 3 highlights the way DB2 will affect the DP staff, including traditional job descriptions, salary structures, and performance appraisal. Further, management issues such as coping with the new breed of data processing professional are discussed.

Section II—DB2 Installation and Implementation. This section focuses on technical issues.

Chapter 4 examines common problems of DP shops that are bringing in DB2 as the new DBMS or are implementing their first application using DB2. Chapter 5 examines similar problems of DP shops that already have DB2 systems installed.

Chapters 6, 7, and 8 cover the many considerations for integrating DB2 into existing I/O subsystem environments. The most common environments are covered, including IMS, CICS, and TSO/PDF.

Section III—Design and Construction of DB2 Application Systems. This section reviews DB2 migration issues as they apply to systems design and implementation.

Chapter 9 highlights hybrid systems that involve interconnecting DB2 with other DBMSs.

Chapter 10 covers converting from another DBMS to DB2. Several common conversion scenarios are discussed, including conversion from IMS,

IDMS, Adabas, and CA-DATACOM/DB. This is supplemented by a consolidated glossary of terms from all of the DBMSs mentioned.

Chapter 11 discusses migration of DB2 systems from test to production. As a part of this discussion, a list of common third-party tools that aid migration is given.

Recommendations on Book Navigation

Readers interested in the changes that DB2 will bring with it are directed to Section I. Chapter 1 covers hardware changes, Chapter 2 focuses on methodologies, and Chapter 3 spotlights people.

Readers interested in common DB2-related problems should read Chapters 4 and 5. Those concerned about integrating DB2 into one of the major I/O subsystems (TSO, IMS/DC, CICS) should reference Chapters 6, 7, and 8.

Readers concerned about implementing DB2 in a multidatabase environment should find Chapter 9 helpful. Those converting from another major DBMS to DB2 should check out the recommendations in Chapter 10.

Finally, Chapter 11 covers moving from Test to Production.

Section I

DB2 Considerations

Chapter 1
Impact on Technology

IMPACT ON EXISTING SYSTEMS

The appearance of DB2 (and its subsequent acceptance by the IBM mainframe community) has caused repercussions in several areas of data processing that up to now were considered unrelated. Much of this impact has been on existing systems. Analysts and designers must now consider whether or not present systems should be upgraded to DB2. This effort may involve several interrelated efforts such as the following:

- Creation of a DB2 DBMS structure to hold the current business data. This structure will probably not be able to mirror all current relationships and functionality managed by the current DBMS. This will require special application logic or nonstandard DBMS structuring.

- Conversion of current business data in file or DBMS form to DB2. This may include coexistence of DB2 and other data for a period of time, necessitating duplicate storage and processing of data.

- Conversion of present applications to access the DB2 data. This may consist of a simple one-for-one replacement of DBMS access code, or may be as complicated as re-engineering all existing applications, including data modeling. Some effort must be spent analyzing current systems programs and their documentation (if any, and if up-to-date). Analysts will encounter the greatest difficulty upgrading transaction processing systems where turnaround time or user response time is critical.

The question naturally arises: Should we upgrade to DB2 at all? This is a difficult question to answer, as DB2 rarely exists in a vacuum. Several conditions must be addressed simultaneously:

- DB2 is a database management system. As such, it is a new possible alternative to VSAM files, IMS-DB, IDMS, Adabas, DATACOM/DB, and other DBMSs. Which is the correct choice? What criteria should be used to determine that choice?

- How does DB2 perform in comparison to other choices? Granted, relational database management systems are considered to be best suited to ad hoc processing; still, what proportion of processing must be ad hoc (as opposed to transaction processing) before DB2 becomes feasible?

- The interface to DB2 is the Structured Query Language (SQL). Supposedly, programmers no longer need to know physical access path information in order to navigate the database. In reality, program specifications must list the tables that the program must JOIN in order to produce the required results, in effect navigating through the tables. Will SQL be efficient? Since there are (potentially) many ways of formulating some SQL statements, how does one decide which should be used?

- Installing DB2 usually means installing an additional DBMS, which affects hardware usage. With some applications using the old DBMS and some the new, how will system and database administrators effect tuning? Will new or additional hardware be required to support CPU-intensive or I/O-intensive processing?

- Installing DB2 usually means installing an additional DBMS, with its attendant backup and recovery processing. DP operations must now handle DB2 system recovery, log file archiving, and a host of additional procedures to support the new DBMS.

These concerns are explored in more detail in the following sections.

Another DBMS Alternative

DB2 is a database management system only; it includes no provisions for data communications. DP shops that install DB2 usually do so in an environment that includes one or more of TSO/PDF, CICS, and IMS-DC. DB2 interacts with each of these subsystems, although the physical interface is slightly different in each case. DB2 is usually presented as database alternative, although many times it is touted as the DBMS of choice.

Several alternative database management systems or file storage strategies exist. Among these are the following:

- *VSAM files.* This is a very common strategy for data storage, usually with CICS as the I/O subsystem. In many CICS shops this was the preferred method over IMS data bases (DL/I).

- *DATACOM/DB* (Computer Associates). This DBMS is structured using databases, areas, and tables, similar to the DB2 concepts of databases, tablespaces, and tables. Coexistence with and conversion to DB2 are much easier than with (say) IMS databases.

- *IDMS and IDMS/R* (now called CA-IDMS and CA-IDMS/R, after Cullinet's acquisition by Computer Associates). A database management system based on the Conference on Data System Languages (CODASYL), or "network" data base model.

- *Adabas* (Software AG). Adabas (pronounced "ay-da-base") is sometimes considered more of a file management system than a database management system. Databases in Adabas contain up to a maximum of 255 *files*, each of which can be accessed using inverted lists (indexes).

Each of these is considered to be a major database management system in its own right. DB2 therefore competes with them as an alternative data storage and retrieval mechanism. (For a list of the considerations involved in converting applications written in these DBMSs to DB2, see Chapter 10.)

Application designers are now faced with an interesting task: deciding which DBMS to implement for new systems or to use in converting old ones. What criteria should be used? Much of the controversy centered around this question involves the word *better*. What does it mean? Faster? More efficient? More cost-effective? Or something else?

Cost Justification

For years I have been asking system design teams, DP managers, Chief Information Officers (CIOs), and other company officials how they justified implementing systems using DB2 rather than retaining the existing DBMS. In rare cases (fewer than 10 percent) the DP shop had done a formal cost/benefit analysis to justify the new DBMS. But in the vast majority of cases DB2 was chosen for more nebulous reasons. (Some of these reasons were mentioned in the Introduction.) Design teams faced with choosing between competing DBMSs should consider the following:

- DB2 is rarely a direct replacement for an existing DBMS. Although it is possible in some cases to substitute DB2 tables for their analogous constructs in the old DBMS, this rarely works. Applications using another DBMS should be redesigned or re-engineered (not a popular word). Remember, DB2 is a relational DBMS, built for the ad hoc query environment. Using it to replace an existing DBMS in a transaction processing environment may not be feasible, efficient, or even possible.

  Redesigning an application means going back to the original data model and business functions that the system was built to handle. (Of course, these things are covered in great detail in the system documentation.) Re-engineering is a fairly new concept, still in its infancy. It involves running application source code and design documentation through a software tool that will generate clean, new, well-documented applications. Not recommended for mission-critical systems.

- DB2 must interface with a teleprocessing monitor system. Which do you have installed? The attachment interfaces are slightly different in each case, with various tricks and traps for the unwary. Probably the most important consideration is performance; that is, how does one tune the DB2 system (and DB2 applications) in each environment?

  With CICS, for example, connection to DB2 is controlled through the Resource Control Table (RCT). Here are defined the connections and threads from CICS to DB2 based on transaction codes. Who controls this table? The DB2 database administrator? The CICS administrator?

- Conversion efforts are sometimes fueled by fears that the old DBMS will not be supported in the future. IMS falls into this category, as IBM has announced that IMS will not be the database protocol used under SAA. Recently, IBM announced a new, updated version of IMS called IMS/ESA 3.2. It contains many new features, functions, and performance enhancements.

  Shops worried about IMS disappearing within a year or two may rest easy: IMS is here to stay, for at least the next 10 years, maybe even longer. During this period DP departments may slowly migrate from IMS to DB2 if they wish. IBM is making their job easier:

it recently announced that the next version of DB2 (2.3) will support a separate feature called the Data Propagator. This feature will propagate updates in IMS to DB2. Later announcements will contain more information.

Performance

Of all the DB2 considerations, the most difficult to understand is that of performance. Early versions of the DB2 Optimizer performed poorly. Later versions included several performance enhancements, including a better sort, additional JOIN algorithms, better index usage, and improved utilization of hardware and operating system features.

Still, performance is called into question when DB2 is presented as a DBMS alternative. How do you define and measure DBMS performance? Several alternatives follow, each with its own advantages and disadvantages.

- *Transaction throughput.* This is usually depicted as a number of transactions completed per unit of time (minutes or hours). Though many feel it is very descriptive, it is very difficult to tie these numbers back to physical (i.e., tuneable) things in the DB2 environment. It is also tied intricately to other things such as availability of DASD for paging, buffer pool size, and CPU usage. This makes it difficult to compare two throughput measurements meaningfully, even when they relate to the same transaction running on the machine at different times. Interested readers should refer to the DB2 V2R2 Administration Guide, Chapter 7-1.

- *Physical I/O.* Touted early in the mid-1970s, designers were told to use this as a measure of program efficiency and to design programs to minimize physical I/O. Designers quickly found that high-level languages and DBMS interfaces (for example DL/I and SQL) isolate the program from the physical environment and make such recommendations of doubtful usefulness. Note that recent versions of DB2 include asynchronous I/O features such as sequential and list prefetch.

- *Standard Work Unit (SWU).* This is another measure from the 1970s. Programs are to be designed so that the Unit of Work, or the work done between synchpoints or checkpoints, was of a standard length or size. Among many methods suggested for measuring SWU inside a program were the following:

- Limiting the number of invocations of the DBMS to a fixed number. In IMS this was accomplished by counting the number of Get, Insert, and Delete calls and multiplying these counts by weighting factors. The sum of the counts was not allowed to exceed a certain threshold. This method rapidly lost favor as later versions of IMS made the correspondence between database calls and actual work done rather tenuous.

- Providing standard interface modules. Modules were written for each possible database call, and were responsible for evaluating the amount of work they did. Such modules were typically written by a systems programmer, and accessed information not usually available (or understandable) to a programmer. These modules took a long time to write, had to be customized for each program or application, and needed to be radically updated when new versions of the DBMS were installed. Maintenance and debugging were also difficult.

The Standard Work Unit concept is even more difficult to implement in a DB2 application. Due to the "atomic" nature of SQL, a single call may cause an entire tablespace to be scanned, along with various sorts and index scans. This may be particularly true of JOINs. Those shops that insist on the SWU concept have taken to modifying some SQL statements so that they are executed multiple times, each execution performing some of the work.

For example, an SQL statement that would retrieve (say) 10,000 rows from a table would be modified to return only the first (say) 1,000 rows using a Cursor. The Cursor would then be closed, the program would COMMIT (perhaps), the SQL statement would be modified to return the next 1,000 rows, and the Cursor reopened. Regrettably, as this example demonstrates, the SQL statement in question may still perform an entire tablespace scan in order to create the result table from which the 1,000 rows are retrieved. DB2 Version 2 Release 3 addresses this problem with the Cursor Hold feature.

- *On-line response time.* This measurement directly impacts the user, is easy to gauge, and is sometimes built into the specifications of the system. Regrettably, predictions about on-line response time for a DB2 application are almost impossible to make prior to implementation. Not only do shops have little or no experience with similar DB2 applications, but on-line DB2 application performance varies greatly with the environment. Such things as buffer pool size, subsystem performance (IMS, CICS, TSO), and CPU utilization can cause such measurements to fluctuate wildly.

The SQL Interface

IBM describes SQL this way:

> *The functional richness of Structured Query Language (SQL) for both programmer and end user enhances the capability to expand applications and reduces the cost of maintaining them. In many cases, additional function can be added to an application with less effort than other data models and with no change to the data base. This means that application extensions which were not justifiable with the existing data base may become justified with the relational implementation.*
>
> *Particular functions found in a relational data base are:*
>
> ***Join**: Operate on multiple tables (files) in a single statement (limited to 15 tables per request in DB2). Data can be correlated among the tables based on any data values in the tables. In DB2, joins can be requested dynamically.*
>
> ***Union**: Treat multiple tables of similar format as a single large table for the purpose of a single request.*
>
> ***Set updates**: The ability to add, change, or delete a selected set of rows with a single statement.*[1]

SQL has other advantages:

- The standards organizations ANSI, ISO, and FIPS have all accepted SQL as the relational data base language.
- With SQL the program is insulated from the physical access path to the data. Programs need not navigate the database to access data.

---

[1]From *DBMS Conversion Guide* (GH20-7564), IBM Application Enabling Marketing Center, June 1989.

Despite these benefits, SQL has several rough edges:

- Insulation from the physical access path is sometimes a disadvantage. Most programmers want their program to execute efficiently, and DBAs support this. But removing database navigation from the province of the programmer makes application tuning that much more difficult.

  The EXPLAIN facility goes a little way toward correcting this problem, though some feel not far enough. As one DBA said to me, "EXPLAIN tells me how a query will attempt to access data on a particular date, at a particular time, with specific catalog statistics ... maybe. It won't tell me how to formulate the query more effectively, what other (perhaps more efficient) options exist for data access, or what effect external factors will have on actual query performance."

- Insulating the program from physical access paths also affects performance when taking into account referential integrity. A programmer coding an SQL DELETE statement in a program has no knowledge of any DELETE rules that may cause rows in other dependent tables to be deleted. Even this knowledge may be of no help, as Primary and Foreign Keys may be added and deleted (using the ALTER statement) without the programmer's knowledge.

- As mentioned previously, sometimes SQL provides several ways of coding the same query. Which is more efficient? Programmers are told to "code queries to take advantages of indexes." Unfortunately, the presence or absence of indexes on certain columns is under control of the DBA. Indexes can be added, changed, or deleted at any time (almost), thus affecting query performance.

Hardware

Many DB2 afficionados consider themselves experts in DB2 performance tuning. What they seem to imply is that they have some expertise in adjusting SQL statements to minimize a factor such as physical I/O, page or tablespace locking, buffer contention, or CPU utilization. The same mindset occurs in some IMS DBAs, who make statements such as "all databases should be HIDAM" or "OSAM is more efficient than VSAM." This phenomenon is commonly termed *micro-optimization.* It ignores the bigger subsystem and system picture to concentrate instead on improving single database accesses in isolated applications. System tuning, on the other hand, concerns itself precisely with the big picture, such as how resources are to be allocated and consumed across the board.

System administrators, database administrators, and application analysts should concern themselves with the methodology described here before tuning an application.

Do MVS tuning. The principle here is that if an operating system is tuned poorly, no amount of application tuning will help it. There are several well-known areas to investigate—and reinvestigate—once you plan to install DB2:

- *Analyze DASD device contention.* With many database management systems (even with applications using flat files) it is common to allocate a database and its index to separate DASD volumes to reduce access arm movement during random access. This practice holds true in DB2 as well. Volumes in a DB2 STOGROUP are used in sequence as DB2 needs the space. Don't assign a table and its associated indexes to the same storage group. Another alternative would be to consider allocating tablespaces using the VCAT option, which allows you to specify VSAM characteristics explicitly.

- *Consider the latest hardware advances and where to implement them.* IBM's latest DASD device is the 3390, which is a bit bigger than the more common 3380 models. The 3390 Model 1 has a track capacity of 56,664 bytes, with 15 tracks per cylinder. It is thus possible to fit 180 control intervals on a cylinder, rather than the 150 that fit on a 3380 cylinder. A common implementation procedure is to install 3390s in *3380 track emulation mode.* This makes the new DASD look like the more familiar 3380s to the system.

  Another consideration is the 3990 cache controller. This device contains a memory cache that speeds up physical I/O. Data written to DASD are first written to the cache. The data originator is then informed immediately that the write has taken place, and the physical write follows. This procedure reduces the total apparent physical I/O time from about 20 milliseconds to about 3 milliseconds. Some IBM 3880 controllers (Models 11, 13, 21, and 23) also have caches.

  A number of uncommon, though certainly interesting, alternatives are available. Some IBM DASD models, such as the 3348 Model 70 and the 3350 Model B2F, have a small number of fixed head cylinders. These cylinders have up to eight dedicated heads per cylinder that remain motionless. Thus they have extremely fast DASD access times. Shops using these DASD models usually allocate these cylinders for highly accessed databases, indexes, and data for mission-critical applications.

- *Reduce CPU usage.* A system chugging along at above 98 percent CPU utilization just can't run any faster, regardless of any application tuning you might do. Try to find ways to spread CPU consumption – either by getting more hardware, by distributing the workload to other mainframes or PCs, by limiting the number of concurrent users and distributing the CPU workload across a wider span of peak time, or by similar practices. As a last resort, upgrade to a bigger CPU.

- *Analyze dispatching priorities.* There are several priorities associated with MVS units of work. The important one here is the address space dispatching priority, which is assigned by MVS at address space creation time. MVS will update this priority when it attempts to balance out the system workload. The job of assigning the CPU to tasks is handled by the MVS dispatcher. Tasks represented by task control blocks (TCBs) and service request blocks (SRBs) that have higher dispatching priorities will be allowed preferred use of the CPU.

  System administrators must consider various priorities for the different address spaces of consequence in IMS, CICS, TSO, and/or DB2 environments. Some of these address spaces are, in approximate descending order of importance,

  The IMS Resource Lock Manager
  The Virtual Telecommunications Access Method (VTAM)
  The IMS Control Region (if applicable)
  DB2 Data Base Services
  DB2 System Services
  TSO performance group 1
  IMS Message Processing regions (if applicable)
  CICS applications (if applicable)
  Other TSO performance groups
  Batch programs

  This order of decreasing priorities will vary greatly across installations, depending on their relative degree of CPU utilization, CPU availability, and the number of applications.

- *Determine if there is sufficient real and/or virtual memory.* Although DB2 does not suffer greatly from virtual storage constraints, often IMS and CICS problems in this area will ripple over to DB2. Another factor to look at is the possibility of acquiring expanded storage. Although it is extremely expensive, it may be the only answer if application performance is paramount.

Do IMS/CICS/TSO subsystem tuning. Once the MVS system is tuned as well as is feasible, its various subsystems can then be tuned. The most common factors to consider are:

- *Buffer pool management.* There is a profusion of various pooled entities in the different subsystems, including the DB2 EDM pool, the VSAM shared resources pool, the ISAM/OSAM buffer pool, the OSAM sequential buffering pool, and so on. Each of these pools is allocated separately and must be tuned in conjunction with the others. Things are further complicated in the DB2 environment by the availability of several buffer pools for data I/O (BP0, BP1, BP2, and BP32K). Some shops, due to early recommendations from IBM, have restricted their DB2 Database, Tablespace, and Indexspace allocation to default to a single, large buffer pool (BP0). Other, more venturesome shops have assigned tablespaces to BP0 and Indexspaces to BP1. Other combinations and permutations are possible.

- *CICS RCT entries.* The Resource Control Table (RCT) is the place in CICS where transaction connections to DB2 are defined. The most difficult part about RCT entries involves defining threads. Should you use *pool* threads or *dedicated* threads? What maximums should be used? Should multiple DBRMs be bound into a single plan, or should we use dynamic plan allocation?

- *IRLM considerations.* It is possible to share an IRLM among many subsystems. Probably the major advantage of sharing is that it takes a long time to get IRLM definition right. There is one minor disadvantage, however. Part of the process of IRLM definition involves setting the "deadlock wait" time (DEADLOK, IRLMRWT). This interval is the time after which the IRLM will wake up and look to see if two or more applications are deadlocked over resources the IRLM is presently managing. Depending on the environment, you may want applications to wait no more than, say, fifteen seconds for an IMS resource or perhaps up to two minutes for a DB2 resource. Setting up this scenario would probably require using two separate IRLMs.

- *Security and authorization systems.* Many shops have extensive, complex security subsystems or products. If these existing products are sufficient for your security needs, you may be able to dispense with IMS/CICS and DB2 security. For example, some shops use RACF security for user sign-on and GRANT privileges on plans to PUBLIC. This procedure has the advantage of streamlining DB2 authorization checking for commonly used plans. (In this case, a plan with access PUBLIC that is already in the EDM pool has a bit that is turned on indicating PUBLIC. When the next user accesses the plan, DB2 will notice this bit and bypass the authorization checking.)

- *Virtual storage constraints.* Although buying more memory may seem to be the only answer, the operations management people should consider various options. For example, TSO is a notorious resource hog. Limit its use by specifying a relatively low MAXUSERS parameter, which is the number of allowable concurrent TSO users. A majority of TSO usage seems to be spent in the ISPF/PDF Edit menu making program changes. Although ISPF is indeed one of the better source code editors for the IBM mainframe, consider offloading this kind of work to PCs. Many shops now use microcomputers as workstations for analysts and programmers. Program analysis, design, and coding – and sometimes even testing – can now be done on a microcomputer. This expedient saves mainframe CPU, memory, and DASD resources.

- *Consider OSAM sequential buffering for IMS.* This feature speeds the sequential processing of databases that use OSAM as their access method.

- *Tune the usage of VSAM.* There are many ways to tune VSAM performance, including allocation of the shared resource pool, choice of control interval size, freespace determinations, and buffer page-fixing.

Do DB2 subsystem tuning. Now that MVS and the subsystems have been tuned, you can address the DB2 subsystem. Part of the reason for saving the DB2 subsystem for last is that most problems with other subsystems, such as virtual storage constraints, seem to ripple over into DB2, affecting it indirectly. Most of these items are beyond the scope of this book, but some are worth mentioning here for the sake of completeness:

- *Understand buffer pool allocation and use.* The DB2 buffer pool has several thresholds associated with it. As the buffer pool fills with buffers marked "in use" (that is, ones with changed data that have not yet been written to DASD), DB2 restricts certain activities. For example, DB2 typically waits until the buffer pool is 50 percent full before attempting to physically write buffers to disk. The pool must reach 90 percent full before the sequential prefetch function is turned off. When it is about 97 percent full, DB2 must devote almost its entire energy to writing buffers.

These maxima are documented in the appropriate IBM reference manuals.

- *Monitor DB2 statistics.* The DB2 Performance Monitor contains statistics that summarize data about DB2 performance. Many shops go quite a bit further and acquire a software tool from a third-party vendor that monitors DB2 in real time.

- *Continually analyze the need to run RUNSTATS.* Optimizer access path selection depends upon the DB2 catalog statistics. If the statistics have not been run, the optimizer uses default values. If they *have* been run, but not recently, the optimizer may end up making decisions based on faulty data. There are many considerations, including those for read-only tables, tables having activity in particular key ranges (so-called hot spots), constantly growing tables, and volatile tables whose size does not vary considerably. Each of these situations demands a different approach to reorganization, RUNSTATS, and application plan rebind.

Finally, do application tuning. Now that all the system and subsystem tuning is done, application tuning may be able to make a difference. It is important to keep in mind that even though your system is finely and professionally tuned and you have thoroughly analyzed all access paths, it is still possible that application tuning will make little or no difference. In fact, the interaction of all the subsystems and their functions and subfunctions is so complex that application tuning may even have a negative effect.

Application tuners should take the following factors into account:

- *Analyze commit frequency.* Taking checkpoints in IMS (or synchpoints in CICS) is easy, but doing it efficiently is an art. There seems to be no standard way of determining exactly how often a program should issue commits, although the reasons for doing so are themselves well known.

- *Decide whether to use conversational or nonconversational programming.* This choice could be made on a subsystem-by-subsystem basis.

In IMS, for example, MPPs communicate with one another, as with terminals, printers, and so forth by using messages. These units contain data for the program or terminal to act upon. Conversational programming goes one step further in allowing programs to exchange additional information not contained in the message itself. These data (up to 32K bytes) are stored in the Scratch Pad Area (SPA).

It is worth noting that IMS conversational programming can be simulated in a nonconversational environment. One method of doing so involves using a *SPA database*. This database would contain the same information that a SPA would, but it would be stored here in a database segment. Programs exchanging messages would then include in their messages the SPA database key for this information.

Another method involves storing information in hidden fields on screens. Many screens contain blank areas – even completely empty lines. These areas of the screen, hence of the screen message, can contain data that would otherwise go in the input message to the program. This information would be displayed with the hidden or nondisplay attribute so that the user would be unaware of its existence. Obviously, the usability of this technique is limited by the amount of empty screen space available and the stability of the screen design.

- *Define IMS databases as nonrecoverable.* This feature is available with IMS/ESA. Databases may be defined as nonrecoverable to IMS. IMS will then not attempt to log all database changes or dynamically back out database changes on program abend. Note that this may preclude on-line updating.

- *Analyze access path selection.* During the bind phase, DB2 selects the access paths for table and index access based on the SQL statement and the DB2 catalog's statistics. Although it is possible to influence DB2's choice by tuning SQL statements, this is now less of a problem than it has been in the past. Certain DB2 Catalog tables have updatable columns containing table and index statistics. These statistics are usually updated by the RUNSTATS and STOSPACE utilities.

  The DB2 Optimizer uses these statistics during bind to calculate the costs of the various applicable access paths to the requested data and chooses the least costly as the preferred method. By changing the values in these columns, the DBA can affect DB2's choice of access path. Doing this requires a high level of expertise and understanding of DB2 catalog dynamics.

SYSTEMS DEVELOPMENT TOOLS

The growth and acceptance of the relational model in the 1980s is now changing the way that we design systems. The development tools and methodologies of the last two decades were dependent on data models that emphasized hierarchical, or parent-child, relationships. With the relational model's accent on *domains* and *attributes*, tools and techniques must be updated.

In this section we will concentrate on the impact DB2 has had on computer-assisted software engineering (CASE) tools and development methodologies. In Chapter 2 we will discuss how these tools and methodologies are used in the DB2 environment.

CASE Tools

As mentioned previously, the appearance of the relational model and its implementations in database management systems has caused CASE tools vendors to rethink how their tools integrate into the application development environment. It is useful to consider how DB2 is consolidated into the two general types of CASE tools and where in the systems development life cycle (SDLC) such tools are used.

Front-end CASE tools. These tools are often called *analysis and design tools*, as they concentrate on the beginning of the development life cycle. The relational model hasn't affected those tools that focus on requirements definition, feasibility, or cost justification. Relational database management systems, however, greatly affect the way that vendors must implement logical and physical design tools.

The existence of DB2 as a physical design alternative causes the tool designer some new headaches:

- *Implementation of relationships.* One-to-many and many-to-many relationships between entities can be implemented in several ways in DB2. One alternative is to use the referential integrity (RI) feature, defining the appropriate Primary and Foreign keys in the tables. This permits DB2 to manage the relationships according to the DBMS-defined Delete Rules. Deletion of a Customer, for example, may cause related Outstanding Orders to be deleted automatically by the DBMS. Another alternative is to manage these relationships in the application logic. Deletion of a Customer, for example, could be followed by code that deleted related Outstanding Orders.

This now requires that CASE tools generating logical and physical design documents be flexible enough to store, analyze, and present solutions to these problems, probably in the form of entity-relationship diagrams. In addition, integrated tools must pass this information later in the life cycle to subtools that generate program source code and test data.

- *Performance problems.* Although DB2's reputation for poor performance has now largely been overcome, it is still true that decisions made during physical design can adversely affect system and application performance. (This sometimes leads to an interesting debate between designers and database analysts: designers will attempt to fully normalize their data to remove redundancies and update anomalies, while the database analysts will selectively "denormalize" for performance reasons.)

  Regrettably, there are no CASE tools currently available that have the skill or intelligence to correctly predict application performance in the DB2 environment. This means that the development effort may proceed as far as the integrated systems test stage before performance problems are detected. This sometimes leads to redesign and, unfortunately, reprogramming.

Back-end CASE tools. Tools in this category concentrate on later life-cycle stages such as code generation and testing. Again, tool designers have had to update, rethink, and sometimes redesign their tools. Among the reasons are the following:

- *Code generation.* Code (or program) generation in hierarchical environments was relatively easy for CASE tools. The main problem for the tool was to analyze the structure of the database and then produce application code that would navigate the structure. (Usually this structure was encoded as part of an earlier tool's output.) In DB2 there is no navigation per se. Instead, all data is readily available in tables. A new problem surfaces, however. Typically there is more than one SQL statement that will fulfill a data request, and each SQL statement may be written in countless ways.

  The code generation tool is now responsible for generating SQL statements that are both correct and, if possible, efficient. This is difficult, because the measures of efficiency may not be present. A common method of determining statement efficiency is to view output of the EXPLAIN facility. This facility may be executed either on-line or as a part of application plan binding. Some of the information returned about a particular SQL statement would include JOIN method (if any), index(es) used (if any), and sorting required (if any).

The code generator may not have access to the DB2 subsystem or, if it does, the specific database tables may not have the appropriate statistics stored in the DB2 Catalog. (These statistics must mirror those to be expected in the Production environment.) This information is required in order to choose the most efficient SQL statement. This means that the generator must be able to simulate or at least understand the DB2 Optimizer in the way that it chooses access paths — not an easy task.

- *Problem detection and correction.* The proliferation of SQLCODEs in DB2 makes the designer's job a bit more difficult. Problems that would cause program abends in other systems are now detected by the DBMS, which then notifies the program. This means that the program is now responsible for checking a wider range of situations and determining if an error action is called for.

  The SQLCODE field of the SQL Communications Area (SQLCA), along with the SQLWARN fields, informs the program about the status of SQL statement execution. In general, an SQLCODE of zero indicates successful execution, greater than zero indicates successful execution with some kind of warning indication, and less than zero indicates unsuccessful execution. Note that "unsuccessful execution" does not necessarily indicate a fatal error in the program. An SQLCODE of -904, for example, indicates that a requested resource was not available. This situation may not require abnormal program termination. Then again, because of business reasons, perhaps it does.

  The code generation tool must somehow be informed of the default actions to take should any of certain situations occur (negative SQLCODEs). Perhaps some of these cases will necessitate error correction; others may require abnormal program termination; still others may mean the program continues execution. This produces additional program code and, as a side-effect, lengthens the program unit testing process.

- *Test data generation.* The proliferation of SQLCODEs now means adding additional test criteria to program test data designed to cover these nonfatal situations. Also, since DB2 may be doing set-at-a-time processing, several different test table combinations may be required to encompass the entire range of test cases. Tools designed to create DB2 test table data may be integrated with interactive debugging tools, allowing programmers to debug with logical data, rather than requiring bothersome replication and copying of test tables.

- *Performance.* Again, application performance is extremely difficult to measure before a system is installed in a DB2 subsystem. As mentioned above, the code generator has a difficult time choosing an efficient SQL statement from the many available to satisfy a particular query. One other situation involves use of a Cursor. (Cursors allow row-at-a-time processing, at least from the program's point of view.) Sometimes a query can be resolved with several forms of an SQL statement, including the correlated subquery, a JOIN, or several queries using a Cursor. These situations will perform quite differently in practice – the code generator will probably not have enough information to make a suitable choice.

In summary: CASE tool vendors have had to reflect on the problems of the DB2 environment and adapt their tools to fit. We will discuss in Chapter 2 how the way we use these tools changes because of DB2.

Development Methodologies

As mentioned previously, the appearance of the relational model and its implementations in database management systems has caused us to rethink how we use systems development methodologies in the application development environment. We will discuss how the methods have changed in Chapter 2. In this section we will consider the changes DB2 and the relational model have made on the software that supports the methodologies.

Software for methodologies. Most of the systems development methodologies of the past few decades have embodied both a method for development and an accompanying diagramming method. These diagramming methods usually depicted either process flow or data flow within an application or system and formed a basis for various *structured programming techniques.* Most of these are still around and are named for the various proponents of the methodology. Early methods, however, were manual ones and were not integrated into software packages until the mid-1980s.

Few of the methodologies needed to be changed because of DB2, since they concentrated on *logical* design rather than *physical* design. Still, these methods tended to be based on hierarchical data structures and emphasized parent-child relationships between entities. As the relational model came into prominence, new tools and methodologies emerged. These new tools have not yet evolved or matured to the point where they are common alternatives for designers.

THIRD-PARTY TOOLS

General Considerations

Most third-party tools built for the DB2 environment take advantage of something uniquely available in the DB2: the DB2 Catalog tables. These tables contain information about DB2 objects in a form that is readily accessible through SQL. Such information exists in IMS, CICS, and MVS, but in highly encoded forms. These forms include IMS PSB, ACB, and DBD libraries; CICS tables; MVS control blocks; DASD Volume Table of Contents (VTOC); VSAM List Catalog (LISTCAT) information; and various other sources. Each of these collections of information has its own special format that is not easily readable, either from an application program or using native commands.

The DB2 Catalog, therefore, gives the tool developer a great advantage in that basic information about DB2 objects is easy to access. Indeed, many initial DB2 tools were nothing more than simple SQL queries against the catalog blended with a primitive user interface.

Advances in Tool Building

It is interesting to note that only one tool developer has taken the next logical step: to design a tool that views information from other subsystems (MVS, IMS, CICS, TSO, and so on) and converts that information internally into the form of relational tables. In this way it would then be possible (in principle) to ask *any* question about objects across multiple environments, expressing such questions in the form of an SQL statement that JOINs the appropriate "tables."

The next logical step would be for such a tool to use SQL update functions to change object definitions. This would involve using an SQL-like statement to make changes to the definitions stored internally in relational tables, then converting such a change into a command or process that affected the object in the real world. Such changes could occur immediately, perhaps in the form of a command. Alternatively, the tool could submit a job to the operating system that would perform the desired function.

This new technology would be difficult to develop initially but would lead to tools with many advantages over conventional tools:

- *They will be easy to develop.* Once the technology is in place that *scans* external information and converts it into the form of relational tables, the tool will have the capability to access information about any and all objects in the environment. Once additional technology is available that takes a request, JOINs the appropriate internal tables, and generates the pertinent command or function, the tool can manage a complete subenvironment.

- *They will meet all user's specific needs.* In principle, such a tool will have access to *all* information about the environment. Thus it can do anything that any other tool can do in the same environment.

- *They will allow the user to leverage the entire DP environment.* Eventually, such tools could be integrated together into a complete workbench. As all the tools store data in a common format, this integration would be relatively painless. The user would then have access to the set of all system objects.

- *They will be relatively unaffected by system changes.* As systems change and new versions and releases of software and database management systems appear and disappear, the only parts of the tool requiring changes will be the interfaces to system information.

- *They will provide an integrated solution.* Users will no longer be in the position of using different tools for each environment, each with its own command syntax and none of them integrated with others. An integrated toolset will provide a common user interface, similar command linkages, common internal data storage, and a standard connection to the DP environment.

Readers interested in this new technology are invited to contact the author for more information (see Preface).

Chapter 2

Impact on Practices

CURRENT SYSTEMS DESIGN METHODOLOGIES

Nondatabased Applications

Many (some would say most) existing data processing application systems do not use a database management system. These systems consist of a mixture of aging batch reporting and master file update systems, sprinkled with a few high-performance systems. (These so-called high-performance systems are sometimes written in machine language or assembler.)

Relational database management systems (RDBMSs) have become another option to flat file systems, although there are several things that make developers worry about this alternative:

- *Performance.* Initial implementations of systems using RDBMSs have acquired a reputation for poor performance. This seems to be due in large part to set-at-a-time relational processing, although execution path length was also a factor. IBM's DB2, in particular, gained an early poor reputation; later releases of the *optimizer* incorporated features for better access path selection, decreased execution path length, and took advantage of specific hardware features.

  Performance is a concern for another, more interesting reason. Many systems implemented using a RDBMS were converted from another DBMS, usually a hierarchical one (IMS is a popular choice). Choosing to convert an existing system to a RDBMS rather than design a new system from the ground up allows the DP organization to compare the two systems in several ways: development time, coding and testing time, ease of installation, amount of maintenance, and performance. Regrettably, in many such cases the RDBMS implementation performs poorly, and management blames this on the RDBMS. A more likely reason is that the original system was designed to take advantage of hierarchical data structures and standard business transaction processing, things that typical RDBMSs handle inadequately.

- *Throughput.* Another version of performance, throughput affects the way users perceive a system. Multisecond on-line response time, crowded batch windows, and high volume transaction processing time are all symptoms.

  Installation of an RDBMS means yet another factor to be taken into consideration when performing capacity planning, workflow analysis, and queue estimation.

- *Tuneability.* Application systems written using relational database management systems are difficult in principle to tune for system-wide performance. With DB2, for example, poorly performing applications can affect an entire system, currency of catalog statistics can influence day-to-day performance of a single program, and buffer pool size can interact in peculiar ways with program usage. This all combines to make the DB2 DBA's job quite tedious.

  Another factor associated with DB2 tuneability is that of DB2s place in the MVS system hierarchy. In general, systems that include DB2 must be tuned from the top down, as follows:

  - First, do MVS tuning. Analyze CPU utilization. If utilization is above 98 percent, then no amount of query tuning or buffer pool management will help DB2. Assess the availability of real memory; consider expanded storage, additional DASD for paging, and so on. Investigate MVS dispatching priorities, and assign priorities according to subsystem importance. Generally, top priority is given to VTAM and the IRLM, followed by IMS Fast Path regions, TSO P1 regions, and so forth.

  - Second, do I/O subsystem tuning. This includes IMS-DC, TSO, and CICS. Make sure that enough VSAM and OSAM buffers are available; adjust TSO MAXUSERS; analyze the configuration of IMS on-line regions and their allocation of memory.

  - Third, do DB2 system tuning. This includes buffer pool selection and sizing, monitoring of lock management, and a historical analysis of catalog statistics. Coincident with DB2 system tuning, do application system tuning. This includes analysis of table and tablespace accesses, EXPLAIN output, and catalog statistics.

Databased Applications

For applications that already utilize a database management system, the installation of a relational DBMS makes the analyst's and systems administrator's jobs much more complicated. Considerations include the following:

- *Metrics.* To calculate project duration, most shops use some type of metrics for estimating program complexity. This usually involves estimating lines of code, function points, or other gauges of logic complexity. Most of these methods rely on a foundation of years of experience of creating similar programs and similar systems.

  Such a basis of information may not be relevant for systems accessing data in a relational DBMS. Using such methods may lead to extended program coding and testing, missed deadlines, and projects over budget.

- *Project management.* Most data processing departments control projects using a project management tool, often installed on a microcomputer. When designing a system that is to use a RDBMS, additional tasks may be required, including the following:

  - *Programmer training.* This includes efficient SQL usage, and the use of coding and testing tools such as syntax checkers and on-line debuggers.

  - *Analyst training.* This includes normalization (and denormalization), referential integrity issues, performance tuning concerns, use of design and prototyping tools (CASE), and the like.

  - *Design reviews.* It is imperative that the system and database design be analyzed and evaluated by competent database administration staff. Only they will be well informed as to the effects a system may have on other applications, the trade-offs between normalization redundancy and performance, and any upcoming hardware or software release features.

- *Program walk-throughs.* Often an overlooked task of application design, the walk-through is even more important in a relational DBMS environment. Often the programmer is responsible for developing the proper SQL statements and program logic. A walk-through that includes a representative of the DBA staff is a must for proper evaluation of query and program performance.

- *Performance measures.* Most designers have enough experience to judge the performance characteristics of a suite of applications prior to design, based on their work with similar systems. For example, consider a program that reads transactions sorted in account number sequence for update of a similarly sorted master file. Valid transactions are Add, Change, and Delete. Most analysts would have little difficulty designing and coding such an application (indeed, most have already done this very thing). Further, these same analysts could estimate the throughput of this application, based on their experience.

  With a relational DBMS, however, analysts have no such wealth of experience. They must rely on "gut feel"; not a comfortable feeling when designing important, mission-critical systems.

- *Testing.* Relational database management systems have become popular in part because of their supposed ability to answer ad hoc queries. How do you test a program that is designed to answer what-if questions? Using exhaustive test cases certainly isn't the answer. In fact, standard testing techniques may not suffice.

- *Conversion.* Some shops have brought in a relational database management system with the intention of converting current applications to the new DBMS. This is much more difficult than it sounds; several chapters of this book are devoted to this very topic. For now, consider that recent surveys indicate that most IS shops devote over two-thirds of their manpower to maintenance and less than one-third to development. With the number of applications steadily increasing, who will be available to convert current systems to a relational DBMS, especially if the systems have no perceived problems?

- *Hybrid systems.* A new RDBMS provides designers with yet another option for systems design—one that uses several DBMSs for data storage and retrieval. Sometimes this means taking database updates in one system and "shadowing" them in another. At other times it means interfacing with different databases from multiple systems.

SYSTEMS DEVELOPMENT TOOLS

Origins

The term *software engineering* in Computer-Assisted Software Engineering (CASE) was first used at a 1968 NATO conference. This was the era of the *software crisis*, when developers had begun to worry about an increasing backlog of unfinished applications. Software engineering seemed the answer to this problem: it would mold mathematics, engineering, and management science into a single exquisite software development process.

As with most new ideas, it took some time for this concept to catch on. The Systems Development Life Cycle (SDLC) became in various forms a template for software engineering. Subsequently, as the field of data processing matured, various software tools were developed to assist analysts, designers, programmers, and maintainers with their work. Thus was CASE as a concept born.

Apart from simply automating repetitive tasks, CASE tools, tool kits, and workbenches allow applications developers to leverage their resources. With CASE, applications managers can allocate staff effectively, increase overall efficiency, and minimize errors. Documentation from the analysis phase of the SDLC can be used as input for the design phase, and design specifications may be fed into code generators. Testing and debugging tools speed the acceptance testing of software. And data modeling documentation aids in maintenance.

For the moment, let's forget about the Computer-Assisted portion of the CASE acronym and concentrate on the tools and methodologies themselves. Which tools and methodologies are really needed? Which are cost-effective? Where will designers and analysts get the most leverage? To decide this, we must first look at the way system designers view the life cycle.

There are now two general categories of such tools: analysis and design tools, often called *front-end* or *upper-case* tools; and prototyping and testing tools, also called *back-end* or *lower-case* tools (see Figure 2.1).

Tool Categories

Certain categories of tools fit best in different portions of the systems development life cycle. Let's review these categories briefly in the order in which they are usually performed.

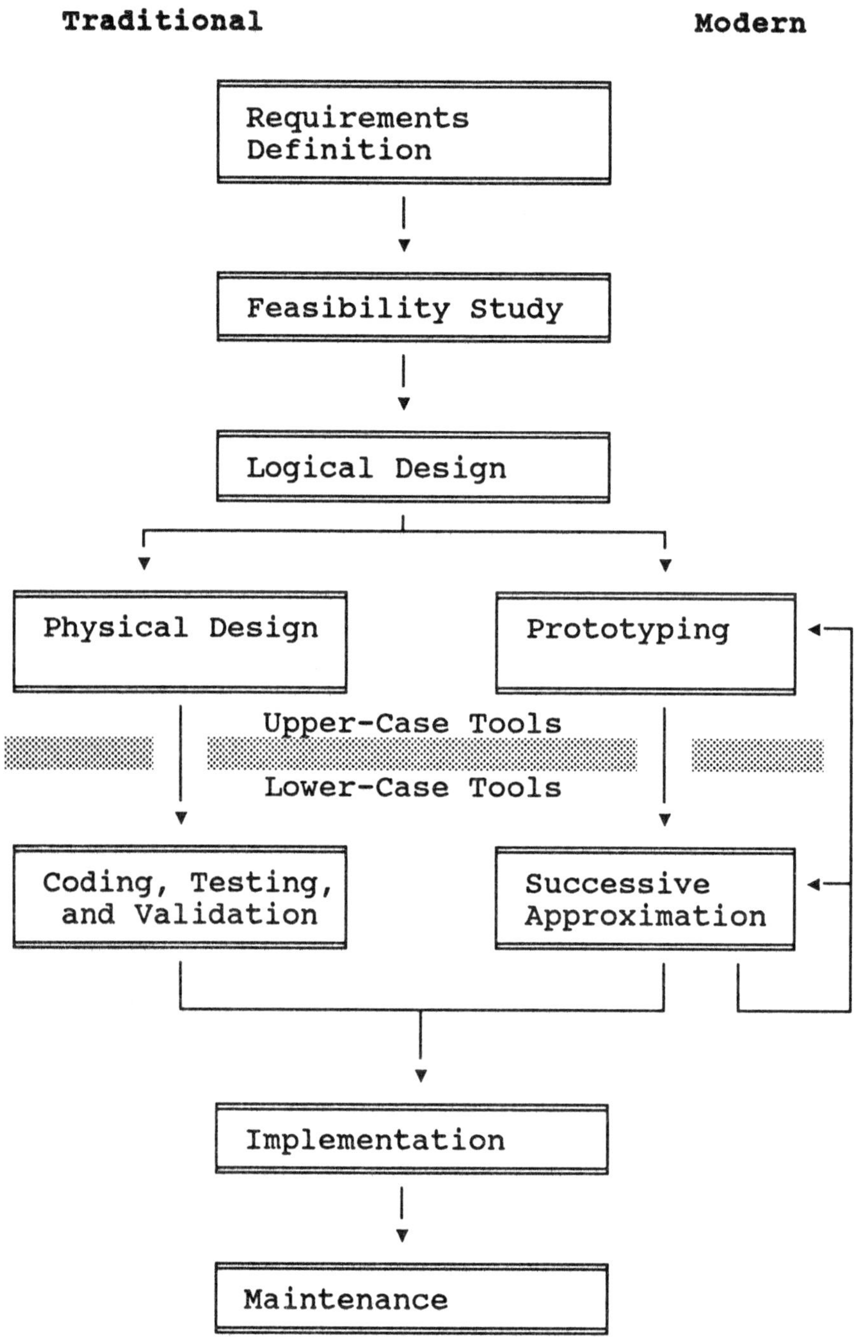

Figure 2.1. The Systems Development Life Cycle.

Requirements Definition. This category includes all manner of strategic planning, data modeling, and preanalysis tools. These tools are used when developing the descriptions of the current and requested systems: they produce reports, charts, and statistics that will be used in the Feasibility Study phase of the life cycle.

Feasibility Study. Under this category are tools for system description, prototype analysis, feasibility assessment, as well as some initial logical design tools. Common tools would include *screen prototypers*, used interactively with the user to develop screen definitions and protocol, and *assessment* tools, used to generate cost estimates for system design and development.

Logical design. This category includes such workbench tools for analysts as diagramming, screen design, documentation, and prototyping. These tools are usually packaged as part of a systems development methodology, and include additional tools such as those used in the Physical Design and Coding phases of the life cycle.

Physical Design. In this category are included tools for DASD space analysis, selection of access methods, database and file definition, and initial performance measurement. As new data storage alternatives arise (such as DB2) these tools must be modified to keep pace.

Coding. Workbench tools for programmers, including editors, syntax checkers, general purpose query facilities, and application generators are in this category. A subset of this area includes various in-house productivity tools and standards for required fields, screen layouts, program boiler plates, security, help facilities, and mail/messaging capabilities. Such tools were probably created during the normal course of development for other, earlier systems.

Testing. Here are included test data generators, on-line editors and debuggers, performance monitors, log and audit processing, and program abend aids. These are sometimes grouped together under the following categories:

- *Fault diagnosis.* These tools, which rely on expert systems, or knowledge-based tools, intercept system error messages and other problems and immediately identify the nature of the problem. These tools essentially automate the time-consuming process of analyzing hexadecimal memory dumps and system error codes. Such information can then be integrated into test plan results. Further, such information facilitates on-line interactive testing scenarios, as it accelerates error detection and correction.

- *Interactive debugging.* Debugging tools facilitate immediate problem evaluation and resolution. They incorporate some sophisticated tools for isolating problems in complex subsystems and application environments. A typical debugging scenario would involve a programmer in an on-line interactive environment "running" a program. Such running includes setting stop or break points, displaying the values of variables and parameters, changing the flow of execution, analyzing the processing of input data, and rerunning the program with different test data. Advanced tools allow the programmer to make immediate program changes to investigate alternative coding strategies and, optionally, permit immediate compile, relink, and retest using the new code.

- *On-line editing.* On-line editing tools permit rapid correction of application programs and data. Most programmers use some kind of editing tool for program coding and modification. Other, more sophisticated tools incorporate program syntax checking and compile/link procedures. Editing is also extended to data as well, including flat files and databases. This permits programmers to create and modify test data.

- *Simulation.* Simulation tools replicate complex network environments. These tools help implementors who need to time-stamp processes in order to identify specific conditions that cause problems. They also help implementors stress test applications to determine the impact of imposing heavy loads on existing networks. A typical network simulation tool can simulate a live, on-line transaction processing environment. This allows programmers to do three things: test applications in environments with thousands of simulated transactions in progress, freeze specific snapshots of actual environments, and modify simulated environments. Regression techniques permit evaluation of the accuracy and replicability of applications in complex environments.

Implementation. This category includes system performance monitors, user-training tools, and documentation aids. Regrettably, many documentation tools are used only at this stage rather than as an integral part of systems analysis and design. Some pundits have even suggested that a *system documentation* industry will spring up, offering a documentation service to companies whose systems are too cryptic to understand.

Maintenance. In this category are system performance monitors, documentation aids, regression testing, and data modeling tools. This portion of the life cycle is often neglected, especially in the DB2 environment, as companies neglect to include this in their planning.

Prototyping. Many DP professionals think this category contains simple screen drawing and simulation tools. There are, however, several others in this class including tools for temporary definition of inputs, processing, calculations, and outputs, as well as graphics and system emulation.

Successive Approximation. This category is usually merged with Prototyping. It refers to a process of iteration performed jointly by the user and the application designer. Beginning with the prototype, the user suggests changes to output formats, input availability, and processing logic. The designer then makes the requested changes and presents the user with the latest version. This process is repeated until the application finally meets the user's criteria.

The New SDLC

The explosive growth of software engineering products has changed the way developers view the SDLC. It can now be viewed as a set of parallel paths traversed by the development team (see Figure 2.2).

Metrics. Metrics are methods of measurement and estimation, including those for estimating programming tasks and testing. This path is one of the fuzziest, with a lack of definition that gives analysts the most headaches. Such questions as these arise: How long will it take to design a data base, code a program, or test a string of applications? Do we measure work in hours, lines of code, tested paragraphs, or by some other standard? The tools that assist the designer in developing metrics for task estimation are most useful in the requirements and design phases. They are frequently used to determine the costs, benefits, or feasibility of a proposed system. Metrics also come into play during maintenance as changes and enhancements to the system need to be prioritized.

Process Flow and Data Flow. These techniques are methods of designing, analyzing, and diagramming the flow of processes and data. Structured analysis and design methodologies usually espouse one or the other. Designers and analysts use this documentation for describing the flow of data through a system and defining how data are processed. These results may then be verified by the user. Some examples of diagramming methodologies include Yourdon, Warnier/Orr, Jackson, HIPOs, Gane and Sarson/Stradis, and Chen diagrams. These diagrams are probably the most important single set of documents produced during the early phases of a development project. Process flow documents are usually the basis for program specifications, whereas data flow diagrams form the elements of records, files, and databases. Unfortunately, during the later stages of a project, especially during maintenance, these documents are often ignored.

Project Management. This stage is a combination of project tracking, forecasting, and control systems. Managers use various methods, such as PERT and GANTT charts, to track work hours spent, compare actual to planned hours, monitor budgets, reallocate resources, and forecast dates for deliverables. In general, projects become more difficult to manage as the number of people assigned to them increases. The transition from the design phase step to those of coding and testing is the most likely period for project staffing to reach its maximum. At this point, methods of tracking, controlling, and allocating resource use become essential.

Performance Measurement. A number of methods of measuring system performance may be required at one stage or another to verify design correctness or efficiency. Some of the measurements are transactions processed per minute, on-line screen response time in seconds, required database reorganizations per week/month, percentage of available free space, and DASD usage statistics. Unless a project involves enhancing an existing system, it is almost impossible to measure performance in early phases.

In later phases, as tested programs become available, developers can use performance measures to tune the system. These measures form a great part of the enhancements (defined later) made during maintenance.

Change Control and Change Management. This path involves a methodology for controlling system changes. Typically security or audit features, these systems are used to verify that changes to a system are controlled, tested, verified for accuracy, and audited. Although the greatest number of changes to a system (usually called *enhancements* rather than *fixes*) come during maintenance, such changes cost the designer much less if discovered in earlier development phases. The single greatest cost saving for a system designer is to be able to detect system changes in the requirements phase so that they may be incorporated into the system design from the beginning. Any changes made later may affect programs already coded or database designs.

It is clear that certain phases and paths through the SDLC are more affected than others by the availability of software engineering tools. Each path has its own unique requirements in staff experience and expertise. Many software tools exist to assist the developer, implemented in either mainframe or microcomputer versions.

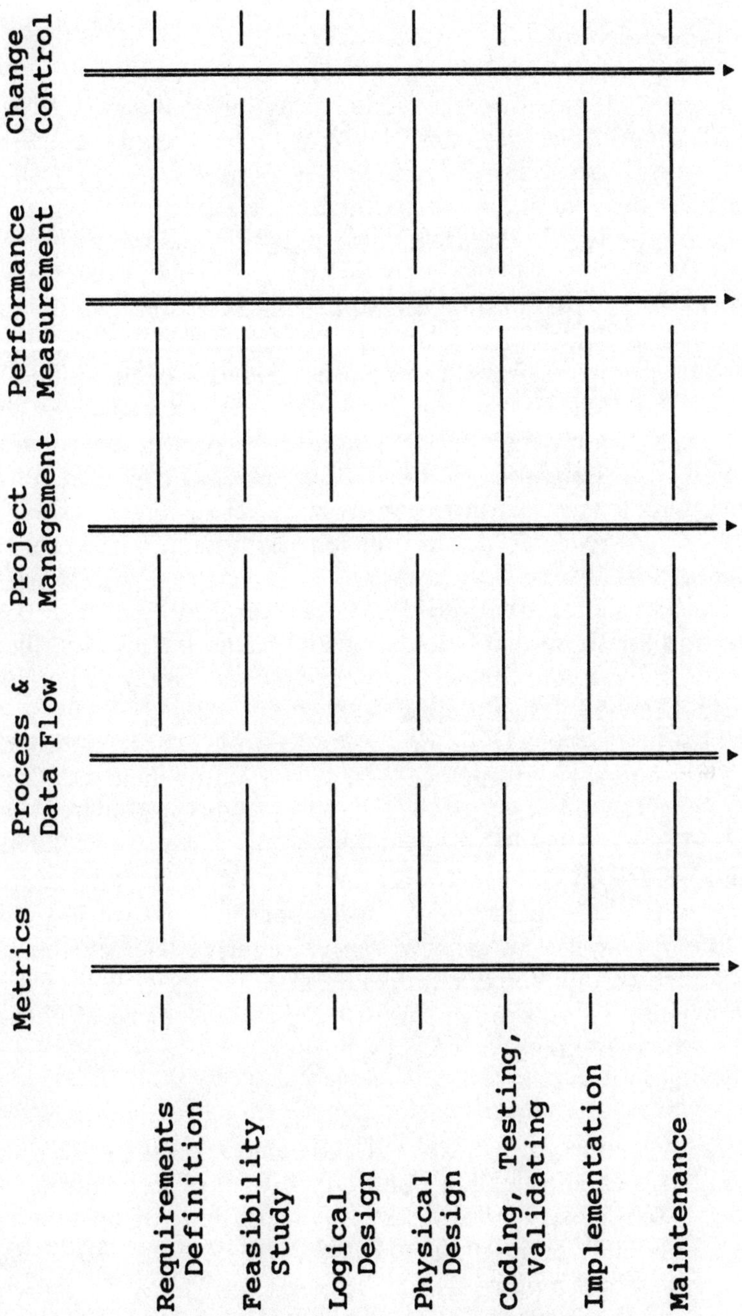

Figure 2.2. Paths in the SDLC matrix.

DBMS Environment

The choice of DBMS is usually made during the analysis and design phase of the SDLC. (Alternatively, this choice may be forced on the application developer by operations management.) Certain categories of tools lend themselves more naturally to particular DBMS environments. Let's concentrate on the big three: hierarchical, network, and relational.

Hierarchical. IBM's Information Management System for Virtual Storage (IMS/VS) is the most widely used mainframe DBMS of this kind. It lends itself will to most business applications, and has been around for several decades. The IMS application developer's biggest challenge comes when alterations to a company's business data model require a regeneration of the IMS data base definitions for the system. This is likely to require extensive programming changes. Conversion from the old database definitions to the new ones can be complicated and lengthy and may require experienced personnel in the systems department.

In the hierarchical DBMS arena, therefore, the most cost-effective CASE tools are those that help define and refine the business data model as early as possible in the SDLC. This would be the *process and data flow* path in the analysis and design phases.

Here are some representative CASE tools that would work well in this area: The Method (Performance Resources); Rapid Analysis (Computer and Engineering Consultants); Information Engineering Facility (Texas Instruments); Telon, Telon/PC (Pansophic); Data Structured Systems Design (Optima); Design (Meta Software); and Design Vision (Optima).

During the analysis and design phases, software engineering tools lower the probability of massive design changes later in the SDLC. The disadvantage (if one could call it that) is that a great deal of time is spent early on planning and organizing the logical and physical data structures. Staffing schedules may preclude this, as programmers wait idly for completed analysis and design.

Network. A mixture of hierarchical and relational (some say), the network DBMS is an interesting hybrid. Computer Associates' IDMS is the best-known product in this area. Typically easier to learn and get up to speed in than either hierarchical or relational DBMSs, the network DBMS can still get complicated rather rapidly.

Using the network DBMS methodology, system designers implement the intricate structure of the business data model directly into the DBMS structure (the *schema*). In particular, they implement many-to-many relationships between "parents" and "children." This requires developers and designers to coordinate their efforts carefully during the analysis and design phases of the project. Accurate documentation of the model is important.

Also, when prototyping applications, developers must react quickly to changes requested in data relationships. Such changes in complex data models put an added burden on the system designer, both to make the changes correctly and to document them fully.

The tools most needed in this area are those that document the business data model thoroughly and support automation of the full development life cycle. Network business data models can be quite complex; clear, concise documentation is required throughout development, implementation, and maintenance. In addition, tools that assist in change control during the maintenance phase are very useful. These tools assist systems planners when changes to the business data model require changes to DBMS internals.

Examples of CASE tools that fit this environment are Foundation (Arthur Andersen & Co.); IDMS/Architect (Computer Associates); Information Engineering Workbench (KnowledgeWare); Pacbase (CGI Systems); and Multi/CAM (AGS Management Systems).

Relational. This newest entry in the DBMS arena holds much promise. IBM's DB2 is the major player for mainframe data bases. In general, developing systems with relational DBMSs follows the prototyping segment of the SDLC. This allows analysts to develop a first approximation of the target system, prototype it, and then tune it to the user's requirements. DB2, for example, allows systems specialists to add to tables without bringing the system down, thus facilitating the successive approximation approach.

With a relational DBMS, the developer needs prototyping tools the most. In addition, as the successive approximation phase is entered, tools that can export usable program code are required. Another set of tools just as important with relational DBMSs are those for project management. These assist the manager in allocating resources. The prototyping environment is a dynamic one, and managers need such tools to track and control large products. Representative CASE tools for this environment are Visible Analyst Workbench (Visible Systems); Excelerator (Index Technology); Silverrun and Goldrun (Peat Marwick Advanced Technology); VS COBOL Workbench (Micro Focus); Project Workbench—Advanced (Applied Business Technology); and MEthod/1 (Arthur Andersen & Co.).

The CASE Bandwagon

Like some other state-of-the-art ideas, software vendors have jumped on the CASE bandwagon. The market is jam-packed with CASE software and development support tools of every sort and description. Just how many of these are really necessary? How can you make an informed decision about which one(s) to use (if any)? Where is the greatest payback? Table 2.1 summarizes the extent of payback developers might expect from software engineering tools. Some of these are further described in the following paragraphs.

Metrics. Tools that assist the designer in developing metrics for task estimation are most useful in the requirements and design phases. They are frequently used to determine the costs/benefits or feasibility of the proposed system. Metrics also come into play during maintenance as changes and enhancements to the system must be prioritized.

Process Flow and Data Flow. This is probably the most important single set of documents produced during the early phases of the development project. Process-flow documents usually are the basis for program specifications, while data flow diagrams form the elements of records, files, and databases. Unfortunately, during the later stages of the project (especially maintenance) these documents are often ignored.

Project Management. In general, projects become more difficult to manage as the number of people assigned increases. The transition from the design to coding and testing is the most likely period when project staffing will reach its maximum. Methods of tracking, controlling, and allocating resource use become essential.

Performance Measurement. Unless the project involves enhancing an existing system, it is almost impossible to measure performance early in the requirements or design phases, for example. In later phases, as tested programs become available, developers can use performance measures to tune the system. These measures form a large part of the enhancements made during maintenance.

Change Control. Although the most changes to a system (usually called "enhancements") come during maintenance, such changes cost the designer much less if discovered earlier. The single greatest cost saving for a system designer is to detect system changes in the requirements phase so that they may be incorporated into the system design from the beginning. Any changes made later may affect programs already coded or even database designs.

Regrettably, no tool (or set of integrated tools) presently fulfills all of a developer's requirements. CASE tool developers take heed: the needs of applications developers are many, but so are their constraints. Budgets,

	Estimating	Project Mgmt	Change Control	Metrics	Performance Measurement
Requirements	**HIGH**	low	low	**HIGH**	low
Feasibility	**HIGH**	low	MEDIUM	**HIGH**	low
Logical Design	**HIGH**	MEDIUM	MEDIUM	MEDIUM	low
Physical Design	MEDIUM	**HIGH**	**HIGH**	low	MEDIUM
Coding	low	**HIGH**	**HIGH**	MEDIUM	low
Testing	low	**HIGH**	**HIGH**	low	MEDIUM
Implementation	low	MEDIUM	MEDIUM	low	**HIGH**
Maintenance	MEDIUM	MEDIUM	**HIGH**	MEDIUM	**HIGH**

Table 2.1. Where do software developers need the most help?

training time, staff availability, and DBMS environment must be factored into tool selection equations. Application managers are looking for cost-effective tools that will increase their leverage and help them deliver systems on time, within budget, and with available staff. Only by concentrating on areas with the greatest return on investment to their customers can CASE tool developers deliver usable, cost-effective software.

REFERENTIAL INTEGRITY

The referential integrity (RI) features implemented in DB2 allow the database designer to embed data processing rules in the database structure. Usually these rules codify a correspondence between business entities having a one-to-one or one-to-many relationship, and describe how (or whether) an occurrence of one entity exists without a matching occurrence of the other. This relieves analysts from the burden of coding rules in programs. Further, as rules change, the database structure can be altered to mirror the new rules.

This ability to automatically handle rules via database structure can cause problems, however, if not properly handled. Some of these problems are described in the following paragraphs.

Systems Design Considerations

The appearance of DBMS-controlled referential integrity as an option now furnishes the DBA with another set of alternatives to consider during database design. Yet, to do this efficiently, the DBA must comprehend the data model created during design. Therefore the database analyst *must* be involved in the systems analysis process. Only in this way can they contribute to an effective implementation of the data model.

The DBA will participate in systems analysis and contribute recommendations regarding what model alternatives can be *realized* efficiently. Such realizations will be the responsibility of the DBA during design and implementation. Part of this duty is advising whether or not referential integrity should be implemented as a part of the database design or as part of the application logic. There are some obvious advantages and disadvantages to each method:

- *Install RI in the database structure.* RI in DB2 tables is implemented using the ON DELETE option for foreign key definitions. Implementing it therefore requires defining all primary and foreign keys during systems analysis. This is both good and bad: good in the sense that it requires analysts to think out the database design thoroughly at the beginning of the project, thus requiring fewer changes later; bad in that it may restrict the design process by precluding the DBA from implementing performance features such as denormalization and index change and deletion.

The major disadvantage of installing RI in the database structure is that later moving of the Delete rules to the application logic may be difficult and time-consuming. This sometimes occurs after implementation as DBAs and systems administrators attempt to tune programs or subsystems. If it is determined that removal of DBMS-controlled referential integrity is required, maintainers must then code (and test) the required application logic.

Another disadvantage involves program testing and maintenance. The most common method of fixing program bugs seems to be to go immediately to the listing of the offending program to make the required changes. Unfortunately, if DBMS-controlled referential integrity is in effect, the maintainer must also analyze the appropriate table relationships, as these will affect the way the program processes in DB2. This problem can be compounded when comments are inserted in the listing such as, "Note: This DELETE will cause additional table rows in other tables to be deleted because of ON DELETE rules in effect." Unfortunately, the Delete rules are under the control of the DBA, not the programmer. They may or may not exist at any particular time, thus making such comments extremely dangerous.

Another consideration is that RI, as implemented in the present release of DB2, has certain limitations. These features are beyond the scope of this book.[1]

- *Install RI in the application logic.* This the most common alternative. DBAs and designers usually choose this route because business data rules can be fully implemented in the program. Development, testing, and maintenance are then made easier, as the program logic embodies the *complete* application. Moving some of this processing outward to the DBMS is possible, although tedious, and will involve removing program logic and extensive testing. The disadvantage of this method is the time and effort taken in coding and testing.

  In general, program-controlled referential integrity is undepen-

---

[1]For a more complete description of referential integrity in DB2 (including restrictions), see *Relational Database Writings (1985-1989)*, by C. J. Date (Addison-Wesley, 1990).

dable. For correct and efficient operation, DBMS-controlled RI is preferable.

Efficiency Considerations

Detailed information about the implications of implementing DBMS-controlled referential integrity are covered in the appropriate IBM manuals. We summarize some general considerations here.

Maintenance. The process of application program maintenance (both fault diagnosis and system enhancement) must include at least an overview of the database design, including table relationships and their correspondence to the enterprise data model. Even a cursory review of the database design should uncover the primary and foreign key definitions. Thus the maintenance effort is expanded beyond the program listing.

Unknown I/O. Implementing primary and foreign keys in effect requests that DB2 manage all I/O involved in maintaining referential integrity relationships. This means that application program queries may no longer be tuneable; in fact, single queries may now begin to take up much more time and resources than previously. This may be an important concern in developing or tuning an on-line system.

Additional program logic. If DBMS-controlled RI is not used, application programs are now responsible for maintaining the relationships. This is usually done by adding the appropriate SQL statement that simulate RI processing. Although the amount of I/O and CPU used will be roughly equal to that DB2 would have used, there is one great disadvantage to this method: the additional SQL statements, SQLCODE checking, and program logic required will make the program longer, leading to a larger load module and larger DB2 Plan. Apart from simply requiring more memory to execute, program testing now becomes more tedious.

Testing and test plans. How does one test whether a program correctly identifies and deals with RI relationships? Clearly, the most complete way to test these conditions is to create test tables with the appropriate data. This task is nontrivial, as it requires the tester to know what the various possible conditions are that might occur in the relationships among the tables, create test data that tests these conditions, and interpret whether the program has in fact performed correctly in each situation.

MAINTENANCE PROCEDURES

No One Seems to Be Ready

Few shops planning on implementing DB2 stop to consider that their maintenance procedures for DB2 programs will be markedly different from standard maintenance. Although this topic is covered in more detail in Chapters 3 and 4, we will discuss some of the basic issues here.

Standard Maintenance

While there is probably no such thing as standard maintenance, we will consider common DP system problems and their solution(s). (System enhancements is sometimes considered a part of maintenance: we will not be covering that topic here.) In general, the most common problem situation and its resolution can be described in the following broad terms.

- *Problem detection.* The term problem detection usually takes the form of an application program abend. Some of my favorite abend codes include S0C4 (addressing exception or storage violation), S0C7 (invalid data), and S0CF (division by zero). I use the term "favorite" because, in this author's opinion, *none of these abends should have occurred* in a properly written program. Another, less common occurrence is for a user to call the developers and complain about a reporting error, or a "screen" error. Such errors can be difficult to replicate.

  Note that problem detection is an *active* process, in that the problem makes itself known immediately (sometimes with catastrophic results). The maintainers are well aware of the existence of the problem and need do little searching for its nature.

- *Change control.* The next step, this involves withdrawal of a program from its Production library to the appropriate Test library for analysis. Hopefully this will be a well-controlled process, as it wouldn't do for several copies of the program to be maintained simultaneously by different maintainers. Only one copy of a Production program should be allowed to exist in the Test environment. As this is often an impossible goal to achieve in a large shop, the solution is to purchase a sophisticated change management product.

- *Problem analysis.* Initial analysis of a problem is usually directed at its symptoms. For example, the typical B37 problem (insufficient DASD space) will probably involve program I/O (always output!), so the maintainer will concentrate efforts on gathering information on allocated DASD space and expected I/O volume counts, rather than program processing logic. More complex problems may involve attempted replication of the problem, running a standard set of test data through the program, and running the program in a Test environment using a debugging tool.

- *Problem solution and testing.* Most DP problems are solved relatively soon after their occurrence, although this is usually eased by standard tools that report on program abends, their occurrence, and their probable cause. Still, once the probable solution is found, the maintainer must test the fixed program. This may involve running the program with a standard set of test data. This is sometimes called *regression testing.*

- *Change control.* This last step moves the program from the Test environment back to Production for execution.

Again, while these steps are not necessarily the same for all common DP problems, they do represent a common methodology of problem detection, analysis, and solution. The DBMS environment, however, has changed this.

DB2 Maintenance

DB2 is one of many DBMSs that are available to DP shops. As such, the following comments apply equally to most DBMS environments. Unique DB2 situations and problems are mentioned specifically.

- *Fault diagnosis.* Today's data processing applications are designed differently from those of the previous decades. Many considerations hold that weren't even considered before, such as the following:

    - *Complete internal data validation.* Most applications are now designed to completely validate all input data. This type of validation includes validity checks, range checks, checks for reasonableness, cross-footing, and sometimes batch totaling. This minimizes or eliminates data exception abends.

- *"Lights out" operation.* Under this theory, applications are expected to be built so that human beings will not be required to intervene in their operation. This means that programs are expected to intercept and handle most error situations and take some default or expected corrective action. This may include printing an exception report, correcting data, or notifying other systems or users of the error.

- *Distributed data and distributed processing.* This means that program data may be spread across several hardware platforms, perhaps across a network. In addition, processing itself may be split or shared among several programs or copies of a single program.

- *On-line, context-sensitive help.* Users of on-line systems are requesting this feature that allows them to get assistance from the program itself (or some other system) if they encounter a problem. Incorrectly entered data should be highlighted, along with an accompanying message explaining the data in error, and examples of valid data or likely mistakes.

- *"Nonfatal" fatal errors.* Interfaces to I/O subsystems or database management systems are usually handled using a subroutine call. After issuing the call, the program is responsible for checking the Status Code returned with the call to determine success or failure. (In DB2 this is handled with the SQLCODE and SQLWARN fields in the SQLCA). Early DBMSs returned three classes of status code: *success, unable-to-process*, and *fatal error.*

  The fatal error status code category embodies much more now. It includes several SQLCODEs that do not indicate fatal errors. Some of these are Timeout, Deadlock, and Resource Unavailable. Programs are now expected to handle these exceptions. In the case of Deadlock, for example, the program may be expected to reattempt the Unit of Work. In the case of Resource not Available, the program may be expected to complete any processing possible without the requested resource.

These additional considerations make it much more difficult to detect the occurrence of errors, inasmuch as it is now a *passive* process. Further, it now becomes the responsibility of the *program* to determine which of many situations now constitutes a fatal error.

- *Multienvironment change control.* This covers several topics.
    - Many shops have more than simply Test and Production environments—they have included a new, intermediate environment, sometimes called Quality Control or Test/Production. This new environment is meant to be a pristine one in which developers can pilot or parallel test new production applications without disruption to current Production. This results in a much more complex Change Control process, as programs must be migrated across several environments.
    - Many shops have networks that utilize distributed processing and distributed data. Several programs, or many copies of the same program, may now participate in data processing. If an error occurs in one of these programs, they must <u>all</u> be included in any problem analysis.
- *Problem analysis.* With passive problem detection, shops now require more sophisticated methods of detecting and analyzing problem symptoms. When a (possible) error occurs, what status information should be kept? Where should it be stored? Should the program or programs be allowed to continue processing?

  Shops now require advanced tools to assist in problem analysis, perhaps using expert systems technology or artificial intelligence techniques.
- *Problem solution.* Problem solving capability is now a complicated mixture of application program logic, expert system tool, and debugging artistry. Problems are rarely the simple ones of the past (see our previous discussion of the B37) and involve data from multiple environments. Once a maintainer develops a hypothesis about the cause of a problem, they must prove that this really *is* the problem.
- *Regression testing.* This is a new name for an old technique. Regression testing involves collecting a complete set of data that *defines* program correctness, and using it to verify that changes made to certain sections of a program have not affected processing in other sections. The tester gathers test data together, runs the program, and stores the results of the test on a permanent media such as DASD.

This allows the results of later tests to be compared using the computer rather than doing it by hand.

- *Multienvironment change control.* As described above, the changed program (or programs) must now be migrated through several environments and placed in the target Production environments. Sometimes additional tests are required. In addition, each environment may have different versions of programs installed.

Many DB2 systems are now being implemented and must take the preceding scenarios into account. The job of the DB2 system maintainer is complex, and DP shops are not anticipating the possible obstacles this may cause to quick, effective implementation.

TESTING

As mentioned in a previous section, the existence of DB2 (and DBMSs in general) in an application system changes the way maintenance and program testing is done. In this section we will discuss the specific modifications required for test plans and test procedures.

Program Logic Changes

Programs must now handle special DBMS status codes, many of which are nonfatal in nature. Among the more popular of these DB2 SQLCODEs are -911 (Deadlock or Timeout) and -904 (Resource not Available). (These were mentioned briefly in the previous section.) These conditions may occur after any executable SQL statement, and must be coded for in the program logic. Many shops have standard program sections that are to be included in every program to handle these conditions in the appropriate manner.

Apart from simply handling these conditions in the code, the programmer must test that they are handled correctly. This leads to an interesting type of testing wherein the programmer (or tester) must somehow replicate or simulate conditions that rarely occur. Deadlock is one of these.

Although it is possible to create other applications whose only reason for existence is to cause timeouts and deadlocks for testing purposes, an alternate way of simulating these during unit testing is to insert special logic in the program that resets the SQLCODE to one of the offending codes on a random basis (say, 5 percent of the time) and does a ROLLBACK. This will cause the program to encounter and handle the simulated errors. Prior to moving the program to Production the code should be "logically" removed, either by commenting-out or by setting a switch. This switch (call it TESTING) should be set to NO in production, so that the error codes will not be generated. It can then easily be set to YES in Test to verify program logic correctness.

Application Test Planning

Test planning, or the creation of formal test plans, is too often included only as an afterthought in the development life cycle. Many so-called DP professionals regard testing as an *art*. Before we review common testing methods, however, here are a few words about *categories* of tests.

Testing is generally thought of as proceeding from the bottom up; that is, first the program is tested, then a string of programs, then the entire subsystem, and so on. Customary terms for these categories of tests are as follows:

- *Unit test.* A test of a single program.
- *String test.* A test of the ability of a set of programs to pass data to one another.
- *Concurrency test.* A test of a program's ability to perform concurrent processing of transactions entered simultaneously from several terminals. This type of testing is very common in the CICS environment.
- *Integration test.* Simultaneously testing several programs in an application when integrated as a system.
- *Regression test.* Testing a system to ensure that a change to one part of the system does not cause an undesired change in another part.
- *Stress test.* Testing the entire system under peak volume conditions to measure system stress.
- *Capacity planning test.* A test to see if an application system can meet desired transaction loads.

High-volume testing such as stress and regression tests requires a different set of capabilities than those needed for interactive unit testing. Such testing requires a structured set of functions to move the test program or programs through the six testing phases. The tester can then use the data of each test phase as the building block for the next. For example, unit test data can be easily replicated to create multiterminal data for concurrency testing. Unit test data from several programs can be easily merged to create integration test data for the entire application.

For thorough system testing and quality assurance, a production environment should be used (or simulated) without using the physical environment. A transaction-driven architecture may be used to recreate the actual production performance characteristics in test, emulating the transaction mix in a multiterminal system.

Test procedures. The ultimate test procedure is one that investigates all possible combinations of input conditions. Usually this is not possible. To approach this goal, one may attempt to assemble a set of test cases that have a reasonable probability of detecting errors, should any exist. One caveat: testing can prove that errors exist—it cannot prove that errors *do not* exist. A test plan should be designed, therefore, to be as comprehensive as possible and feasible in attempting to detect errors.

A single test case should have three properties:

- *Sufficiency.* The test case should completely and fully test for the presence of errors (*bugs*) either in a specific portion of the program logic or in a subset of possible input data or conditions.

- *Necessity.* The test case should specifically test one or more of the *user requirements* making up a part of the design specifications.

- *Informative.* The test case should unambiguously provide results that allow the tester to conclude that *no errors* exist either in the section of program logic or subset of input data or conditions tested.

What follows is a review of the three most common unit test plan methodologies, and some recommendations as to how DB2 application considerations should be integrated into them.

Equivalence partitioning. With this strategy, testers separate (*partition*) the complete set of possible input data conditions into two or more sets. Each set would contain values (or sets of values) that have the following property:

- *Equivalence.* All values (or sets of values) in the partition are equivalent in the sense that if one test case detects a certain error, all other cases in the same partition are expected to detect the same error. Conversely, if one test case does not detect a possible error, no other case in the same partition would be expected to detect that particular error. This set of test cases is called a *class.*

To generate test cases with this methodology, first one must identify the equivalence classes. This is driven by the program or system specification. Each requirement of the specification differentiates between valid and invalid inputs, valid and invalid outputs, or valid and invalid processing. The test planner uses this distinction to identify equivalence classes by stating all possible conditions, then dividing them into valid and invalid cases.

Sometimes cases will overlap. For example, consider an input field where valid inputs are in a certain numeric range. In this instance, the test planner would consider all values within the range to be in a single *valid equivalence class.* Values outside the range, however, may either be placed in a single *invalid equivalence class,* or in two such classes, one class of values below the valid range, one class of values above the valid range. In situations like this, we recommend using two equivalence classes.

Equivalence partitioning has some disadvantages. This method tends to overlook certain types of test cases that test several conditions at once. It also sometimes fails in situations where data or conditions are mutually dependent.

Boundary value analysis. Similar to equivalence partitioning, this method concentrates on dividing test cases into classes that test similar conditions. Each class is then considered to represent a set (or *space*) of all possible test conditions, and data are prepared that test the *boundaries* of that space. Examples should serve to clarify this.

- If an input field requires valid values that fall within a specified range, the values within that range are included into a class. The boundaries of this class would then be the lowest and highest valid values in the class. Test cases would then include both the highest and lowest values (those at the boundary), an invalid value slightly lower than the lowest value, and an invalid value slightly higher than the highest value (those immediately outside the boundary).

- If a process consists of one or more repetitions of a specific condition (reading a record from a file, for example), the various conditions (one record read, two records read, and so on, up to some maximum allowable number of records read) are grouped into a class. Test cases would then include occurrences of a single record, and of many records (conditions at the boundary). Additional test cases would include *no records* and some number of records greater than the maximum allowed (conditions immediately outside the boundary).

Boundary value analysis is most practical when test cases are clearly defined and unambiguous. It fails when combinations of input data or processing events overlap. The last method attempts to solve these thorny problems.

Cause-effects lists and graphs. A cause-effect graph is a diagram that is developed from program or process specifications. It is an extension of an old friend, the program flow chart. Many CASE tools include these as options when designing applications, and allow the tester to divide programs (or systems) into manageable, testable pieces. Each piece is then analyzed for *causes* and *effects.* A cause is a distinct input condition or an equivalence class of input conditions. An effect is an output condition or a system transformation (a lingering effect that an input has on the state of the program or system). For example, if a transaction causes a master file to be updated, the alteration to the master file is a system transformation; a confirmation message would be an output condition.

Causes and effects are identified by reading the program or system specification and recognizing words or phrases that specify causes and effects. Each cause and effect is then identified as a distinct test case and included on a list. The lists of programs that interface with one another should overlap. These lists may then be compared for matching conditions, resulting in a combination of overlapping lists. This allows us to reduce the total number of test cases.

A total test planning strategy. These test planning methods may be combined into an overall strategy. Each will contribute its own individual set of useful test cases, with no one method being sufficient in and of itself. Testers should link the appropriate methods together, following these guidelines:

- If the specification contains mixtures of various independent input conditions, start with cause-effect lists.

- Use boundary value analysis. This method will produce a set of additional test conditions, many or all of which can be merged or derived from cause-effect lists.

- Identify valid and invalid equivalence classes for input and output conditions.

- Compare test conditions across interfacing programs, combining cause-effect lists so that multiple programs may be tested at the same time (in sequence).

DB2 application testing considerations. As DB2 is a database management system, applications that access DB2 must consider the following general situations common to DBMSs:

- *Status code checking.* In DB2 this refers to the SQLCODE and SQLWARN fields of the SQLCA. Programs should check these fields after every *executable* SQL statement. Test cases must generate possible codes for each equivalence class.

- *Handling nonfatal "fatal" errors.* Many SQLCODEs indicate system errors that may not be considered fatal. These include indications that resources are not available (-904, -923, -924), that a deadlock or timeout occurred (-911, -913), or that some error has transpired that does not preclude the successful execution of further SQL statements (-901). These errors should not cause program abnormal termination and may require special coding.

- *Synchpoint processing.* This refers to the externalization of database updates, and the logging of the current unit of work as being complete. In DB2 programs this is done using the COMMIT statement. Note that COMMIT is invalid in IMS or CICS programs, as the IMS Checkpoint and CICS Synchpoint commands perform this function. Certain types of programs may need to be coded as *restartable,* meaning that synchpoint processing must be tested to see if the program and the associated I/O subsystem and database management system (if any) coordinate the synchpoint or rollback process correctly.

In addition to these general considerations, the following are some of the DB2-specific circumstances that should be tested:

- *Referential integrity.* This refers to the case where business data relationships have been included in the application logic. Examples include testing for the existence of rows in one table with foreign keys that correspond to the primary key of a row in another table, this check taking place before table update (or row deletion).

- *Connection failure.* It is possible for programs to begin execution without either the DB2 subsystem or the connection to it already established. This is particularly true for IMS batch message programs (BMPs). In this case, the program will be informed of the problem (via SQLCODE) after invoking the first executable SQL statement.

- *Deadlock and timeout.* DB2 applications may be informed at any time (via SQLCODE) that they have been chosen as the "victim" of a deadlock, and that the current unit of work has been rolled back. This results in all DB2 updates being undone, along with all IMS database and CICS-related work also rolled back. In addition, all DB2 cursors are closed. This is not a fatal situation; generally, all that is necessary is to re-execute the current transaction from the beginning of the program logic or from the most recent checkpoint, synchpoint, or commit point. Still, this condition may occur at any time, so test cases should be developed that verify that programs can handle this condition.

Creating DB2 Test Data

Test data for DB2 is more difficult to create than are standard files for simpler program tests. Not only must testers create and modify tables, they must also consider testing for possible referential integrity situations. Many on-line editing tools now exist for creating test data and test files (ISPF, for example). For DB2 programs, testers have the following alternatives:

- *Use SPUFI.* In this scenario, the tester uses SPUFI and one or more CREATE and INSERT SQL statements to create test tables and populate them with data. Regrettably, the syntax of the INSERT statement requires that data be inserted to a table column by column. This can be very tedious, especially if the data already exists on flat files somewhere.

- *Use a utility.* Assuming you can learn the syntax of either LOAD utility or DXT control statements, this allows you to copy data from a flat file to a DB2 table. This assumes that you have the appropriate authority to do so, and that you do not require complicated data subset processing such as record selection based upon multiple fields or data conversion. Such things are still possible, but the control statements to do this are cryptic.

- *Use an on-line editing tool.* By far the best choice, several third-party tools exist. They allow a full-screen edit capability, so that you can edit and browse DB2 table data and make changes on-line. Several tools come equipped with formatted data presentation schemes that display column attributes, and allow copying and moving of blocks of rows.

- *Download data from the mainframe.* Assuming you are developing in the microcomputer environment and have a micro-to-mainframe connection available, you may choose to store your test data on the mainframe, perhaps as a subset of production data. When required, you access the host through a network connection, download the data to your microcomputer, and test there.

- *Use a test data generator.* Several CASE tools are available that generate the appropriate test data based on a system or application design. Some of these tools have options that generate DBMS-specific test data as well, and even provide written test plans to follow.

These are the chief alternatives for generating DB2-specific test data. As mentioned above the best alternative is using an on-line editor that allows full-screen edit of DB2 tables. This provides the tester with a way to customize test data and interactively modify test conditions and program logic.

Testing DB2 programs

Testing in general is a laborious process. Typical test plans (mentioned above) require the tester to run a series of tests, check the results, run another series, and so on. Adding a DBMS into this equation means both providing DBMS test data and checking database updates for correctness. As before, the tester's best tool is an on-line editor for DB2 tables.

Another useful tool is the Interactive Debugger. This tool allows the tester to analyze a program interactively during the testing process. When errors occur the tester may validate input and output data, display the values of program variables and data areas, make changes to the program logic (either temporary or permanent), recompile the program, and continue testing. Such tools are becoming extremely popular in the microcomputer-based development environment, as DB2-, IMS-, and CICS-simulation software matures. (For more information on this environment see Chapter 4.)

Chapter 3

Impact on Staffing

THE IS STAFF: EVOLUTION, OR REVOLUTION?

A Shifting of DP Staff Roles

RDBMSs already exist for microcomputers. Indeed, several PC products are available that can be used to code, debug, and test COBOL DB2 applications that may then be ported to the mainframe. This change in the way database applications can be developed means changing the way we allocate resources (people) to a project.

In addition to the arrival of DB2, computer-assisted software engineering (CASE) is now coming of age. Soon, integrated tools will be available that automate every phase of the systems development life cycle. Developers will use these tools on microcomputers along with fourth- and fifth-generation languages, local area networks (LANs), and distributed systems.

All of these changes mean that programmers and analysts will require less skill in the following traditional areas.

- *Procedural programming.* As integrated CASE tools come of age, computer programming practices will change radically. Fewer and fewer programs will be written using procedural languages such as COBOL and PL/I. Programs will be written using fourth-generation languages, or generated using the code generation facilities of CASE tools. As programmers migrate from COBOL to 4GLs and CASE tools, programming skills will become less useful.

- *Applications expertise.* Many data processing professionals consider their expertise in one or more application areas as a critical success factor. An analyst, for example, may have several years of experience developing payroll applications or inventory systems. This type of experience will be less useful in the future, as prototyping tools and "application generators" become available.

- *Human-to-human communications.* Speaking and listening skills are usually lumped together and called "oral communications skills." These skills are usually used by analysts as they meet with users to solve the users' business needs. As users and analysts communicate with one another, they jointly develop some kind of system request document describing the functions of the required system.

  In the future, analysts and users will not require these skills. Replacing them will be prototyping and distributed processing. Prototyping is a relative newcomer to the systems development life cycle. In this phase, the analyst (or the programmer) meets with the user to acquire a preliminary description of the target system. By means of an interactive prototyping tool, this rudimentary system is then constructed and demonstrated to the user. The user analyzes the prototype and makes suggestions regarding system changes. Based on the user's feedback, the programmer or analyst updates the prototype. Continuing in this manner, the user and analysts iterate the enhancements to the prototype. During this process the prototype functions as a go-between; it serves as a model of the target system; communications about requirements are couched in terms of the prototype, and the user and analyst need not create tons of documentation.

  Distributed processing will allow the user to control his or her access to data. One form of this involves downloading data from a mainframe database to a local network or personal computer. The user then invokes a local software package to manipulate the data, and then (optionally) uploads the (changed) data back to the mainframe. All this can be done without the intervention of the programmer or analysts. All that is required is for the user to purchase an appropriate software package.

- *Business systems skills.* Every business has some automated systems. As employees work for a company over a period of time they become acquainted with many of these systems, either by developing or by maintaining them. This experience with particular systems (or programs) serves the DP staff well in that expertise in some systems is transferable to other systems. The input files to one system, for example, may be output files from another system. Many analysts on development projects use their past experience with similar systems to do several things: estimate work effort for programming tasks; develop file and database designs; and conform to various standards such as report layouts, screen designs, and service-level agreements.

In the future, this experience will be far less valuable. At the moment, DB2 systems are being developed by people with little DB2 applications expertise. This is partly due to the fact that brand new systems are being developed.

In the future, therefore, more emphasis will be placed on prototyping, PC-based software, data modeling, and third-party software. This applies to the present staff as well as to future staff. This upheaval in the knowledge and skill profiles of DP personnel will require revolutionary ways of dealing with them. Some of these problems are discussed in the following sections.

The Changing DP Staff Profile

As we mature into the 1990s, we must alter the stereotypical way we view DP job titles and job descriptions. What follows is a short list of standard DP job descriptions from the early 1980s and some notes on how they will change (or already have changed).

Manager of Data Processing

Old: Reports to the VP for administration.

New: In more and more progressive companies the manager of data processing reports to a new position: the chief information officer (CIO), who reports directly to the president of the company.

Old: Manages the supervisor of systems analysis, supervisor of programming, supervisor of machine operations, supervisor of production control.

New: Many organizations have moved away from a totally centralized DP shop approach toward a more division-centered or user-centered one. This typically includes companies whose user communities are geographically spread out, as well as multinational corporations. This decentralization allows each division or department to develop specific expertise in developing systems and relieves upper management of the burden of maintaining a single, massive DP organization.

As the users become decentralized, so does the DP organization and its supporting hardware. This sometimes leads to separate, distinct DP organizations, each servicing one particular user or set of users. Each organization may then consist of a manager, supporting supervisors, and other DP personnel.

Further, as we march into the networking and distributed processing world, the manager of DP will probably manage the *supervisor of network control* and the *supervisor of distributed database services*. These positions are somewhat self-explanatory; however, please note that both must be concerned with intercommunication among multiple hardware platforms, multiple DBMSs, and perhaps trans-border data flow.

Old: Responsibilities include management specifics of DP activities. Technical duties include review and evaluation of computer systems, requests for additional services, new equipment or vendors' proposals, equipment and personnel utilization, education, and training.

New: In addition to the above, the manager of DP will review and evaluate requests for outside services. This includes contract programming, consulting, outsourcing, and system integration. Also, as DP organizations have grown, it has become apparent that there is a need for ongoing training, both technical and business related. These needs are sometimes handled by an internal training organization headed by a manager of technical training. Occasionally this will include a provision for the acquisition of training from outside vendors.

Old: Administrative duties include budgeting, personnel recruitment, evaluation, policy matters, departmental coordination, and planning.

New: Although the typical manager's duties have not changed much, the new DP manager must take into account the personalities and egos of computer people. Much has been written on this subject recently, and managers are becoming increasingly aware of some of these new management techniques.

Old: Desirable qualifications include a business-oriented degree, specialized training in the currently installed hardware system, if possible, and five to ten years of directly related experience.

New: Managers are becoming less dependent on specific hardware platforms and their attendant software and DBMSs. There will be many different hardware platforms in the DP shop of the future (mainframe, minicomputer, and micro). To combat the dependence upon a specific machine, IBM has proposed a set of standards, interfaces, and protocols called Systems Application Architecture (SAA). As we move into the 1990s, the DP manager will need less specialized knowledge about hardware.

To counterbalance this, the DP manager must have a broader business background. Initially, data processing systems supported only a very narrow spectrum of applications: at first accounting; later, personnel and payroll. Today, DP applications span the gamut of business systems from the traditional (general ledger, payables, receivables, materials management, payroll) to the modern (point of sale, electronic data interchange, airline reservations, industrial process control, CAD/CAM) to the futuristic (multimedia imaging systems, Strategic Defense Initiative (SDI) battle management, voice-actuated data input). Such areas of business that a company enters will require the DP manager to acquire a background of knowledge and expertise in order to better manage personnel and resources.

Supervisor of Systems Analysis

Old: Reports to the manager of DP.

New: As hinted previously, this supervisor may not exist as a single individual; rather, systems analysis, design, and development will be bundled into a single group of people that is in toto responsible to a particular user community. Using matrix management techniques, this group may then be responsible to several supervisors.

Old: Supervises two or more senior systems analysts.

New: The job of senior systems analyst (described next) has changed radically in the last decade. As analysts have taken a larger role in multisystem applications, networks, distributed database, and micro-mainframe usage, they may now report to several managers. Using matrix management techniques, supervisors of systems analysis now cross-report to one another and direct the work of many subgroups.

Old: Responsibilities include providing technical and analytical assistance in the identification and solution of data systems problems; defining information requirements and prescribing procedures; organizing studies on systems matters, including resource costs of time, personnel, and money; and evaluating the advantages of and alternative efforts to management.

New: With the explosion of new data processing hardware and software of the past decade, supervisors of systems analysis now rarely provide specific technical assistance unless it is within their own area(s) of expertise. More and more this supervisor is responsible for budget analysis, analysis of vendor proposals, and management of external resources such as outsourced vendor personnel and system integration staff.

Old: Desirable qualifications include a business-oriented degree, specialized training in systems and pertinent hardware capabilities, and four to seven years of direct experience.

New: Again, this supervisor needs less specialized hardware or software training, and more knowledge and experience in managing people. In addition, a business-oriented degree helps when attempting to integrate a wide set of diverse applications into the specific company's environment.

Senior Systems Analyst

Old: Reports to supervisor of systems analysis.

New: As described previously, new areas of expertise are forcing senior systems analysts to specialize in particular hardware platforms, application areas, and even specific software packages. This and the concept of *matrix management* dictate that analysts may report to several superiors. For example, a senior systems analyst with expertise in DASD capacity planning and financial systems may support data center operations and financial application development, thus encouraging reporting to both the manager of operations and a supervisor of systems analysis for financial systems.

Old: Supervises one or more systems analysts.

New: Little has changed in this area in the past decade. Many data processing development projects are managed with a standard hierarchy of line management and technical support. In a few cases, though, the concept of Joint Application Development (JAD) leads to a single systems analyst supervising a team of analysts, designers, database analysts, users, and managers. This relatively new methodology has received some attention in the trade press.

Old: Responsibilities include providing technical and analytical assistance in analysis and design of data processing systems; assistance in defining information repositories and data flows; help in conducting studies on systems matters, including resource costs of time, personnel, and money; develops and presents alternatives to management.

New: These responsibilities have been expanded to include attention to matters typically left to management, such as performance appraisal, proposal preparation and presentation, and evaluation of hardware and software tools.

Old: Desirable qualifications include a business-oriented degree, specialized training in systems and pertinent hardware capabilities, and two to five years of direct experience.

New: The business-oriented degree is becoming more important, as companies acquire other companies and expand internationally. This forces middle management to become more aware of what the business is about, in terms of both integrating diverse applications and consolidating disparate or dissimilar business data models.

Supervisor of Programming

Old: Reports to the manager of DP.

New: This was the standard in many organizations where the data processing department was organized traditionally. In a more modern, decentralized organization, there may not be a single manager of DP. Further, programmers and senior programmers may work for several teams on several projects simultaneously. Programmers will then typically report to one or more project leaders, who will manage their work.

Old: Supervises two or more senior programmers.

New: The title "senior programmer" is an old one. In the modern data processing shop, programming itself has taken on a wide variety of meanings, covering a broad base of knowledge, skills, expertise, and experience. A supervisor of programmers has almost become a contradiction in terms.

Old: Responsibilities include providing technical and administrative assistance in the development of new programs and the maintenance of operational programs. Also schedules revisions to operational programs.

New: These responsibilities have been shifted to several kinds of technical specialists, including network analysts, database analysts, system administrators, and quality assurance staff.

Old: The candidate for this position must be knowledgeable in the details of the databases, programs, and products of all systems. Qualifications may specify a business degree as desirable but not mandatory, specialized training in appropriate hardware systems and programming languages, and four to six years direct programming experience.

New: As this position has diffused into those of several other staff members, these qualifications are no longer relevant.

Supervisor of Machine Operations

Old: Reports to the manager of DP.

New: In traditional organizations this reporting structure is sound. In more modern DP shops (especially those that have decentralized or distributed DP operations) each hardware complex may require separate management. These supervisors may report both to a divisional data processing manager and to a central point (probably a chief information officer).

Old: Supervises shift leaders, tape librarians, data entry and support equipment supervisors, software support activities (in some instances), database administration (in some instances), computer performance monitors, and distribution personnel.

New: This still holds true, with the addition of new hardware (such as magnetic tape cartridges, CD-ROM storage, terminal networks, and satellite communication networks) and new software (such as distributed database management systems, I/O subsystems, and third-party application packages).

Old: Responsibilities include supervision of the I/O control function; ensuring effective utilization of EDP equipment and personnel in accordance with schedules, operation run books, standards manuals, and equipment operation manuals; maintaining logs of operation, equipment utilization, downtime and maintenance, tape library controls, and input/output.

New: Also includes managing and evaluation of hardware alternatives, parallel testing various hardware and software configurations, and monitoring network activity.

Old: The candidate must be acquainted with file structures, procedures, and products of major applications systems. Qualifications should include some college courses as desirable, specialized training in the current hardware system, as well as four to seven years of directly related experience.

New: College courses are becoming less important for operations staff as the number and complexity of hardware platforms and software packages increases. Far more important is specialized training.

The Salary Barrier

Question: How will managers structure salaries if two-year people have more valuable skills than twenty-year people?

The entire issue of salary administration is commonly tied to the performance appraisal process. In most IS shops, appraisals (or evaluations) are performed once a year, with salary changes depending on the outcome. Measurement and judgment of a data processing professional's performance are usually based on objective criteria such as tasks performed on time or quality of work completed.

It will be extremely important for management to review the performance appraisal process with regard both to how employees are measured and how the results are used to judge their performance. The measurement mechanism may need to be revised to reflect an emphasis on behaviors rather than results. This somewhat paradoxical idea causes supervisors to concentrate on managing what employees *do* rather than on the results they produce. Results themselves cannot be managed—supervisors are limited to *reacting* to results after the fact, restricting their ability to improve an employee's performance. Behaviors, on the other hand, *can* be managed. A supervisor can observe and document an employee's behavior, gauge its appropriateness to the situation, and recommend any corrective action.

For more information on management of results and behaviors, see any recent book on performance appraisal.

The Training Issue

Question: Which staff members will be trained, and in what?

Training budgets are usually limited. Installation of a new RDBMS will strain these budgets even further as programmers must learn SQL and relational programming basics, analysts must learn DBMS features such as referential integrity and performance issues, database administration staff must incorporate relational databases into the corporate data model, and system administrators must acquire third-party tools.

Part of this problem revolves around the issue of how the staff is allocated to the development and maintenance operations. (This is covered in the following section.) The greatest training problem appears to be a budgetary one, although the political question of which employees will get advanced training remains.

Development or Maintenance

Questions: How should the maintenance and development efforts be managed? Should they be in separate departments or the same department? Should they have different managers? What mixtures of staff expertise should be assigned?

With two-thirds of the data processing staff already devoted to the maintenance activity, perhaps this question seems irrelevant. Yet, with the advent of applications that access relational databases, the performance of the maintenance staff will have an ever-increasing effect on the ability of the data processing department to deliver systems that work. This puts a lot of pressure on the development staff, for they must now be responsible for higher quality products. The maintenance staff feels pressure too, as they must support a rapidly growing number of relational applications.

Here are the two most common alternatives for managing these two diverse sets of employees:

- *Development staff, maintenance staff.* In this scenario, the development staff will need training in any CASE tools used for analysis, design, and prototyping. If few (or no) CASE tools are being used, the development staff must learn the shop's development methodology in addition to coding standards and testing procedures. Along with basic SQL they must also learn any rules of thumb (heuristics) regarding database design and query efficiency.

  The maintenance staff must be fluent in fault detection and diagnosis, sometimes requiring the use of third-party tools. They must also be aware of the business data model, so that changes to the model may be reflected in the application software. Occasionally they are called on to make enhancements to an existing system that may involve performance tuning. This may require considerable experience in efficiency techniques, including SQL coding alternatives.

  One disadvantage of this division is a political one: in many companies that have tried this option, the development staff seems to cultivate a we-are-better-than-you attitude toward the maintenance staff. This affects everyone's ability to get the job done, and sometimes even causes more capable staff members to gravitate out of the maintenance environment.

- *Maintenance by application area.* Here, each application area (financial, inventory, sales, and so on) develops systems and then accepts responsibility for maintaining them. Expertise developed during design, coding, and testing thus remains and is available during maintenance. No particular individuals are designated as maintenance staff.

  In many cases, companies find that this method causes each application area to develop pockets of internal expertise that are not transferable to other areas. Database administration support also tends to be local, with each area developing its own DBAs and systems administrators. These DBAs and administrators then find it difficult to coordinate their efforts, especially in system performance tuning.

Summary

Managers must plan for these changes before implementing a relational system. The entire applications development procedure will be changing, and this will affect staff skills, training, and performance.

Section II

DB2 Installation and Implementation

Chapter 4
Common Preimplementation Problems

As of this writing (Spring 1991), over 5,000 sites worldwide have installed one or more DB2 subsystems. Many of these IS shops encountered problems, 8either when first installing DB2 or during the design or implementation of the first DB2 application systems. These problems typically fell into the categories described in the following sections.

CHOOSING A RELATIONAL DBMS FOR THE WRONG REASONS

Many businesses choose a relational DBMS because it is the "thing to do." Many choose DB2 because DB2 is IBM's database manager of choice for the future, or because IBM recommended that they do so. The most enterprising shops are able to cost-justify installing DB2, although they sometimes forget to factor in the costs of staff training, additional required database administration overhead, necessary third-party tools, and additional DASD. Still, there is no doubt that relational database management systems are here to stay.

However, simply because a database management system is relational (or claims to be relational) does not necessarily mean that it is the correct choice, either for a set of application systems or as a standard for a business enterprise. Even the definition of the term *relational* is hotly debated. Opting for the more conservative course, we look to the father of the relational model, Edgar F. Codd.

Defining the Relational Model

In 1969 and 1970, Edgar Codd wrote two important papers[1,2] that formed the bases for what we now call the relational model. It is this model that so-called relational database management systems are measured against to determine whether they support the full functionality demanded.

In 1986, Codd[3] suggested 12 rules that determine to what extent a database management system is relational. These rules (along with a primary rule called Rule 0) were stated approximately as follows:

Rule 0: *Foundation rule.* Any system that is advertised as or is claimed to be a relational DBMS must manage databases entirely through its relational capabilities.

Rule 1: *Information rule.* All information in a relational database must be represented explicitly at the logical level in exactly one way by table values.

Rule 2: *Guaranteed access.* Each and every data value in a relational database must be guaranteed to be logically accessible by resorting to a combination of table name, column name, and primary-key value.

Rule 3: *Representation of null values.* The database management system must have a consistent method for representing null values.

Rule 4: *The system catalog.* The description of the database is represented dynamically at the logical level like ordinary data so that authorized users can apply the same (relational) language to its interrogation.

Rule 5: *Comprehensive data language.* No matter how many languages and interactive modes are supported, at least one language must

---

[1] Codd, E. F., "Derivability, Redundancy, and Consistency of Relations Stored in Large Data Banks", IBM Research Report RJ599 (August 1969).

[2] Codd, E. F, "A Relational Model of Data for Large Shared Data Banks", CACM 13, No. 6 (June 1970).

[3] Codd, E. F., "The 12 Rules for Determining How Relational a DBMS Product Is", TRI Technical Report EFC-6, May 1986.

be supported, expressible as character strings by some well-defined syntax that supports interactively by program: data definition; integrity rules; data manipulation; views; transaction boundaries; authorization rules.

Rule 6: *View updatability.* For each view, the DBMS must have a way of determining at view definition time whether the view can be used to insert rows, delete rows, or update which columns of its underlying base table(s) and store the results of this decision in the system catalog.

Rule 7: *Set operation.* The capability of operating on whole tables applies not only to retrieval but also to insertion, modification, and deletion of data.

Rule 8: *Physical data independence.* Interactive operations and application programs should not have to be modified whenever changes in internal storage structures or access methods are made to the database.

Rule 9: *Logical data independence.* Interactive operations and application programs should not have to be modified whenever changes to the base tables involving no loss of information are made to the database.

Rule 10: *Integrity independence.* Interactive operations and application programs should not have to be modified whenever changes to integrity rules defined with the data language and stored in the system catalog are made to the database.

Rule 11: *Distribution independence.* The data language implemented by the database management system must support the ability to distribute the database without requiring changes to be made to application programs.

Rule 12: *Nonsubversion.* If a DBMS has a low-level (procedural) language, it should not allow it to subvert or bypass the integrity and security rules expressed in the high-level relational language and stored in the system catalog.

In *The Relational Model for Database Management: Version 2* (Addison-Wesley, 1990) Codd described the latest form of his relational model, called

RM/V2 (relational model version 2). It consists of 333 features. Readers interested in the latest foundations of the relational model are invited to study this book.

Choosing a Database Management System

Choosing DB2 as a company's DBMS simply because it may follow most of the rules of the relational model is like buying a hammer and then looking for things to pound in, whether they be nails or not. As with most things, one must choose the right tool for the right job. What are relational database management systems good for?

The relational DBMS. Relational DBMSs work best in the ad hoc environment. Here, users typically ask what-if questions. Systems are designed to accept queries whose form, content, and syntax cannot be predicted during systems analysis. Such systems may even process queries *dynamically*, determining data access paths and database navigation criteria at the time of the query. The database management system provides set-at-a-time processing, permitting applications to be ignorant of data retrieval details.

Traditional DBMSs (hierarchical and network) work best in a transaction processing environment. Here, single queries are batched into similar queries, either by function or by application. These batches may then be sorted and matched against master databases. This record-at-a-time processing is very common in current systems, and would lead one to think that most (if not all) current systems would not run efficiently in an ad hoc environment.

DBMS purchasers, therefore, should first define what job they want to accomplish and then, after such an analysis, determine which products to buy. Cost-justification of a DBMS can be a long and difficult process but is a necessity for the enterprise.

An analogy can be drawn here to the difference between cars and transportation. What kind of car should you buy? Some people would only consider choosing between a Chevrolet and a Cadillac. These people are purchasing *cars*. Other people might choose between riding the bus, buying a Chevrolet, or acquiring a Chevrolet and a chauffeur. These people are purchasing *transportation*.

In terms of a DBMS, what are you buying? Are you buying a DBMS, or are you buying an efficient, effective method for storing and retrieving information that assists your company in meeting its business goals, both immediate and long-term? The answer to this question should help to determine your DBMS needs.

THE EVOLUTION OF THE INFORMATION SYSTEMS STAFF

Computer-Assisted Software Engineering (CASE) tools are now appearing on the scene. Soon, integrated CASE toolsets will be available that automate every phase of the systems development life cycle. These advances in software are matched by similar advances in available hardware. Application developers will use CASE tools on microcomputers along with fourth- and fifth-generation languages, local area networks (LANs), and distributed systems.

These advances will radically change the makeup of the IS staff. In particular, the following skills may no longer be needed:

- *Procedural programming.* Integrated CASE tools are taking the place of programming languages. Many of these tools contain code-generation facilities that create programs based on parameters set during systems design. While it is true that current system maintenance will require some programming expertise, this expertise will be limited to basic coding skills. Further, code re-engineering tools are beginning to appear that generate designs based on program code. Such designs then form a basis for system changes.

- *Applications expertise.* Many data processing professionals consider their expertise in one or more functional areas as a valuable skill. Knowledge of current financial systems, for example, is deemed an advantage for the analyst designing a new application that interfaces with the financial systems. These skills may be less valuable in the future as prototyping tools and Joint Application Development (JAD) shift the burden of system knowledge from the analyst to the user.

- *Human-to-human communications.* Determining and documenting user needs and system specifications has traditionally required both oral and written communications skills. In the future these skills will be less important as users design and build their own systems. Along with prototyping tools and JAD, users will utilize microcomputers to access and retrieve corporate data through networks for temporary storage locally. This data can then be massaged and processed using microbased software such as spreadsheets, word processing packages, and database management systems.

In the future, then, more emphasis will be placed on the following skills:

- *Use of CASE and re-engineering tools.* These tools will integrate automated functions that support the entire systems development life cycle. Analysts and designers will input requirements, costs, benefits, and feasibility information, and tools will output measurements of system interfaces and paybacks. This information may then be used as input to the analysis and design stages, as data and process flows from user requirements are compared with the corporate data model, producing program and module specifications. These specifications then automatically generate the required programs, test data, and implementation procedures.

- *Data modeling.* An adjunct to CASE tools, analysts will now be responsible for the creation and maintenance of the corporate business data model. This model, including a data dictionary of data items and relationships, will serve as a base for current and future systems.

- *Joint Application Development (JAD).* A process wherein users, analysts, designers, and management meet to jointly develop application requirements and specifications, JAD speeds up and organizes the development process. Some training is required for participants, but the results justify this initial investment.

- *Microcomputers and microbased software.* Probably the most obvious point, microcomputers have taken the country by storm. They serve as workstations for programmers, "smart terminals" for users, and sophisticated system monitors for operations personnel. A profusion of software is available, including database management systems that act like their mainframe cousins.

This upheaval in the knowledge and skill levels and profiles of DP personnel will require revolutionary ways of dealing with them. Some of the problems will be:

- How will managers structure salaries if two-year people have more valuable skills than ten-year people? What does "valuable" mean?

- Which staff members will be trained, and in what? Will advanced DB2 training be necessary?

- Should the staff be separated into maintenance and development departments, should they be commingled, or should each functional area maintain its own applications?

Managers must plan for these changes before implementing a relational system.

TRAINING FOR THE DB2 ENVIRONMENT

Although it is generally recognized that it is easier to learn SQL coding than (say) IMS coding, this is a far cry from saying that less *total* training will be required after implementing DB2. Organizations that use DB2 for new applications must now change the way they develop and maintain systems. Using the ad hoc environment is new and different, and is quite a change from the transaction processing systems to which the DP staff is accustomed.

What Is Changing

The relational model is not new. Unfortunately, few shops have really bought into such a nonhierarchical way of looking at data and processes. The result may be the development of hierarchical systems using DB2 as the DBMS. In this way any benefits of the relational model are somewhat negated. Therefore, before implementing a relational DBMS, an organization must acknowledge the usefulness of the relational model and find that it actually models their business needs. In addition, since little training is available in this area, organizations must be prepared to make a commitment to developing internal education or to searching out what is available in the marketplace. Some of the more important new concepts are described in the next section, along with recommended teaching methods and suggested audience.

DB2 objects and general concepts. This would encompass all DB2 objects and relationships that programmers, analysts, and DBAs would come into contact with, including the following:

- Storage Groups, Databases, Tablespaces, Tables, Views, Synonyms, Indexes, Database Request Modules (DBRMs), and Plans.

- Data Definition Language (DDL) for creating and altering such objects, including CREATE, ALTER, and DROP.

- Basic Data Manipulation Language (DML) for accessing these objects, including SELECT, UPDATE, and DELETE. Optionally include cursor processing (OPEN, FETCH, CLOSE).

- The DB2 Catalog Tables, sample queries for accessing them, and their relationship to the bind process.

- DB2 Utilities, including RUNSTATS, STOSPACE, LOAD, COPY, and REORG.

- Basic DB2 security, authorities, and privileges.

The suggested audience for these topics is everyone who would come into contact with DB2. This includes not only programmers, analysts, and DBAs, but also management and the user community. Such grounding in the basics is essential if users are to be included in application design, and managers are expected to appraise the performance of their subordinates.

The relational model and database design. Sometimes dismissed as merely theoretical, the relational model is the basis for the DB2 relational database management system. It provides an entirely new and different way at looking at data, data relationships, and data access. This causes changes in the way we look at the process of systems design. Many development methodologies require viewing the data in a hierarchical fashion, thus sometimes precluding the use of a relational model.

SQL efficiency and EXPLAIN. In general, queries issued from an application can be coded in several different ways. Some of these differences are trivial, such as the order of the columns retrieved from a table. Others are strikingly different, such as choosing a correlated sub-select rather than a JOIN. With several alternatives available, the programmer finds it difficult to choose the most efficient or best performing query. Therefore programmers and analysts should be aware of the various advantages and disadvantages of query types.

In addition to this, programmers, analysts, and DBAs should be familiar with the EXPLAIN feature. EXPLAIN may be invoked in several ways. It allows one to "ask" DB2 what methods will be employed to satisfy the query, as well as what access paths will be used to retrieve the data. This information includes index access, JOIN types, sorting, and tablespace access. Interpretation of EXPLAIN results is extremely useful, as it allows one to compare the results of several queries and choose the most appropriate one for a given situation.

Advanced SQL. Beyond the simple SELECT statement lies the arena of advanced SQL. Some of these concepts include simple JOINs, complex JOINs (such as the *outer JOIN* and *theta JOIN*), simple subSELECTS, correlated subSELECTS, and *dynamic SQL.* These statement types are very powerful in that they allow a user or application program to access multiple tables simultaneously in a single statement, with the database management system doing most of the work. Sometimes these statements are the most efficient choice for a particular data request. Programmers, analysts, and DBAs must be aware of the various combinations and how to interpret them.

Performance and tuning. Although system and database tuning is usually the territory of the system administrator or DBA, programmers and analysts can assist them in their quest for high performance. This requires the training described below.

- *DB2 data storage.* This includes page formats, including page header information, row storage and overhead, row identifiers (RIDs), space map pages, and freespace parameters; index structure, including leaf and nonleaf page usage, leaf subpages and locking considerations, and creation of index levels; and tablespace dataset allocation.

- *Plan optimization.* This includes the DB2 Catalog tables and what columns are updatable by users and utilities; the RUNSTATS and STOSPACE utilities, and when they should be used; the LOAD, COPY, and REORG utilities, how they work, and what they affect; the bind process (the Optimizer) and how it uses Catalog columns to choose data access paths; and the EXPLAIN feature, and how to interpret its results.

What Other Training Is on the Horizon

Although this was examined closely in Chapter 2, we will summarize here what training the DP staff will require in the future, as hardware, software, and methodology advances change the way we develop and maintain systems.

Systems development methodologies. As relational modeling becomes more common, and as systems get more complex, designers must depend more and more on using a set of standardized methods to develop systems. These methods, called *methodologies,* have been around for several decades (some were discussed in Chapter 1). As businesses move into the future, analysts and designers will require extensive training in these methodologies.

CASE tools. Mentioned in Chapters 1 and 2, CASE tools automate the systems development life cycle. At the time of this writing, no set of integrated tools has appeared that completely manages and automates systems analysts, design, construction, and implementation. Several well-known packages exist that automate major phases in the SDLC, but they are neither completely integrated nor easy to learn. This situation will influence which staff members get training for these packages.

Communications skills. Long overlooked in the scheme of things, basic oral and written communications skills may not be required in the early stages of requirements definition. This will be usurped by prototyping tools that allow the user to interactively define system specifications. Later phases in the development life cycle will also be heavily automated, limiting the need for human-to-human interaction.

Where communications skills will be *critical* will be in the business data modeling process. Developing a data model for the business enterprise requires an understanding of current systems, future trends, national and international businesses and economic trends, and so on. Acquiring this information will require a broad base of oral and written skills. Communicating the data to others will require this as well.

DASD USAGE IN THE DB2 ENVIRONMENT

In any type of system installation or conversion, developers make allowances for extra DASD requirements. These include the need for copies of production files, sort work space, database image copies, and the like. Implementation of DB2, however, requires just a bit more thought.

DB2 DASD Usage Differences

Many DBAs and system administrators seem to agree that DB2 implementations take up more DASD space than those using other database management systems. (Rumors of a "standard" conversion factor of 130 percent were common.) Why should this be so?

DASD tricks. Conventional wisdom asserts that DB2 database designers and implementers are using some favorite tricks to make systems run faster or perform better, resulting in additional required DASD capacity. These tricks include the following:

- *Denormalization.* A favorite heuristic of the DBA, this technique assumes that designers and analysts have been taught to fully normalize their database designs. It is rare that this full normalization is an efficient one to put into practice. DBAs usually manage to convince the designers to live with a bit of data redundancy in order to greatly reduce Joins and Tablespace Scans. This redundancy translates into more DASD space taken up by the tables.

- *Unusual space allocation.* DB2 database analysts and systems administrators have several options for allocating space for tables within a tablespace. Freespace can be distributed on a page-by-page basis, can be strewn across the tablespace in the form of empty pages, or both. As these parameters are respected only during running of the LOAD and REORG utilities, over time free space tends to fragment, causing performance problems. DBAs sometimes try to avoid this by allocating "a bit more" free space than would be required.

  Another interesting special case is when a table consists of rows that are frequently accessed or updated. To prevent one application's access from locking out other programs from other rows on the same page, the DBA has the option of defining the rows in such a way that only one row fits on a page. (This can be done by adding a column to the table that increases the row length beyond about 2,000 bytes.) The net effect is that only one row will fit on a 4K page, thus maximizing concurrency. Regrettably, this tactic is sometimes incredibly wasteful of DASD space.

- *Fooling the optimizer.* It is possible for someone with the proper authorization to change those columns in certain tables in the DB2 Catalog that are used by the DB2 Optimizer during *bind.* These columns (called *statistics*) contain values that allow the Optimizer to estimate how many rows will be accessed by a query, how many tablespace pages are expected to contain rows that satisfy the query, and how many I/Os will be required. During optimization DB2 makes certain assumptions about the distribution of data values in a table as it attempts to calculate a *cost* for each data access method.

  Occasionally these assumptions are invalid, and DB2 chooses an inefficient access method (perhaps it chooses a tablespace scan when indexed access would seem to be preferable). In some of these cases the DBA or system administrator may decide to change the statistics to reflect a more accurate picture of reality. Alternatively, they may decide to change the statistics to something wildly different from reality in order to force the Optimizer to choose a preferred access path. Warning: this extraordinary procedure should not be attempted without a great deal of DB2 expertise, including an in-depth understanding of the catalog.

Such fooling of the Optimizer sometimes requires that table rows be stored in the tablespace in some evenly distributed fashion. This may dictate that the DBA allocate extra free space, so that rows are more likely to be stored on preferred pages.

Other Differences

Another difference DBAs notice between IMS and DB2 is the relative sizes of the buffer pools. In IMS a two- or three-megabyte buffer pool is considered average. In DB2, however, buffer pools of 25 or 30 megabytes are not uncommon. This order of magnitude difference in buffer pool size really comes into play when the implementers must allocate DASD space for paging.

Another common occurrence when implementing DB2 is that organizations typically wish to convert databases from IMS-DB to DB2 tables. This may not be as simple as running DXT. Because several systems may interface to the databases in question, it may be necessary to have *both* IMS and DB2 versions of the database coexisting until the conversion is complete. This coexistence will require both DBMSs with their own logs, catalogs, database image copies, backups, and so on.

(A new product available along with DB2 V2R3 called the Data Propagator allows MVS/ESA to "shadow" IMS database updates in the DB2 environment within the same unit of work. This will assist developers that require support for IMS/DB2 coexistence. Still, additional DASD is required.)

In other words if you plan on implementing DB2 and converting IMS databases to DB2 tables, your long-term DASD requirements may need some looking into. Plan on plenty of cushion in your estimates.

SYSTEMS DESIGN IN THE RELATIONAL ENVIRONMENT

The relational model and its implementations will require systems developers to rethink the way they design systems.

Structured Techniques

Most analysts are familiar by now with the traditional structured design and programming methodologies and their attendant diagramming techniques. Among these diagraming techniques are Warnier-Orr, Yourdon, Jackson, HIPO, DeMarco, and the like. Most of these methods had the following in common: (1) They assumed that the system being designed or modeled had files that were accessed sequentially or randomly (with keys). (2) They assumed that the logic processes that acted on the data files were essentially hierarchical.

With the appearance of the relational data model and relational DBMSs, these assumptions are no longer universally valid. Systems based on the relational model can not be efficiently designed using these older methodologies because the fundamental assumptions are no longer true. What is needed are newer methodologies to define relational systems.

Such methodologies exist today; however, organizations are only slowly beginning to use them. This is due partly to a resistance to change and partly because such systems have not yet displayed track records to speak of. By far the major reason, though, is that most organizations' budgets preclude making the necessary investments in hardware, software, and personnel.

Before implementing a relational DBMS, look long and hard at the way you intend to develop relational systems. If you planned on using a set of standard systems development tools, determine if they will handle relational systems.

TAKING ADVANTAGE OF MICROCOMPUTERS

This is a tremendous opportunity that most organizations should take advantage of. Today, more and more systems are on-line or real-time and require 24-hour availability. Some examples are automated bank teller machines, airline reservation systems, and industrial process control.

In this environment application developers may threaten the performance of the production system by their very existence on the mainframe. This may be either because they consume valuable CPU cycles, allocate or lock necessary DASD, or cause other system bottlenecks. These situations are easily remedied by providing developers with PC-based tools for design, coding, and testing.

Many microcomputer-based tools exist now and are being used for systems development. Common integrated CASE tools assist users and analysts in prototyping applications, developing program logic, and sometimes even generating program code. Other tools permit developers to copy production files and databases to the PC, thus allowing programmers to test programs there with actual data. This relieves the mainframe CPU, lessens the need for DASD test files and databases, and protects the mainframe from inadvertent outages due to overzealous testing.

In addition, PC-based tools can provide the DP staff with such productivity-enhancing facilities as local area networks for code and data sharing, intraproject communication with electronic mail, automated task and project management reporting, and word processing facilities.

USING THIRD-PARTY PRODUCTS IN A DB2 ENVIRONMENT

One of the most common mistakes made by DP shops that implement DB2 is the failure to realize that implementing a database management system requires implementing all of the associated security, authority, performance monitoring, and auditing systems that go with it. In general, such systems used on any other DBMS are not transferable to the new one.

These systems are not bundled with DB2, and must be purchased from third-party vendors. In this section we will describe several tool categories and summarize with recommendations for selecting the proper set of tools.

(The following categories of tools are adapted in part from a presentation given by Terry Mason of the Bank of Montreal, during the meeting of the 1989 International DB2 Users Group. Further information is available in the IDUG proceedings for that year.)

Catalog Information

Tools in this category were the first to arrive on the DB2 scene. Since the DB2 DBMS environment is described in the DB2 Catalog tables, a catalog information or navigation tool is relatively easy to develop. Before these tools became widely available, DBAs began to accumulate their own collections of tools. These included SQL queries against Catalog tables, sometimes enhanced by CLISTs or ISPF/PDF panels.

Typical catalog information returned by these tools includes the following:

- *Space allocation.* This includes information gathered by the STOSPACE utility, although it is usually not limited to this. STOSPACE updates the following Catalog table columns:

SYSTABLESPACE	SPACE
SYSINDEXES	SPACE
SYSSTOGROUP	SPACE, SPCDATE

- *Object structure.* Tables SYSSTOGROUP, SYSDATABASE, SYSTABLESPACE, SYSTABLES, SYSTABLEPART, SYSVIEWS, and SYSCOLUMNS can be Joined in various ways to produce detailed lists or charts of all tables in a database, etc.

- *Statistics.* This usually involves the data collected and updated by the RUNSTATS utility, including the following Catalog table columns:

SYSTABLES	CARD, NPAGES, PCTPAGES
SYSCOLUMNS	HIGH2KEY, LOW2KEY, COLCARD
SYSTABLESPACE	NACTIVE
SYSINDEXES	CLUSTERED, CLUSTERRATIO, FIRSTKEYCARD, FULLKEYCARD, NLEAF, NLEVELS
SYSTABLEPART	CARD, NEARINDREF, FARINDREF, PERCACTIVE
SYSINDEXPART	CARD, NEAROFFPOS, FAROFFPOS, LEAFDIST

- *Referential integrity relationships.* Tables SYSTABLES, SYSCOLUMNS, SYSKEYS, SYSFOREIGNKEYS, and SYSRELS (among others) can be Joined in various ways to describe RI relationships between tables.

- *Plan information.* Catalog tables SYSDBRM, SYSPLAN, SYSPLANAUTH, SYSPLANDEP, and SYSSTMT provide plan and DBRM data.

This is only some of the information available in the DB2 Catalog tables. Tools that query the Catalog have access to all the knowledge DB2 has available to it about objects under its control. (This isn't precisely true; the DB2 Directory contains additional information, but it is beyond the scope of this discussion.)

In addition to simply retrieving information, these tools should be able to predict the effects of changes to the Catalog—for example, using the ALTER, REVOKE, or DROP commands. Additional facilities might include the ability to generate DDL for object creation, counts of objects by category, and integration of statistics.

Migration

These tools claim to assist the DBA in migrating DB2 data and object definitions from one environment to another. Regrettably, at this time they seem to limited to movement only. What is required is a more robust tool that can analyze the target environment and warn the DBA of impending problems such as out-of-space conditions, duplicate object names, and similar conditions.

Additional useful information about migration would include a cross-reference of affected Views, Plans, Aliases, and Synonyms; an interface to dataset allocation information (VTOC and VSAM Catalog); and lists of required authorizations.

Space Management

Tools in this category analyze the DASD space taken up by DB2 objects and (perhaps) reallocate them. Other tools provide a fix capability that allows DBAs to modify space allocations, fix broken pages, move objects, reallocate automatically based on predefined thresholds, display extents and free space data, and be independent of DB2 operation.

Performance Monitor

The most useful tools (and those most often purchased) are the monitoring and performance tools. These may monitor system performance, application or transaction throughput, or other system attributes. Some of these tools do their reporting on an after-the-fact basis, reading SMF and RMF information, and reporting on what has already happened. Other tools work in real-time and provide colorful graphics of system and program performance.

Real-time tools should report lock activity, thread and trace information, buffer pool and EDM pool status, and DB2/IRLM parameter values.

Fast Copy, Reorganization, Load

The DB2 utility programs COPY, REORG, and LOAD are not known for their blazing speed. In this case several third-party products have arisen to take their place. These products sometimes provide a fourfold decrease in execution time, assisting shops having narrow batch windows.

Database Editor

Constituting a popular category of product, these tools provide full-screen edit facilities for table columns. Some products have the option of displaying data column by column, including heading information describing column attributes. Another option describes table data in terms of a COBOL or PL/I record layout. These tools are very useful for creating and modifying test data, and for viewing the results of program execution.

Security Management

Another set of tools does security management and may coordinate granting and revoking authorities to access databases, programs, or terminals. Many shops purchase one or more of these tools, hoping to be able to manage the complexity of DB2 security and authorization options. Almost as many soon give up on DB2 security, grant all users PUBLIC access to DB2 objects, and use some other method of security.

Audit Reporting

These tools capture DB2 object definition changes (CREATE, ALTER, and DROP commands) and store them in a history file. This allows administrators to keep track of system modifications.

Plan Analysis

Such tools model DBMS structure or access path strategies, giving analysts and programmers helpful advice for program and subsystem development. Sometimes EXPLAIN-like output is included, allowing the DBA to analyze across Plans or DBRMs to anticipate access or performance problems in advance.

In Conclusion

Organizations implementing a relational DBMS should include the investigation and acquisition of all of these types of tools in their budgets.

PLANNING AHEAD FOR SYSTEM ENHANCEMENTS

Maintenance happens. DP departments recognize this fact of life by forming maintenance teams or by allocating varying percentages of their budgets to maintaining current systems. Somehow this seems to be forgotten when a new DBMS is brought in-house, however. If you begin developing systems using the relational model and a relational DBMS, you must sooner or later plan for upgrades and enhancements to these systems.

A New Type of Maintenance

You must not only plan for maintaining these new applications, but also realize that this maintenance will be different from that of older systems. In general, new versions of IMS (for example) have not necessitated significant changes in older IMS applications. New versions of DB2 (from V1R2 to V1R3 to V2R1 to V2R2 in about three years) involved numerous performance improvements, additional features, and a wealth of third-party products. This meant a radical shift in the way DB2 applications were maintained.

There are several unique features of DB2 that require rethinking maintenance. Some of these are mentioned in this section.

Referential Integrity

The referential integrity features of DB2 involve the definition of Primary and Foreign keys for tables. This definition may take place during table creation, or they may be added at a later time. In either case, programs typically have no knowledge of whether referential integrity is in effect for a particular table or set of tables. Further, an application deleting (say) a row from a table will not be informed as to whether additional rows in other tables were deleted because of referential relationships.

Maintainers will no longer be able to go directly to the program listing to make program changes or enhancements. They must now also analyze the current database design, including Primary and Foreign key definitions. Perhaps the most interesting case would be when these key definitions are added or removed. In this case no application coding changes may be made, but the consequences of the change may radically affect program results. Testing, therefore, becomes extremely important in this environment.

CASE Tools

There are currently no integrated CASE toolsets that completely automate the software development process. Soon, however, these tools will be available. Most of the work of application development will take place during requirements gathering, analysis, and design. From that point on the CASE toolset will generate the appropriate documentation, program code, test data, and test procedures. This shift of work from the back end of the development life cycle to the front end means that system changes and enhancements will focus on making the appropriate design changes and regenerating the application. Maintainers must become aware of the system design and acquire training in the pertinent CASE tools.

Distributed Processing and Distributed Databases

Another consideration is that of distributed database systems. DB2 was designed with this in mind, though the current release (Version 2 Release 2) does not support all types of distributed requests. Still, future systems will most probably support some level of distributed systems. This raises several questions, especially in the maintenance environment.

Question: If you implement a distributed system, what mechanisms will be in place for local DBAs to communicate performance information?

For systems that access data in multiple locations, efficiency will be an important factor. This includes both local performance and total network performance. To correctly analyze global efficiency, database administrators at the local level must gather facts and information about local levels of performance and communicate it to some authority in charge of the entire network. One way to do this is to use the network itself, storing performance data in tables accessible from a central location. Another alternative is to allow a central DBA to gather information from across the network.

Question: How will local outages affect the network?

For mission-critical systems, the failure of local hardware or software should not lead to total system failure. This may require that vital data be duplicated across several locations (called *local copies*). These copies serve two purposes: they allow local (hence quick) access to critical data; and the failure of one network node will not preclude other nodes or distributed applications from functioning.

Question: Who will be in charge of maintaining (and paying for the maintenance of) distributed applications?

This may be a political question rather than an economic one. Consider a network node that stores a local copy of some important data. Should the local site be responsible for purchasing or leasing sufficient DASD for storage, and should that DASD be high-performance? What if this leads to degradation of local systems? Who will be responsible for refreshing the local copy with new information? How about backup and recovery?

Another consideration is maintenance. Distributed applications may exist where multiple copies of application programs are installed in several sites. Imagine the case where two such sites detect dissimilar errors in a program, and each site fixes one of the errors. Who moves what to Production? The coordination of application maintenance, including change control, must somehow be centralized, even though the actual maintenance may be performed at multiple local sites.

Question: How about microtuning versus macrotuning?

We visited this question in another form when we discussed query tuning versus system performance tuning. In that case, the DBA was often caught in an untenable situation: system administration would clamor for better system performance, while developers would cry out for better application performance. Many times these situations are interdependent, and appeasing one group leads to antagonizing the other.

This situation becomes even more sticky in a distributed processing environment. Tuning on the network level becomes tremendously important, especially in an on-line or real-time environment. Local DBAs must somehow come to terms with network performance concerns in addition to those local concerns already mentioned.

TRANSACTION PROCESSING USING AD HOC QUERIES

The real power of relational systems lies in their ability to organize and respond to what-if questions, the so-called ad hoc environment. In this environment, users ask ad hoc questions of the system, needing no understanding of the underlying physical database structure. Despite its lure, the ad hoc environment is not an efficient one for doing transaction processing.

What Causes Ad Hoc Inefficiency?

Two things have slowed the realization of this concept.

- Systems designers seem to be developing typical transaction processing systems in the relational environment. Part of this problem lies in converting existing systems using hierarchical or network database management systems to DB2. Naturally, developers have encountered performance problems. Although the later releases of DB2 addressed performance and optimization concerns, developers are still wary of using a relational DBMS.

- The suboptimal performance of the environment to date makes genuine ad hoc systems perform poorly. Relational database management systems are still in their infancy. By comparison, IMS has been in use as a production DBMS for about twenty years. Another concern is DASD access speed. Since relational DBMSs tend to access data using set-at-a-time processing, many ad hoc systems contain queries that are serviced by retrieving entire tables. Since these tables exist on direct access storage, DASD I/O performance and buffer pool allocation are paramount concerns.

These two developments led to inefficient systems and to on-line users with the power to bring systems to their knees. Users had to fight for DASD space and CPU cycles and struggle with poorly designed systems. Recent advances in DASD and CPU technology may counteract these problems. The IBM 3990 Cache Controller has the capability of *caching* DASD write requests in a memory cache at the device. Instead of a typical 20- to 30-millisecond time lag for I/O to take place, the caching takes place in about one-tenth the time. The channel is informed that the write request has taken place in two to four milliseconds. Meanwhile, the device controller handles storing the cache on the physical media.

If you intend to implement a relational DBMS, anticipate and prevent these problems. Design ad hoc systems with the relational DBMS, and leave the transaction processing systems on the old DBMS (if possible).

MISUSING THE ON-LINE ENVIRONMENT

One major feature of relational DBMSs is called set-at-a-time processing. Answers to queries may consist of an entire set of table rows, where the number of rows requested is unknown prior to request submission. In the on-line environment it may not be possible to present a requester with an entire solution at once, however.

Most user on-line interaction uses 24 line screens, either IBM 3270-compatible or a microcomputer or workstation. These devices have a limited display area. As a consequence, the application must present a limited amount of information to the user. How do users access the additional information, and what performance penalties do they incur?

Scrolling Alternatives

Screen scrolling, for example, may be implemented either by saving the entire solution somewhere (thereby consuming DASD or other resources) or by reissuing the request for each screen, displaying only a portion of the entire solution at a time. Some of the possible alternatives follow.

- *Store the entire solution.* During request processing, store all of the retrieved information somewhere. This may take the form of a temporary DB2 table, an IMS database, several logical pages of an MFS, or CICS temporary storage or transient data queue. Presenting the information to the user can now be done without incurring I/O across all of the retrieved data. Scrolling consists of remembering the key of the last record processed, then using this key to access the stored information directly. Sequential I/O may then be used to retrieve a screenful of data.

  This method has three serious drawbacks. First, all of the retrieved data must be stored, meaning that sufficient DASD or memory must first be allocated and the storage area may need to be preformatted. Shops may not have the luxury of this much space.

  Second, what happens to the data if the application abends? Developers must come up with some mechanism to "clean out" leftover data. Also, applications must check for the existence of such data before storing their own.

  Third, the retrieved information has a limited useful life. As time goes on, the data becomes less and less current. This may not be a problem in some systems, but in ones where data currency is important this method allows users to see old (and perhaps inaccurate) data.

- *Store a partial solution.* In this scenario, the request is deemed satisfied after a predetermined amount of information is retrieved. One common method is to store only (say) 10 screenfuls of information and allow the user to scroll backward and forward through this subset. Should data not within that range be necessary, the user must reissue the request.

- *Reissue the request.* Perhaps the least efficient, this method does have the advantage of always presenting the user with up-to-date information. Here, every time the user attempts to scroll to the next screen, the application reissues the entire request. During retrieval (or, perhaps, as part of the request itself) only information that logically follows that currently displayed is either retrieved or displayed. Although this causes much resource consumption, it is sometimes the only feasible solution.

Such inefficiencies in scrolling alternatives can affect other mission-critical applications in an enterprise's DP environment. Keep this in mind when converting older on-line transaction processing systems, or when developing new applications.

Chapter 5
Common Post-Implementation Problems

After a shop installs DB2 there is typically a pilot or acceptance period. During this time, there are written and implemented one or more applications that use DB2 tables. This is usually a time of education, of trial and error, and of frustration for programmers, analysts, and DBAs alike. The many problems that surface during this period are called *learning experiences*. Still, after the initial plunge, when things become settled, the shop has become accustomed to designing DB2 application systems. It is at this point that many shops encounter yet another class of problems. These are described in this chapter.

WORRYING ABOUT PERFORMANCE (TOO LATE!)

The problem with system performance measurement is that numbers are absolute, whereas perceived performance is relative. Some of the more common performance measures for on-line application systems are as follows:

- *Average user on-line turnaround time*. This is the amount of elapsed time from the moment the user presses the Enter key (or some other key that generates an interrupt) until the moment the terminal returns a response to the user. This average time is periodically included as a requirement in the system specifications, with the intent that the delivered system will perform at least that well for most of the time.

  This concept, sometimes called the *service level agreement*, is becoming more and more common, as on-line users become responsible for accessing mission-critical systems. It is easily estimated after installation (perhaps with a stopwatch and a calculator) and provides a rather visible measure of perceived system performance. Its one disadvantage is that tuning an application for fast turnaround may adversely affect other systems.

- *Number of transactions processed per second.* Used for both on-line and batch systems, this metric attempts to measure system *throughput.* It is valuable when comparing program or system performance at different times or with differing resource mixes. Its main disadvantage is that it gives little indication of what resources, hardware options, or software parameters must be changed to improve performance.

- *Number of lines of code executed per second.* This is a simple measure of program execution speed. It is most useful during the testing phase of the life cycle as programmers search for inefficient modules or code fragments. Many interactive debugging and fault diagnostic tools provide information about program execution, even down to the level of how many times each line of code is executed.

  This metric is valuable for measuring raw program speed but is not as useful when attempting to measure overall application or system performance.

- *Number of standard units of work processed per second.* The *standard work unit* concept is a simple one and is related to the concept of the *transaction.* A transaction is a sequence of zero or more operations on a database that ". . . transforms a consistent state of the database into another consistent state, without necessarily preserving consistency at all intermediate points."[1] The database management system guarantees that, should a transaction fail, all of its updates will be *undone.* Thus no transaction will ever partially complete or partially fail. Each program or application defines *transaction initiation* and *transaction termination* to the database management system. (In IMS, for example, this is accomplished with the Checkpoint command, in DB2 with the COMMIT command, and in CICS with the SYNCHPOINT command.)

  If these work units are the same *size* (that is, they perform approximately the same amount of work and utilize the same number and amount of system resources), then this metric provides a measure of how well the program or application is able to complete transactions. Its main disadvantage is that work units across programs are rarely the same and cannot be compared.

---

[1]Date, C. J., *An Introduction to Database Systems: Volume I,* (fifth edition). Addison-Wesley, 1990. Page 402.

Until you define it, then, performance is an elusive animal—hard to catch and, once caught, difficult to tame. The basic problem is one of definition: How much performance is "good"? What do we measure? If performance is "poor," what can we do to improve it, and by how much?

Concern about performance of relational DBMSs is justified, as few installations seem to install systems that live up to their perceived expectations. Benchmarks do not tell the whole story either. Until the RDBMS is installed, it may be impossible to predict performance. Until the application system is in place, it may be impossible to get an accurate picture of how well it will work.

Anticipate that performance will not be quite as good as you expect. In addition, be prepared to do MVS tuning and I/O subsystem tuning before tuning the DB2 subsystem or any DB2 applications. (See Chapter 2.) Insufficient DASD for paging or 95 percent CPU utilization will give poor DBMS performance regardless of the DBMS chosen.

NOT ACQUIRING OR USING THIRD-PARTY TOOLS

Some specialized third-party software tools that complement DB2 are available. (Many of these were discussed in Chapters 1 and 4.) The main tool categories are as follows:

Catalog information
Migration
Space management
Performance monitor
Fast copy, reorganization, load
Database editor
Security management
Audit reporting
Plan analysis

Tools in these categories are essential for getting the best use out of DB2.

Why Every Category?

Although many shops budget for a few tools in what they consider are the most important categories, most large DP organizations find themselves purchasing one or more tools in each category. There seem to be several reasons for this. IBM has not seen fit to include many such tools with DB2, possibly because DB2 itself is changing so quickly and possibly because the functionality in some of these tools is expected to be incorporated into the base DB2 product at some future date.

Another consideration is that each category of tools provides either functionality, performance benefits, or organization of information that DB2 itself does not. Granted, a lot of information is available to authorized users using queries against the DB2 Catalog tables; however, this is not enough.

What to Expect

The DP organization may allow only a certain number or category of tools to be purchased, usually because of budgetary restrictions. How do you choose the best set of tools for your situation? The following recommendations should be useful:

- *Integration.* Tools should be integrated; that is, the output or results from one tool should be accessible to the others. For example, a space management tool that returns a list of DASD volumes that are over (say) 90 percent full should present the list of volumes in such a way that it can be used by the fast copy tool to copy DB2 datasets on those packs to other volumes. The better-integrated toolsets provide a central command screen or interface from which each of the tools can be accessed.

- *Internal information storage.* The best tools store DB2 information they have gathered as tables internally. This allows them to process requests using an SQL-like interface. Further, changes to DB2 or other systems will require only minor changes to the tool's interface to DB2. These vendors can respond quickly to changes or upgrades.

- *CUA-compliant user interface.* IBM's System Application Architecture (SAA) is a compilation of interfaces and standards that IBM software and hardware will conform to in the future. One interface, Common User Access (CUA), specifies the standard way that users may access systems and applications. As most on-line systems of the future will conform to this standard, tools that follow the standards now will not require a retraining effort in the future.

- *Optionally microcomputer-based.* As the use of microcomputers has grown in the business enterprise, so has the software. Many applications are now being developed to run on several different hardware platforms. It is becoming more and more common to see application developers writing, compiling, and testing programs on microcomputers, and later uploading them to the mainframe where they will be executed. Tools that manage security, data migration, test data creation (database editors), and performance monitoring will need to execute in some form on the microcomputer in order to manage this form of application development.

- *Relevant to installed hardware and software.* Many businesses are migrating from one hardware platform to another, and changing database management systems as well. In some cases, the old DBMS will coexist for quite a while with the new one. In these cases, third-party tools can not restrict themselves to the DB2 environment alone. Further, they must be relevant to multiple hardware platforms and several different software combinations. It would be annoying, for example, for a DP shop with five slightly different hardware and software environments to purchase five different versions of the same tool (or five different tools in the same category).

- *Require a trial period, a formal review, and vendor-supplied training.* Most reputable vendors offer their software for a trial period and include product training. During this trial period you should test the tools provided, paying close attention to any statistics gathered about problems encountered, or tool use. Midway through the trial period meet with the vendor and analyze progress to date. Is anyone using the tool? What problems are they having? What problems are the tools solving?

A Final Concern

One last concern in regard to training. The data processing operations staff must be trained to use any DBMS or system performance monitoring tools. Such tools are simple to use, but required detailed system internals knowledge to correctly interpret their results or recommendations.

LACK OF DASD SPACE

This problem reared its ugly head before implementation, and now it returns. Installations that planned on additional DASD requirements before implementing DB2 found that they had underestimated their requirements, sometimes by a factor of two or more. Why was this?

The Art of DASD Capacity Planning

There are several ways to predict future DASD capacity expansion. Most of these assume that the users and analysts doing data modeling for systems design are aware of current and future storage needs and can forecast based on those needs. While it is generally possible to approximate future capacity needs, planners seem not to take into account the following common occurrences:

Users underestimate needs. One of the most common errors made in storage estimation is underestimating activity. Users and their management are usually accurate in their predictions of (say) the number of accounts that will be added to a master file or the number of inventory storage locations for parts. Where they commonly falter is in measuring data storage involved in *activity.* Some examples of this might include some of the following:

- Open orders files.
- Transaction logs.
- General ledger and general journal entries.
- Traffic activity, including carrier information.
- Text, such as engineer's comments, problem descriptions, or address information.
- Database management system log files and archive logs.

In these cases, information that is considered temporary (compared to other information on the database) must still be stored on DASD. Users typically have little in the way of historical statistics on this type of data.

DBA not involved in requirements or analysis. Here, in another common scenario, the DBA is not included in either the user requirements definition or analysis phases of the development life cycle. Instead, analysts and designers complete a (normalized!) data model and hand it over to the DBA. The DBA's sole task is then to issue the appropriate CREATE statements for the listed DB2 objects.

This is unfortunate. The DB2 DBA is the best source of information about DB2 performance options, DASD usage, and CPU utilization; it should be included from the outset of the development process. By the time the designers force a particular design on the DBA it is usually too late—there is not enough time to make more than minor changes to the design. The result is a poorly performing system and overuse of DASD.

For example, the DB2 DBA is aware that DB2 row storage involves eight bytes of overhead per row. A table with columns totalling eight bytes of data already has 50 percent overhead! In addition, DB2 Version 2 Release 2 limits the number of rows per data page to 127. In the case of our eight-byte rows, this limits the total actual data per 4K page to 1,016 bytes!

Involve the DBA from the beginning, or you can count on needing lots of additional DASD.

Duplication across DBMSs. Many shops are either migrating from one DBMS to another or are allowing data to coexist in both DBMSs. During the migration or coexistence period (which may take many years), data may be duplicated and exist in two forms on two databases of differing types. Migration from IMS to DB2, for example, may require some IMS databases to be "duplicated" onto sets of DB2 tables, as application designers parallel test the new systems. In effect, a production database will exist both in IMS and DB2 for a period, and will take up twice the DASD it could, along with all of the associated overhead.

Interesting Choices

Some installations got around certain performance problems by taking advantage of some special DASD features. Some IBM 3350 DASD models, for instance, have several *fixed-head* cylinders. These cylinders can be accessed with no delay associated with head movement because special fixed-position read/write heads are included in the hardware. Another example is the IBM 3990 DASD cache controller. This controller can hold several tracks of data in a cache for later writing to the disk, while allowing the channel to continue with data transfer. These creative DASD solutions are temporary, however, as they do not directly address the problems mentioned previously.

FAILURE TO INVOLVE THE VENDOR

Too many systems departments have one or more gurus with an "I can do it myself" attitude. While sometimes laudable, this can lead to unacceptable system downtime as these experts attempt to solve problems. In some cases the hardware or software vendors have encountered such problems and are aware of the solutions.

A typical example is CICS dynamic plan allocation. This features allows DB2-related CICS transactions to transfer control to other transactions while automatically changing the DB2 plan they are using. Setup for this should take only a few hours with the help of IBM. Some shops, however, took several weeks to experiment with different configurations of parameters before informing the vendor of their situation.

In general, vendors have knowledge of other shops that are encountering the same problem you are. Use this expertise to your advantage, by involving the vendor from the beginning.

System Tuning

Another area where vendors should be involved is system tuning. Vendors have a stake in system performance—they want their products to look good and perform well. Involving vendor personnel in application or system tuning takes a load off your staff and may be a valuable learning experience. One additional point: if performance is still poor, perhaps the vendor can be convinced to take its product back and offer your a full refund.

LACK OF OUTSIDE TECHNICAL SPECIALISTS

Businesses need to manage risk. Managers, faced with a large backlog of applications to develop, sometimes resort to outside services such as outsourcing or consultants. The advantages of these services include the following:

- *No permanent office space need be assigned.* Many consulting or contract programming firms will work out of their own offices. Businesses need not allocate valuable office space and do not incur additional overhead costs such as telephone calls, secretarial services, and supplies. In some cases, these firms will be able to use their own computing resources to do work. This relieves the business of CPU and DASD resource usage and prevents development work from adversely affecting the production environment.

- *Such firms often warrant or guarantee their work.* This can be a big benefit when systems must be delivered on time.

- *DP departments can get qualified help quickly.* They need not resort to a recruiting, hiring, and training process and the corresponding learning curves.

- *Specific applications experience.* Many outside services specialize in providing help in certain technical areas. DB2 consulting services in particular are hard to find, except in certain regional markets. Part of this is due to DB2 having existed for only a few years.

There are disadvantages to using these services, however. Any experience gained by the service may leave with its personnel when the task is finished. Also, such services may cost more than some companies are willing to pay.

Implementing new applications that use DB2 may require that developers come up to speed quickly. The best way to get systems developed quickly using new technology is to begin the development process with the current staff and import the required coding and testing expertise from an outside service. With many relational DBMSs (including DB2), few qualified personnel exist. This makes it difficult for businesses to develop new relational applications quickly.

Before committing your staff to a large amount of new development, check into the availability of services that can provide personnel with experience in DB2, including analysis and design expertise, and coding and testing experience. Although they may be expensive, they will help you manage risk and assist you in justifying acquisition of the new technology.

ATTEMPTING TO FOOL THE RDBMS

Too often in the recent past developers have been forced to outthink the DB2 optimization software. This is the part of the database management system that analyzes relational requests and determines the optimal database access path. The optimizers of most earlier versions of DB2 were not very efficient. This led to developers having to structure their queries in ways that they felt would be most efficient. This is called *micro-optimization.*

As DB2 has evolved it has become much more efficient. Unfortunately, the state of the system developer's art has not kept pace with this trend. Except for the most recently published books, efficient relational query tactics and strategies are still being published and discussed. Many present relational systems have embedded queries that may become *less* efficient as the tricks used to fool the optimizer became less efficient.

In general, let DB2 and the optimizer do their work. Structure relational queries using common sense, and resist the temptation to add anything to "make the optimizer more efficient."

BOTTOM-UP PERFORMANCE TUNING

The first place some system programmers and DBAs look for performance enhancements in a relational system is in the applications. This is backwards.

Good performance in DB2 database management system is dependent on good performance in the operating system and the teleprocessing and I/O subsystems. These must be tuned first.

First, the Operating System

The first step should be operating system tuning. Specifics include the following:

- *Reduce DASD device contention.* Consider additional DASD if necessary; analyze strings and channel usage.

- *Reduce CPU utilization.* Consider a larger CPU or an attached processor if required. If current CPU utilization is over 95 percent, all the query tuning in the world won't help your DB2 applications.

- *Check dispatching priorities.* VTAM and the IRLM should have the highest priority. After that, use monitoring facilities to determine how much CPU and I/O resources these two hogs are taking. A system with the IRLM swallowing up 25 percent of the CPU is ripe for a lock management and analysis tool.

- *Analyze memory usage.* Consider expanded storage or tuning virtual storage allocation.

Problems in these areas will greatly affect DB2 as well as other systems.

Next, the Teleprocessing Systems

Next, analyze IMS, CICS, and TSO performance. Consider use of IRLM and/or DBRC and their associated parameters. Investigate security and authorization schemes. In general, CPU, memory, and DASD problems with these systems will spill over onto DB2.

Next, the DB2 Subsystem

Next, check the DB2 subsystem. Study buffer pool allocation and usage, DASD usage for work space, and available sort space. Determine whether any special features can be used, such as sequential prefetch or list prefetch.

Finally, Analyze Application Performance

Finally, study application performance. This should be the last area checked. Problems in the areas above may make any application performance enhancements ineffective or useless.

CONVERTING HIERARCHICAL SYSTEMS TO DB2

Because they are not familiar with the relational model, many developers think that conversion from (say) IMS to DB2 will require minimal programming changes. (After all, we're just converting from one DBMS to another.) Unfortunately, hierarchical systems are not readily convertible to relational ones. Some of these problems are discussed here.

Common Problems

Access path selection. The most common problem is one of access path selection. Hierarchical DBMSs require that the application specify the access path as part of the request. This is usually determined by the application at execution time. DB2 has an Optimizer that resolves the access path for the user, usually at bind (compile) time. Thus converting from a hierarchical to a relational DBMS may be impossible (or at least incredibly difficult).

Data integrity. Hierarchical database structures contain implicitly some basic referential integrity. When you delete an IMS root segment, the children are automatically deleted (by definition). This corresponds to the DB2 Delete Rule of ON DELETE CASCADE. DB2 has other delete rules (such as ON DELETE RESTRICT) that are not implemented in hierarchical database structures but must be handled by application program logic. In this sense, DB2 has capabilities that IMS lacks.

Converting from IMS to DB2 applications that have these business rules built into the code will force developers to either convert the code to that appropriate for the DB2 environment or remove the code and build the correct referential integrity rules into the DB2 tables.

Optimization. In hierarchical systems, navigation of the database is the responsibility of the application. In DB2, navigation is specified by the Optimizer. In addition to mere selection, the Optimizer also determines which of the several possible access paths has the lowest *cost.* (The term *cost* is not precisely defined by IBM, although it will admit that the cost of a query is a function of the estimated I/O required, the I/O device(s) used, the estimated CPU required, and the CPU model itself.)

Chapter 6
Integrating DB2 into an IMS Environment

DB2 AND IMS COEXISTENCE

How do IMS and DB2 coexist, and which is in control? As more and more sites come to employ them simultaneously, data integrity and timely response become paramount concerns.

Peaceful Coexistence

DB2 is IBM's relational DBMS for the MVS operating system. With DB2, users perceive the data as being stored in a collection of tables. Applications then manipulate these tables, using Structured Query Language (SQL) to make inquiries, produce reports, and derive further tables. The strength of DB2, as well as other relational DBMSs, lies in its ability to handle ad hoc queries. Some other DBMSs, such as IBM's IMS/VS and Computer Associates' CA-IDMS, have generally proven superior for transaction processing applications.

Many new systems are being developed to combine DB2 tables and IMS/VS databases, using IMS/DC as the data communications subsystem. IMS/DC users communicate interactively with IMS/VS applications, which then access IMS/DB databases, DB2 tables, or both. An inventory control application, might, for example, access an IMS/DB inventory database, update a vendor DB2 table, then produce a report on-line.

How do IMS/VS and DB2 coexist? Do application programs exist within both environments at once? This chapter addresses these questions and presents solutions to some common problems. First we will see how the IMS/VS and DB2 subsystems communicate with one another.

Connections and Threads

The DB2 subsystem allows other subsystems, such as TSO, CICS, and IMS/VS, to access its DB2 resources. IMS/VS does so by establishing a communication path (called a *connection*) to DB2 by using the DB2-IMS/VS Attachment facility; other facilities are used for TSO and CICS. IMS/VS may then create one or more of what are called *threads* on that connection. A connection is analogous to a railroad right-of-way between two cities in that it establishes a two-directional pathway between subsystems. Using this analogy, the threads correspond to the railroad tracks. They connect specific subsystem users (origins) with specific DB2 resources, or destinations. One or more threads may be present on a given connection.

The Attachment facility creates two kinds of threads on connecting IMS/VS to DB2. First, it creates a *command thread* from the control region to DB2 once the initial DB2 command is entered from an IMS/VS terminal. Terminal operators use these command threads to issue DB2 commands such as −DISPLAY THREAD. Second, the Attachment facility creates a *transaction thread* once an application has issued its first SQL statement. The transaction thread connects a single IMS/VS application to DB2.

During IMS/VS start-up, the control region attempts to connect to DB2. The IMSVS.PROCLIB dataset contains a member that informs the control region of the necessary DB2 connections. It is possible to have several connections simultaneously between IMS/VS and DB2, each to a different DB2 subsystem. At region start-up time a connection is established to all the DB2 subsystems that have been defined in the dependent region's subsystem member (SSM) of IMSVS.PROCLIB. Dependent region connections require that a connection already exist between the control region and DB2.

Before completing the connection, the Resource Access Control Facility (RACF) or its equivalent checks the DB2 subsystem's name to authorize the connection. If RACF does authorize the connection, a connection is completed between IMS/VS and the particular DB2 subsystem. Connections for Message Processing Programs (MPPs) are therefore created before the execution of application programs.

Alternatively, a Batch Message Processing (BMP) region will establish its connection to DB2 when the application executes its first SQL statement. This procedure may result in having a BMP begin execution without having an active DB2 subsystem. BMPs must consider this possibility by checking the SQLCODE after the execution of their first SQL statement. (Note that "first SQL statement" refers to an *executable* statement, such as SELECT or OPEN CURSOR.) Some of the possible SQLCODE values are -922 (Connection Authorization Failure), -923 (Connection Not Established), and -924 (DB2

Connection Internal Error). BMPs and MPPs both create transaction threads when issuing their first SQL statement.

Should either DB2 or IMS/VS fail, the connection will also fail. The failing subsystem must then be restarted and the connection reestablished. If only the connection fails, however, then only it will need to be reestablished. An abnormal termination of an IMS/VS transaction will cause both DB2 and IMS/VS to back out any changes made to their respective resources.

Two-Phase Commit

IMS/VS does not finalize database updates immediately when it is in an on-line environment. Instead it holds them until a synchronization point (synchpoint) occurs. At that time all database updates are committed, and any IMS/VS resources held by the application are released. The application may at this time explicitly generate synchpoints by using the CHKP call, for example. Synchpoints may even occur naturally at program termination or on receiving the next message from the message queue.

For DB2 the corresponding term for synchpoint is the *commit point.* In a TSO environment, for example, DB2 holds table updates until they are committed, using a COMMIT SQL statement.

Application programs in IMS/VS cannot issue a COMMIT statement. How then can DB2 resources be committed and locks released? How do IMS/VS and DB2 coordinate what are referred to as their points of consistency: that is, their synchpoints and commit points?

DB2 table changes are committed during IMS/VS synchpoint processing. This commit process consists of two distinct phases, with IMS/VS acting as their coordinator. Table 6.1 summarizes the sequence of events during this so-called two-phase commit process, described in the following paragraphs.

IMS/VS Commit: Phase 1. IMS/VS first writes a *Begin Commit* record to its log. It then informs DB2 and other subsystems, such as Fast Path, that they are to *Prepare to Commit.* Each subsystem informs IMS/VS whether or not it can continue with the commit process by returning a *Ready to* Commit response. If a subsystem is unable to continue, IMS/VS informs all the subsystems that the current Units of Recovery (URs) are to be rolled back. If DB2 fails, on restart it will back out any changes made to DB2 resources, without needing to connect to IMS/VS.

DB2 Commit: Phase 1. Next, DB2 logs table updates, writes an *End Phase 1* record to its log, and ensures that this record is externalized. DB2 thus assures

Table 6.1. The two-phase commit process.

IMS/VS Commit: Phase 1

IMS/VS writes a BEGIN COMMIT record to its log.
IMS/VS begins Commit protocol.
IMS/VS issues PREPARE TO COMMIT to DB2.

DB2 Commit: Phase 1

DB2 logs all table updates.
DB2 writes an END PHASE 1 record to its log.
DB2 ensures that log buffers are written to the logs.
DB2 retains all locks and returns a READY TO COMMIT response to IMS/VS.

IMS/VS Commit: Phase 2

IMS/VS commits all its resources.
IMS/VS writes a CROSS OVER SYNCHPOINT record to its log.
IMS/VS ensures that the log buffer is written to the log.
IMS/VS issues a COMMIT to DB2.

DB2 Commit: Phase 2

DB2 writes a BEGIN PHASE 2 record to its log.
DB2 ensures that the log buffers are written to the logs.
DB2 commits its resources and releases locks.
DB2 writes an END PHASE 2 record to its log.

IMS/VS End of Two-Phase Commit

IMS/VS writes an END OF COMMIT record to its log.

---

itself that the log is complete. It then returns a *Ready To Commit* response to IMS/VS. For a brief period beginning at this point, the DB2 Unit of Recovery is referred to as in-doubt. Should either IMS/VS or DB2 fail now, the failing system must be restarted and the connection be reestablished. IMS/VS will then inform DB2 whether or not to commit or roll back resource changes found to be associated with the in-doubt unit of recovery.

IMS/VS Commit: Phase 2. If all subsystems have responded as being ready to commit, IMS/VS logs a *Cross Over Synchpoint* record. It then ensures that this record has been written to the log and issues a *Commit* message to the other subsystems.

DB2 Commit: Phase 2. Just prior to this point, the DB2 unit of recovery was classified as in-doubt. Now, DB2 writes a *Begin Phase 2* record to its log and ensures that the record becomes externalized. Should DB2 fail after this event, on restart it will commit changes without needing to connect to IMS/VS. After committing its resources, DB2 next logs an *End Phase 2* record. IMS/VS then logs an *End Of Commit* record. This step ends the two-phase commit process.

In-Doubt Units of Recovery

Either IMS/VS or DB2 or both may fail during a two-phase commit process. If so, each builds a recovery list for DB2 units of recovery that have not been committed. The list built by DB2 is called an in-doubt list. The list built by IMS/VS is called the Residual Recovery Entry (RRE) list. IMS/VS logs these entries during checkpoint processing. During the resolution process the IMS/VS Attachment facility compares the lists built by IMS/VS with those from DB2 and deletes those it can resolve. Both systems then either back out or commit the unit of recovery.

At the end of the process some URs may remain in-doubt. If so, IMS/VS informs the Master Terminal. The database administrator must now resolve these URs manually by listing the appropriate IMS/VS and DB2 log entries. In DB2 the command -DISPLAY THREAD TYPE(INDOUBT) identifies these URs. The DBA then uses the DB2 command -RECOVER INDOUBT to either back out or commit the resource.

MPP Programming

Let's explore some specific problems associated with the IMS/VS-DB2 environment. First we will consider message processing program concerns.

Deadlock ("the deadly embrace"). IMS/VS resolves a deadlock in an MPP environment by selecting one of the contending programs as the offender (sometimes called the victim). This will usually be the program that has, according to IMS, done the least amount of work. IMS halts the offender by generating a U777 pseudoabend. This step allows the other contender to have access to the locked resource. The IMS/VS database management system dynamically rolls back the offender to its most recent point of consistency and requeues it there. This process is completely transparent to the application program.

Nonresponse MPP usage. An MPP need not communicate with a terminal but may be invoked from another MPP by using a *message switch.* These MPPs are called nonresponse ones because they cannot respond to a terminal. These MPPs should not be used to update DB2 tables used by on-line processes. Should either DB2 or IMS/VS fail, the table updates may become part of an in-doubt unit of recovery. Until DB2 and IMS/VS then resolve the unit of recovery problem, the data in the table will not be consistent and may adversely affect on-line processes.

DB2 resource allocation. Thread creation and application plan allocation occur in DB2 when the MPP executes its first SQL statement. Until then, the MPP has no way of obtaining information about the status of DB2. All that the program can assume is that a connection does exist. If the application plan does not in fact exist or is somehow invalid, the SQLCODE returned for the first SQL statement will probably be -923 (Connection Not Established: DB2 Allocation Error).

Inquiry-only MPPs. MPPs can be defined in IMS/VS as "inquiry-only" by specifying INQUIRY=YES on the TRANSACT macro in the IMS/VS Sysgen. This means that the program is therefore not able to update any IMS databases. One side effect is that in the DB2 environment an MPP defined as being inquiry-only cannot issue any of the following SQL statements: INSERT, UPDATE, DELETE, CREATE, ALTER, DROP, GRANT, or REVOKE. Any attempt to do so will result in an error return code (SQLCODE) of -817. In other words, the MPP is also inquiry-only in DB2! (For more information on this topic, see the DATABASE 2 Messages and Codes manual.)

Batch Message Programming

Now we can look at the second IMS/VS-DB2 environment, batch message processing (BMP). As with MPP programming, certain specific concerns crop up.

DB2 resource allocation. DB2 connection, thread creation, and application plan allocation occur when the BMP executes its first SQL statement. Until then the BMP has no way of obtaining information about the status of DB2. Should a BMP begin to execute without there being an active DB2 subsystem, the SQLCODE returned after the execution of the first SQL statement will be nonzero. Some of the possible codes are -922 (Connection Authorization Failure), -923 (Connection Not Established), and -924 (DB2 Connection Internal Error). If the application plan does not exist or is invalid, the SQLCODE returned will probably be -923. Note also that BMPs are usually bound with ACQUIRE(ALLOCATE) and RELEASE(DEALLOCATE), which ensure that all tablespace locks are available at the start of execution. This prevents the program from getting a -904 SQLCODE (resource unavailable) on a SELECT against table A when it is table B that is unavailable.

Use of OS/VS datasets. IMS/VS and DB2 do not log the changes made to OS/VS files. Therefore BMPs that access OS/VS files may not be restartable. This limitation is particularly important if the BMP contains a long-running internal sort. Such programs may have to be rerun from their beginning. To be restartable, however, the checkpointing must not interfere with the creation or sorting of the Sort file.

When IMS/VS restarts the application, the program becomes responsible for repositioning any OS/VS datasets. This step is usually accomplished by retaining a counter or key that indicates the last record processed, then using this information to skip forward through the input file until the correct record is found.

DB2 cursor processing during checkpoint. During checkpoint processing, DB2 closes any open cursors. To simplify program logic, all applications should explicitly close all cursors before doing a checkpoint and also explicitly open them afterward. It is thus necessary for SELECT statements contained within cursor definitions to provide for this. In most cases the program can use one or more host variables to keep track of the last row returned by the FETCH statement for the cursor. The host variables are then included in the WHERE clause in the SELECT SQL statement for the cursor. Figure 6.1 shows one example of such cursor control.

Choice of output media. BMPs are frequently used to print reports. Thus application designers should design applications that are restartable but do not adversely affect report generation. In particular, using an OS/VS file or a standard output file (SYSOUT=x) may preclude restart. Neither IMS/VS nor DB2 log changes to these media, so if the BMP fails it must be rerun from the beginning to produce a complete report.

Several alternatives for report output are available to allow the application to be restartable. Applications may use either General Sequential Access Method (GSAM) or Simple Hierarchical Indexed Sequential Access Method (SHISAM) databases, Fast Path databases, or DB2 tables to hold

```
EXEC SQL
  DECLARE PART_CURSOR
  CURSOR FOR
     SELECT PART_NUMBER, PART_QTY, PART_COST
        FROM PART_TABLE
        WHERE   PART_NUMBER > :LAST-PART-NO
        ORDER BY  PART_NUMBER
END-EXEC.


EXEC SQL
  FETCH  PART_CURSOR
  INTO  :IN-PART-NO, :IN-PART-QTY,
        :IN-PART-COST
END-EXEC.


IF  SQLCODE  EQUALS  ZERO
    MOVE  IN-PART-NO  TO  LAST-PART-NO.
```

Figure 6.1. Sample SQL showing cursor control.

report records for later processing and/or printing. Each of these methods involves special—sometimes bizarre—considerations.

GSAM databases provide a convenient way of importing and exporting OS/VS files to and from IMS/VS. Although GSAM database changes are not written on the IMS/VS log, IMS/VS still keeps track of the relative record being processed and stores this information during the checkpoint or synchpoint process. On program restart, IMS/VS uses this relative record information to position the GSAM database at the proper record. GSAM databases defined with VSAM as their access method cannot, however, be repositioned by IMS/VS during restart; BSAM must therefore be used instead of VSAM.

SHISAM databases provide an even more secure form of report output media, because IMS/VS writes SHISAM database changes to the IMS/VS log. SHISAM allows the application designer to use the database's indexing capability to route or otherwise separate reports by type, depending on the value of the index. SHISAM databases can also be used for small reports produced by MPPs.

Fast Path databases may appear to offer a speedy method of storing large quantities of data, but not many technicians are familiar with them, and few applications exist as examples. Therefore, unless enough supporting technical expertise exists, I would recommend not using Fast Path.

Applications may be designed to store report records in a DB2 table for later printing or access. Users could then access portions of the report on-line. Employing a DB2 table allows the application designer great freedom in designing report delivery criteria, as well as in designing security considerations.

It is probably not wise to store large reports in DB2 tables. If doing so becomes necessary nonetheless, a fast way is to preload the table with empty rows, using the DB2 LOAD utility. Records can then be placed in the table using UPDATE rather than INSERT SQL statements. UPDATE is significantly faster in this situation because VSAM would not have to format control intervals and control areas. In addition, index maintenance will not be necessary. Such formatting and maintenance is done during the insertion of records during LOAD execution.

Deadlock detection and resolution. We now come to the most interesting feature of BMPs in the IMS/VS-DB2 environment.

In a BMP environment IMS/VS resolves a deadlock situation by rolling back IMS/VS and DB2 resources and returning control to the application. If the application was trying to access an IMS/VS resource, the call would return an *FD* the status code for the Program Control Block (PCB) used in the call. If, instead, a DB2 resource was being accessed, the application would receive an SQLCODE of –911. In both cases, IMS/VS and DB2 would roll back database updates to the previous point of consistency, the synchpoint, before returning control to the application.

In a CICS/VS-DB2 environment the deadlock situation is even more interesting. CICS applications that access DB2 are defined in the Resource Control Table (RCT) with a parameter specifying whether or not CICS and DB2 should roll back resource updates to the previous synchpoint before returning to the application. If so, an SQLCODE of -911 is returned. If not, the SQLCODE is -913. CICS application designers therefore have more options available for handling deadlock situations.

Application designers must take these particular deadlock situations into account. They signify not fatal errors but simply that the application has encountered a deadlock, which may no longer even exist. If not, the program may be able to retry processing and continue with execution with no further problems. However, the lock causing the deadlock may be a long-term one. In this case, the program will enter an infinite deadlock and rollback loop. To avoid looping in this fashion, application programs should keep track of the number of times they encounter a deadlock situation, indicated by an IMS/VS FD status code or a DB2 SQLCODE of -911. After a suitable number of occurrences, the application should terminate with an error condition.

It is not clear from IMS/VS and DB2 reference manuals whether GSAM databases are in fact repositioned when execution resumes after a deadlock. In general, GSAM databases are repositioned only after a restart due to program abend. The program may then issue an XRST call, which will explicitly reposition the GSAM database as of the previous checkpoint. Unfortunately, trying a subsequent XRST call to force repositioning may result in a U102 abend.

When continuing an execution after a deadlock, IMS/VS restores the values of variables stored in the checkpoint work areas. The program may, however, be knee deep in logic. In other words the program must explicitly check for deadlocks in any program section that attempts to access an IMS/VS or DB2 resource. The very same check is required in sections at higher levels that also invoke such sections. Being able to perform this check requires that application designers anticipate the logic needed to monitor the situation, along with the significant amount of effort required to test this logic.

Summary

Here we have covered some of the most important aspects of the IMS/VS-DB2 environment. Three stand out as most significant:

- Resolution of any in-doubt URs
- Alternatives for storing report data
- Necessity for batch message application programs to handle deadlock situations

In-doubt URs are created by IMS/VS or DB2 failure, or the failure of both, during commit processing. Application programs can be made less vulnerable to this problem by judicious selection of checkpoint procedures and resource allocation. Although no hard-and-fast rules exist, programs should get their checkpoint frequency from an external source. This practice will make program testing and tuning easier. The impact may also be lessened if you design resource access to minimize table and tablespace locks and database record enqueuing.

Several alternatives for report media can be found in the IMS/VS-DB2 environment. In general, small reports should be produced by non-response MPPs and stored in DB2 tables. Doing so allows for maximum flexibility. Use BMPs for somewhat larger reports, and place them on GSAM databases. Reports with multiple routing or their own breakdown requirements can be stored on a SHISAM database, with an application program using the index to perform subsetting.

Deadlock is usually the exception rather than the rule. However, in a large on-line system the possibility of deadlock may be significant. BMP application designers must consider deadlock resolution as part of necessary program overhead. The need for it will change estimated programming and testing times and may require some creative testing procedures. The maintenance of such programs may be especially difficult, because adding a single IMS/VS database call or SQL statement may require massive coding changes. Program and design documentation must take this difficulty into account.

Finally, the implementation of recovery coding for deadlock situations may be difficult to test. Consider the problems involved in creating a situation where two applications are forced into a deadlock. One brute-force method of testing an update application is to go first into the Query Management Facility (QMF) and issue a query that retrieves all the rows in a given table. Assuming that the table contains more than about 25 rows, this query will require several screens in QMF. Until the last screen has been reached, or until the QMF user issues a RELEASE QUERY command, QMF holds a "share" lock on the table. The update application will now be locked out of updating the table, and it should encounter either a deadlock or a "resource not available" condition.

Application design in the IMS/VS-DB2 environment is more complicated than in either environment alone. Designers must therefore keep their wits about them and be cautious and thorough.

SQL TECHNIQUES IN IMS PROGRAMS

This section deals with using SQL in IMS programs. Although most of the information herein deals directly with DB2, IMS application designers also should take it into account, because future business applications may be converted from IMS to DB2. Worse still, potential systems may even require concurrent access to both IMS and DB2 databases.

Checkpoint Logic

Many IMS programs include checkpoint logic, either to release held resources or to handle recovery or restart after the abnormal termination of a program. An IMS program that contains DB2 statements must deal with an additional complication, the allocating and releasing of DB2 resources. Such resources are usually acquired through the use of locks, which are released when DB2 does a commit. In an IMS-DB2 program, the DB2 commit happens during an IMS checkpoint. This step takes place as part of a two-phase commit (discussed earlier in this chapter). The major concern for the application analyst is that commit processing forces all open cursors to be closed.

The DB2 cursor is the method used in application programs to access single rows of a result table. Remember that DB2 processes such queries using set logic, under which all results passed back to applications are in the form of tables. Rather than requiring some kind of variable-length mechanism for a program to secure the results of a query, DB2 permits the following process:

1. As part of static storage, the program defines a SELECT statement, using a DECLARE CURSOR statement.

2. During program execution the cursor is OPENed. This stage then causes DB2 to begin evaluating the original statement defined by the cursor. At this time DB2 may or may not create the complete result table.

3. The program next issues a FETCH command against the opened cursor. This procedure causes DB2 to return the first row of the result table to the program.

4. Succeeding rows of the result table are now obtained, using a FETCH command.

5. After the last row is fetched, DB2 informs the program through the value of the SQLCODE that the end of the result table has been reached. The program now CLOSEs the cursor.

This process becomes much more complicated if a checkpoint must be taken after cursor OPEN and before cursor CLOSE. Because the cursor must be closed for the checkpoint (commit) to take place, it must then be reopened after the checkpoint. If the cursor is simply OPENed, however, the entire result table is recreated. This function is, after all, what the program is requesting by opening the cursor.

Imagine an SQL SELECT statement that returns a result table of 10,000 rows. If a checkpoint is taken every 1,000 rows, the 10,000-row result table will be recreated ten times. This practice is noticeably wasteful of resources.

To avoid this scenario, the original DECLARE CURSOR statement must be expanded. Typical applications for this purpose define the query by giving it an additional predicate in the WHERE clause specifying that it create an ordered result table having key values greater than the value in some host variable. This variable is then set to the value found in the last row FETCHed. Thus, in our imaginary example, result tables of 10,000, then 9,000, and so on, to 1,000 rows will be created. This result is somewhat better, but not much. Another alternative would be to save the entire result table in either an IMS database or a permanent DB2 table before going ahead with processing. In this case, however, a program abend at any point could create recovery and restart problems.

There is no completely satisfactory answer to this problem, but application designers can still avoid most of its attendant problems by being careful in their query formulation.

Locking and Data Contention

There are several options regarding the way locking is implemented in IMS and DB2. The usual arrangement seems to be to use the required IMS Resource Lock Manager (IRLM) for DB2 and Program Isolation (PI) for IMS/VS. If IMS resources need to be shared among applications and other subsystems, however, IMS usually uses IRLM. In this case DB2 and IMS can share the same IRLM, though doing so is sometimes not recommended "for performance reasons." Although these reasons are not explicitly stated, they include considerations of lock duration and timeouts. (A detailed discussion of lock managers and how they work is beyond the scope of this book. For a more complete treatment, refer to the appropriate IBM manuals.) System administrators wanting different parameters used for IMS/VS and DB2 resources will use two IRLMs. Note that defining an IRLM takes lots of tedious grunt work. I personally don't recommend doing it twice.

Adding DB2 to the equation changes the way that locking and contention are handled. Now programs can be informed through a status code or SQLCODE that a deadlock has been resolved and the program's database updates have been rolled back to the previous commit point. This situation, discussed earlier in this chapter, must be handled by additional program logic or database and table structuring.

One way of reducing the threat of deadlock is to use collision fields. A collision field is a special field in an IMS segment, or a column in a DB2 table, whose value indicates whether the remainder of the data in the segment or row are available for use. An application requiring one or more segments or rows first accesses and changes the values of the collision fields to some value indicating that it is in use. Once this has been done successfully the application can continue, knowing that all the necessary data will be available. The collision fields would be reset back to "available" after processing has been completed.

The disadvantages of collision fields include the following:

- They take up additional space, which can be prohibitive in large segments or tables.

- Using them may almost double the amount of I/O done by the DBMS, because segments are retrieved more than once.

- Program size increases because programs are required to hold segments or rows in memory for simultaneous updating.

- Collision fields may create deadlocking on the collision fields themselves.

Another solution to the contention problem is that of using control tables. A control table implemented in DB2 would contain one row for every requested resource in the system. Programs wishing to access these resources would proceed as follows:

- By accessing rows of the control table corresponding to required resources for update purposes.

- Setting each row to indicate "resource in use."

- Storing the rows back in the control table.

- Releasing locks on the control table, perhaps by doing a checkpoint.

At this point the control table is now available to other users, and it is indicating that some resources are in use. Regrettably, there are many disadvantages to this method:

- A program abend during resource processing leaves the control table indicating "resource(s) in use" when in reality they are not.

- The control table becomes highly volatile, making performance and recovery a problem.

- These tables can cause contention problems.

Despite these disadvantages, having a control table appears to be a popular method in some shops for reducing or avoiding resource locking problems. I strongly recommend against using them, however. Instead, use good application design.

Ad Hoc Processing in an On-Line Environment

In general, IMS systems are designed with transaction processing in mind. Most of the common structured design methodologies consider work both in terms of process flow and data flow. Relational modeling and ad hoc processing are concepts foreign to most IMS professionals.

The best advice concerning whether or not to do ad hoc processing in an on-line environment is simply *do not.* Although DB2 is admittedly still in its infancy, on-line performance suffers because there is such a profusion of interfacing subsystems and such a lack of well-optimized access path selection. There are several alternatives to developing on-line ad hoc systems:

- Take production data, offload it to a separate system, and use ad hoc queries in this system. In this manner, any query performance problems will not adversely affect other on-line systems. IBM's Query Management Facility (QMF) can be used in this regard.

- Use the Resource Limit Facility to limit the hogging of resources by ad hoc queries.

- Prohibit on-line updating. This is not as terrible as it sounds. Allow updates to be entered on-line, but batch them for processing at a later time, presumably when the system is less fully loaded. This option may be unacceptable in a 24-hour on-line environment.

- Give users distributed processing capabilities. IBM's Enhanced Connectivity Facility (ECF) and Host Database View (HDBV) program products allow, say, PC users to download production DB2 tables to a microcomputer, select the required data for processing, update the tables locally on the PC and, finally, upload the result tables to the mainframe. The point is that offloading CPU and DASD consumption from mainframe to PC isolates other on-line systems from the process, allowing them to perform better.

Time and Date

The addition of DB2 and its associated built-in SQL functions to a program permits it to access time-of-day and date information from DB2. If at all possible, using this feature should be avoided. Not only is it inefficient to use a powerful database management system to get today's date, but DB2 must return it as the response to a query. Since the FROM clause is required in the DB2 SELECT statement, getting the time of day or date requires accessing a DB2 table, despite the fact that the table is never referenced. (Some shops that still insist on getting the date in this fashion have defined for themselves a special table called the STUPID_TIME table to use for this purpose.)

There are several alternatives available for accessing the time and date. Most programming languages have their own facilities or reserved words for accessing these. The I/O-PCB in an IMS program will return the date and time when a message was queued for a given transaction. Perhaps the best solution would be having an in-house assembler subroutine that would invoke the appropriate operating system routine.

Variable-Length Data

Although IMS allows databases to have variable-length segments, they are not common. Shops using DB2, however, always seem to define some columns with the VARCHAR attribute. This means that table rows are implicitly understood to be of variable length. This characteristic has a great impact on the way DB2 does its logging.

A general rule for DB2 logging of table updates is that DB2 logs the first changed byte through the last changed byte in the row. Because a row containing a VARCHAR column has a Row Length Prefix field at the beginning of the row, we thus conclude that changing the length of a VARCHAR column causes DB2 to log from the beginning of the row (remember that the Row Length Prefix has changed) through the last changed byte (the end of the row, since the length change has shifted succeeding columns one way or the other).

Referential Integrity

Referential Integrity (RI) usually is not a problem in IMS. By default, deleting a segment automatically means also deleting its physical children. However, in DB2 this is not always the case. DB2 tables can be defined using primary key and foreign key relationships having *delete rules* so that some new options become possible:

- Deletion of a parent row in one table may be prohibited if any related child rows exist in another table.

- Deletion of a parent row in one table may cause a related child row in another table to have its key value set to NULL.

- Deletion of a parent row in one table may cause one or more related child rows in another table to be deleted. This effect may be cascaded, causing further rows in other tables to be deleted, and so forth.

These options are discussed more fully in the appropriate IBM DB2 manuals. The important thing to remember here is that IMS-based applications are usually written with the built-in assumption that the DBMS will handle RI issues. The addition of DB2 tables and associated logic may then mean that applications must hard-code this logic. This requirement is especially true in hybrid applications with related IMS and DB2 structures.

Using the EXPLAIN Facility

The EXPLAIN facility of DB2 gives the designer and programmer a look at the access path that DB2 has chosen for a selected SQL statement. The EXPLAIN statement is commonly used in the SPUFI environment for single SQL statements. Alternatively, one can specify EXPLAIN(YES) during plan binding to explain all SQL statements for a particular plan.

Before using EXPLAIN it is necessary to create a table into which DB2 will put the results of the process. After execution, this plan table will contain a row for every query or subquery in the original SQL statement. The meanings of the columns in the EXPLAIN table are interpreted in the IBM DB2 manuals as well as in various DB2 books on the market. Here, let us concentrate on the things EXPLAIN will *not* tell you.

Indexes and foreign keys. EXPLAIN will not inform you if a plan will use a particular index to access a foreign key. (For definitions of primary and foreign keys, see the discussions of Referential Integrity in the DB2 Application Programming manual.)

Predicate evaluation sequence. Some SQL queries have multiple predicates in the WHERE clause in the SELECT statement. EXPLAIN will not tell you the order in which it evaluates the predicates to determine the access path chosen.

Statistics and assumptions. The DB2 catalog contains statistical information about all the tables in the system. In particular, it keeps data regarding key cardinality, or the number of unique values in a column, the number of rows in a table, and other measurements. These statistics are not updated automatically; to create them you must run the RUNSTATS utility. Until you do, DB2 will continue to use certain assumptions regarding the range and distribution of values of certain columns.

These statistics are then used by the optimizer at bind time to determine the chosen access path to be used by queries. Invalid or out-of-date statistics, or none at all, may cause the optimizer to select an inefficient or costly access path. EXPLAIN does not inform you which statistics or assumptions were used by the optimizer.

IMS-TO-DB2 MIGRATION

Some IS shops currently using IMS-DB as their database management system are now considering migrating from it to DB2. This change is not as straightforward as it might seem. Replacing hierarchical databases with DB2 tables is uncomplicated, though tedious, but unfortunately DB2 does not perform well yet in a purely transaction processing environment. Furthermore, present application systems were originally designed with hierarchical or network/plex database structures in mind. As a relational DBMS, DB2 thus requires an entirely different mindset, a completely different approach to system and application design.

To understand fully the complexities involved, let us review the various features of IMS, CICS, and DB2, with the different environments in which they are used. This analysis will lead us to a projection of future IS staff makeup and how it will affect application development.

IMS, CICS, and DB2 Release Features

It is instructive to compare the features of the various releases of IMS, CICS, and DB2 (see Table 6.2).

As can be seen, recent IMS and CICS releases have concentrated on functionality, whereas DB2 has emphasized performance. The reputation DB2 had for poor performance in early releases has by now been mostly overcome. Although DB2 is designed for the ad hoc environment, as in fact are most relational DBMSs, it is now able to perform fairly well in a transaction processing environment.

As companies find that DB2 will generally perform well in most environments, they will inevitably begin to migrate their database environment over to DB2. This process may take decades, for several reasons:

Table 6.2. CICS, IMS, and DB2 release features.

CICS Version 1, Release 7: July 1985

Virtual Storage Constraint Relief (VSCR) for
Auto-Install
Resource Definition On-line (RDO)
Startup/Init processes made more concurrent
Files now "open on first use"
TempStore and Transient Data formatted more efficiently
Local Shared Resource (LSR) pool now the default for VSAM buffers

CICS Version 2, Release 1: March 1989

Extended Recovery Facility (XRF) now above the line
Future releases will be MVS/ESA
Removal of support for macro level coding, BTAM, direct block addressing
Special CICS internal security (RACF)

IMS Version 1, Release 3: February 1984

DASD logging
Use of LAST for checkpoint-ID
Enhancements to Fast Path

IMS Version 2, Release 1: March 1986

Enhancements to Database Recovery Control (DBRC)
Various DASD log enhancements
BKO parameter available for dynamic batch backout
Support for CICS 1.7
Use of MVS/XA for IRLM

IMS Version 2, Release 2: July 1987

VSCR for IMS-DC
OSAM Sequential Buffering (SB)
Support for CICS/MVS 2.1
Off-line dump formatting
Changes to HD locking
Future releases will be MVS/ESA

IMS Version 3, Release 1: October 1988

VSCR for DL/I
Log reduction and compression

Table 6.2 (continued)

DB control blocks and buffers above the line
VSAM and OSAM buffer pools above the line
High Speed Sequential Processing (HSSP) for DEDBs
Time Controlled Operations (TCO)
Split into Data Manager and Transaction Manager

DB2 Version 1, Release 3: June 1987

DATE, TIME, TIMESTAMP, and associated functions
Utility performance enhancements
Optimizer enhancements
VSAM Linear Dataset (LDS) support

DB2 Version 2, Release 1: October 1988

GRANT to groups of users
Dynamic SQL governor
CICS dynamic plan selection
Optimizer and lock manager enhancements
User update of system catalog columns
DBMS-controlled referential integrity
Segmented tablespaces
"Distributed processing"

DB2 Version 2, Release 2: September 1989

Distributed processing enhancements
Optimizer enhancements
Use of Data Facility Hierarchical Storage Manager (DFHSM)

- Hierarchical and network (CODASYL) databases cannot be easily converted to relational databases.
- Most IS shops have a backlog of applications in various stages of development, so they have no staff left to do database conversion or the massive application rewriting required.
- Many common hierarchical and network database management systems have special features not available in DB2.

On the other hand, as discussed earlier in this chapter, DB2 has several features of its own that make it suitable for IS applications of the future:

- DB2 includes referential integrity, at least up to a point.
- DB2 Version 2, Release 2, includes the beginnings of distributed processing features. These advances will be enhanced in later releases.

The most common scenario will no doubt be that companies will decide to migrate their IMS databases to DB2 tables over a period of several years. New applications will be written using DB2 whenever possible. Maintenance and enhancements to existing applications will then involve converting databases and rewriting programs.

The IS Shop Moves into the Future

The DB2 environment of the future will be quite different from the IMS and CICS DP environments of today. What will such an environment be like, and what problems will an IS staff then face? What follows is a foreshadowing of things to come (see Table 6.3).

The future production environment. Today's production environment is one of transaction processing. It is here that IMS and CICS excel. Indeed, it is estimated that several trillion lines of code are currently invested in COBOL transaction processing programs alone. However, the future will see a rise to prominence of the ad hoc environment. In it packaged software and modular systems will replace standard application development. What will be left to develop will be expert systems, perhaps based on artificial intelligence, to help business planners answer what-if questions. Relational database management systems are specifically designed for this environment.

Future staff responsibilities. An estimated almost 80 percent of a DP staff's hours are spent maintaining and enhancing existing software. This will change as more and more development tools become available, shortening the system development life cycle. System designers and application analysts will use such tools as rapid analysis, logical data modeling, prototyping, storyboarding, joint application development (JAD), and integrated CASE tools to speed development. As systems shift from transaction processing to an ad hoc environment, systems development will accelerate.

Table 6.3. Comparison of IMS, CICS, and DB2 information systems environments.

Category	CICS and IMS	DATABASE 2
Production environment:	Transaction processing	Ad hoc queries
Staff primarily doing:	Maintenance	Development
Database environment:	Static	Dynamic
Sample applications available?	Many	Few
Third-party software available?	Much	Little
Tuning aids available?	Many	Few
PC tools and applications available?	Few	Many

The future DBMS environment. Most hierarchical and network/plex database structures share a common characteristic: they are relatively static. Therefore database structural changes or data relationship changes require system redefinition. For IMS, changing a database structure by adding or lengthening a segment, rearranging the hierarchy, and the like require something like the following procedure:

- Define the new structure.
- Bring the system down.
- Unload the current database in its appropriate form: image copy or a flat file, for example.
- Delete the original structure's definition.

- Create the new structure's definition.
- Allocate DASD space for the new database.
- Run the required reload, reorg, and resolution utilities.
- Bring the system back up.

All these steps may not be necessary in every case; nevertheless, having them still leads shops to create standards and procedures such as "system changes will be made only every other Saturday, and only if we receive the proper paperwork by the preceding Wednesday."

The DB2 database environment is, by contrast, markedly different. In DB2, columns can be added to tables while the system is up. The ALTER and DROP statements can be used to change various parameters affecting referential integrity, indexes, and the like. This dynamic environment is essential for the IS shop of the future. Even now we hear about 24-hour system availability. As more shops make IMS data available on-line, the need for batch programs and the corresponding batch window dwindles.

Sample applications. Analysts designing new IMS or CICS systems have at least one great advantage over their DB2 counterparts: there are almost always other, similar applications available for comparison. Often an existing IMS application can provide a designer with information regarding performance, development time and cost, degree of user satisfaction, skill levels of analysts and programmers, and other useful information.

By comparison, the DB2 analyst has few if any such systems to study. This scarcity makes it difficult to estimate development time and system performance. Furthermore, since the risk of making mistakes from inexperience is higher in DB2, the developer must allow for an additional "fudge factor" in development time and consider the costs and disadvantages of delivering the system late and over budget.

Third-party software and tuning aids. Over the past two decades many software and hardware companies sprang up offering tools for IMS and CICS systems that IBM did not provide. Some of these offerings later became IBM program products and others, such as Abend-AID, exist to this day. These tools and tuning aids assisted DBAs and system administrators in monitoring system performance, analyzing problems, and cataloging and organizing system information.

Until recently there were few such tools available for DB2 systems. This shortage was due in part to the rapid changes in succeeding releases. In the future, more and more such tools will appear to support the DB2 environment.

Microcomputer-based tools and applications. In today's environment there are few microbased applications, and not many PC tools. This does not mean they do not exist, just that many companies are simply unaware of them or are unwilling to use them. Remember that IBM came out with their first PC in 1981, after IMS and CICS had been around for more than a decade.

Remember that DB2 is a relational database management system. Relational systems, based on set-at-a-time processing, are fundamentally different from transaction processing systems. As a consequence, systems analysis and design are done quite differently in relational systems. PC development tools will assist designers in carrying out this responsibility.

PC-based software packages, especially CASE tools, are becoming more and more common in the business environment. Some experts feel that these tools will become a necessity if businesses are to survive in the future.

Section III

DB2 Conversion and Migration

Chapter 7

Converting Applications Using Other DBMSs to DB2

In 1989, IBM published a set of manuals intended to assist users of other database management systems in their conversion efforts from that DBMS to DB2. These DBMSs included Adabas (Software AG), DATACOM/DB (Computer Associates), IDMS, or CA-IDMS (Computer Associates), and VSAM files. See the end of the chapter for a list of these manuals. (Interestingly, IBM's Information Management System—IMS—was not included in this effort.) This chapter summarizes some of the considerations and scenarios, including straightforward migration, database coexistence, and system conversion.

OVERVIEW OF THE CONVERSION PROJECT

Conversion or migration of a set of applications from one database management system to another is not necessarily a productive effort. There are, however, a number of relational advantages that justify the conversion of existing applications with little or no change in function. In the case of converting to DB2, these reasons are essentially the reasons that caused the choice of DB2 for new applications. Typically, the choice is to do new application development and major rewrites with DB2 and permit existing applications to atrophy. There are several additional factors that come into play:

- The cost and effort of maintaining two database managers
- Maintaining skills in multiple database management systems
- Assigning system resources such as memory to multiple systems
- Maintaining currency of code on multiple systems

Data interchange and consistency between the two systems can also be costly and complex.

The following sections are excerpted from the IBM DBMS Conversion Guides listed at the end of this chapter and will give the reader an idea of why IBM feels that conversion to its new DBMS (DB2) is cost-justifiable.[1]

The Relational Model

The relational model provides significant value for an application implemented in DB2. It can be shown to add value and reduce cost.

Conceptual simplicity. The tabular relational model is a very simple concept. That fact reduces training costs of personnel who will be working with the model. It also means that data processing analysts can communicate readily with the application users on data base issues such as content and relationships. These capabilities extend to end-user support, as we will describe.

Normalization. Two of the primary purposes of a database system are to reduce redundancy and ensure integrity of the information. Normalization provides a mathematically proven technique for ensuring nonredundancy and ensuring that no information will be inadvertently lost due to the deletion of associated data. This reduces the requirements for data maintenance, ensures data consistency, eases application extension, and avoids the loss of information.

Functionally rich language. The functional richness of Structured Query Language (SQL) for both programmer and end user enhances the capability to expand applications and reduces the cost of maintaining them. In many cases, additional functionality can be added to an application with less effort than other data models and with no change to the database structure or definition. This means that application extensions that were not justifiable with the existing database may become justified with the relational implementation.

The following particular functions are found in a relational database:

- *Join.* Operate on multiple tables (files) in a single statement (DB2 contains a current implementation limit of 15 tables per request).

---

[1]Portions of this chapter reprinted by permission from these publications by International Business Machines Corporation.

Data can be correlated among the tables based on any data values in the tables with either a static or dynamic request.

- *Union.* Treat multiple tables of similar format as a single large table for the purpose of a single request.

- *Set updates.* The ability to add, change, or delete a selected set of rows with a single statement.

- *Views.* The data in a view is not maintained as a separate table but is derived from the underlying table(s) each time it is required for data access. Each user may have a different retrieval requirement from the data contained in the tables of the database. Views provide the data elements required for each user's specific purpose. Views are also an effective way to implement data security. They can be used to restrict access to sensitive information contained in the database by granting user access to specific columns (fields) of a table, instead of, as in the case of VSAM, access to the entire record.

- *Ordering.* In SQL, an ordering clause puts the rows of the result table in order by the values of the columns identified.

Industry direction. The data processing industry has embraced the concept of the relational database and has accepted it as the current direction in database technology. The American National Standards Institute (ANSI), International Standards Organization (ISO), and FIPS have all accepted SQL as the relational database language.

New applications from the PC to the largest mainframe are being developed using the relational model. This trend has several impacts on an installation. As end users look for new applications on personal computers, they will often be using relational databases. As departmental computers are installed, they will use relational databases. Conversion of host applications to a relational database provides a common foundation and format that is familiar to users.

If older applications are to interact with new DB2 applications, either locally developed or purchased from vendors, the older ones will need to be converted to DB2.

For data processing personnel, working with the most popular MVS relational database ensures them of a valuable skill. New personnel will recognize the value of learning and using this database technology.

Courses and seminars are readily available for acquisition and exchange of information. DB2 user groups exist in most major cities for the sharing of experiences and knowledge. Groups of active DB2 projects exist within the national IBM user groups, GUIDE and SHARE.

Design productivity. As normalization isolates data to the lowest common denominator, the addition of new data or relationships need not impact existing applications while retaining minimal redundancy and data consistency and integrity. Relational database is more "forgiving" of design errors and omissions. Designs may be built more quickly with less future planning required. As a result, application development may start sooner. New applications sharing data with existing applications benefit as well.

Referential integrity. The relational concept of referential integrity allows the database administrator to define relationships between tables with integrity constraints. This concept removes the enforcement of such constraints from the application program and puts them in the database system definition. This means that the addition of new data and relationships need not impact the existing applications to enforce data constraints. Further, as the system maintains the relationships, end users may be given authority to update selected data with the knowledge that the system will ensure that no damage is done to the overall data consistency.

Extensibility. The relational model permits the addition of new data into a system or even into a table without the requirement for reorganization of the existing data.

Current applications can be readily extended without database changes requiring changes to existing programs. Additional function that could not be justified in the past due to the impact on existing programs or data will be more feasible on converted applications.

Recovery management. DB2 has a comprehensive and integrated recovery scheme that includes dual disk logging, automatic recovery on restart, and extensive utility support. Most important, though, DB2 recovery is fully integrated with the recovery of the CICS transaction manager with which it operates. DB2 communicates with CICS so that problems in any part of the system can be resolved while retaining the integrity and consistency of the data. DB2 protects data from three types of failure: subsystem, media, and application program. Applications and transactions that use DB2 data operate across subsystem boundaries. DB2 supports fully synchronized recovery across multiple subsystems. The points at which changes to the database are committed are synchronized so that recovery can be coordinated between subsystems if a failure occurs at any point.

On subsystem failure, a restart of DB2 automatically restores data to a consistent state by backing out uncommitted changes and completing the processing of committed changes.

If CICS is attached to DB2 at failure, DB2 coordinates restart with the transaction manager, keeping data consistent across all subsystems.

DB2 makes provision for media recovery (failure of a disk device or failure of a read or write to disk) by providing logging. DB2 tracks log activity in separate data sets so that recovery is simplified. DB2 uses the information on the log (both from online and batch update processing), reducing the requirement for manual control of update activity. DB2 utilizes an image copy and applies the updates gathered on the log (since the last image copy) and applies the changes to create an updated database, using the DB2 recovery utility.

If an application program ends abnormally, DB2 isolates the work associated with the failing program. It then dynamically backs out all uncommitted changes to data, without interfering with other subsystem activities.

DB2 also permits you to back out uncommitted changes. For example, this capability allows an application programmer or other user to perform a series of hypothetical updates to the database, explore the effects of the updates by using SQL statements, and then restore the database to its original state.

Concurrency. DB2 allows more than one application process to access the same data at essentially the same time. However, the integrity of the data could be exposed if DB2 did not apply the proper controls. On the other hand, too much control could impede access to the data. A proper mix in DB2 of "locking" and "concurrency" is the answer.

A lock associates a DB2 resource with an application process in a way that affects how other application processes can access the same resource. DB2 uses locks to ensure that no other application process accesses data that has been changed by another application process but not yet committed. To preserve data integrity, DB2 acquires locks implicitly under DB2 control. It is never necessary for an application process to request a lock explicitly to conceal uncommitted data. In DB2, the IMS Resource Locking Manager (IRLM) acts as a traffic director to control updates to the data, both from the on-line CICS, or batch. Therefore you can still run batch jobs while the DB2 on-line system is up and not have to worry about the integrity of the data.

Security. DB2 offers the ability to protect various levels of data, from an individual data value (column, row) up to an entire table and provides a leveled authorization mechanism for allowing functional capabilities related to DB2 databases. Therefore you can keep all your data in a centralized file (table) and still have the flexibility of restricting access to sensitive fields (columns/rows) within the table. DB2 provides these security and authorization levels through two mechanisms: views and the GRANT/REVOKE statements.

In a view, the user is dealing with a controlled subset of the data. The security control is provided by authorizing access to a view (i.e., selected columns and/or rows) and not the entire table.

The basic unit of functional security in DB2 is the *authorization ID.* A single user may own one or more authorization IDs or several users may share a single authorization ID. In turn, each authorization ID is granted privileges to use any one of the varied DB2 capabilities. Each privilege applies to the ways a user can affect a DB2 database object, whether it be a single element in a table or an entire data base. The GRANT and REVOKE functions of SQL are used to specifically authorize these privileges to an authorization ID. More specifically, these statements provide tighter security because no user can perform any operation unless the user is explicitly authorized to do it.

Availability. The requirement for continuous operation is a recognition of a need that DB2 helps address.

First of all, DB2's utilities can be invoked on-line and can execute upon data without requiring that the DB2 system be quiesced. Further, changes to DB2's environment (for example, alterations to tables, adding and dropping of indexes, etc.) can be made dynamically without requiring that the DB2 object being changed become unavailable to other users.

Non-DB2-related outages (for example, power interruptions or hardware failures), while outside the scope of DB2, can be reduced in their impact through the use of DB2's simplified and expedited emergency restart procedures.

The basic design of DB2 as a separate MVS subsystem isolates it from potential failures in other related software components. As a result of this architecture, DB2 can remain active while other system components are being recovered or restarted.

Nulls. Any field value in a table, regardless of its data type, may have the special value "null." Null represents a value that is unknown or not applicable. A null value may be thought of as an empty space, or a space reserved for later insertion of data. Nulls can occur in a table by explicit user request through an insert or update operation, or implicitly when a new column is added to an existing table. Null values can be prohibited for specific columns when a table is created. In VSAM, nulls must be part of the program logic, thus making application development much more complex. The ability to discern between unknown and zero (0) values in calculations in an important consideration in application development.

Programmer productivity. The relational model removes a number of functions from the programmer. There is no structure to be maintained by the programmer, no paths to be navigated to the data. Access of the data is the responsibility of the database manager, not the programmer. Referential integrity maintained by the DBMS relieves the programmer from the responsibility of writing and testing the code for the function.

In addition to the relational model, DB2 also utilizes current state-of-the-art technologies both in software and hardware. These technologies provide benefits to existing applications that would be converted.

Optimizer. Relational database has as a fundamental rule that the programmer or end user must be isolated from the physical storage of the data. The corollary to this is that if the user is isolated, then the system must be responsible for navigation (finding and selecting the records for the application). In the case of DB2 it is the optimizer component that is responsible for the navigation of the individual request. This expert system analyzes the current structure of the data, which indexes (if any) are present, and statistics about the data organization. The optimizer attempts to select an access path that will minimize that amount of work to fulfill a request. As the data changes, as the database administrator changes designs, or as technology changes the hardware that the system runs on, the optimizer will adjust the execution so that it is still optimized. Converted applications will gain the benefits of new technologies without rewriting code.

MVS/ESA utilization. DB2 uses all of the appropriate features of the MVS/ESA operating system. Operating in several address spaces with a large number of tasks, DB2 uses the superior scheduling of MVS/ESA and the enhanced cross-memory services.

Multiprocessor utilization. DB2 was built with the assumption that it would run on a multiprocessing computer. The architecture selected is not limited to any number of processors, but is driven by the number of users. Even CICS, with a single-task architecture, benefits from the design. Each CICS transaction operates as an independent operating system task when performing DB2 functions. Thus 100 concurrent terminal users would drive 100 independent tasks with the potential for driving 100 processors if such systems existed. Benchmarks have proven the effectiveness with the six-way processors available today.

Since DB2 does utilize all the potentially available processors, there is no need to run multiple copies of the database manager for system utilization. Data may be truly shared among applications. Conversion to DB2 delivers the ability to use the multiple CPUs and the simplification of managing only one copy of the database management system.

Storage management system utilization. DB2 is integrated with the IBM storage systems products and uses their facilities. This includes the Data Facility Storage Management Subsystem (DFSMS) capabilities for data control and the Hierarchical Storage Manager (DFHSM) for data archiving and staging. DB2 operates below the external interfaces as a privileged user of services providing a shorter path length requesting I/O directly from the media manager.

System Application Architecture

System Application Architecture (SAA) provides a common set of facilities across the hardware architectures that support user functions in OS/2 EE on the PS/2, OS/400 on the AS/400, and VM and MVS on a S/370 host. SQL has been designated as the database interface for SAA. In MVS, DB2 is the product providing that interface.

Connectivity. SAA defines connectivity between the different system platforms. Users connected to one platform can communicate with another platform to access data. When the data is in DB2, the SAA systems will be able to ensure the integrity of the transactions without regard to where they are executed.

Distributed data. SAA has introduced Distributed Relational Data via SQL. The function defined allows for access and update of data across platforms. A user will be able to access and update data on multiple systems with a single transaction without knowing where the data exists or the type of system on which it exists. Security, integrity, and performance will all be built into the implementation. DB2 will provide this capability for the MVS platform.

Data converted to DB2 will be able to participate in SAA distributed. This means users on other systems and other architectures such as OS/2 EE will also be able to utilize the data.

Portability. Applications written using SAA SQL and an SAA language such as COBOL or the SAA 4GL Cross System Product can be readily ported from one environment to another. They may be developed on an interactive environment such as VM and executed in another environment such as MVS.

Applications converted to DB2 can then be extended through development in the environment most appropriate for the development process.

Distributed Data

The relational model is ideally suited to data distribution. The following specific capabilities support distributed data.

Select. The relational select operation permits the user to restrict the data to be transmitted to only that required. Extensive Boolean and comparative operators limit the data selected. Subselects to qualify the request based on data in the same or other tables further reduce the amount of data to be transmitted.

Project. The project operation of relational data permits the restriction of data transmitted to only that required by the application. Data not required is not transmitted, improving communications performance.

Join. Joins permit the user to have extensive intertable manipulations done at the location of the data before transmitting the resultant matched data to the user. This may result in significant communications reduction, as no unmatched data need be transmitted.

Set operations. The fact that relational operations are performed on sets permits a distributed data system to respond to a single request with a number of rows of data in a single transmission. The reduction in the number of requests and the blocking of the response both serve to optimize the system.

End-User Support

The requirements specific to an end user were key when the relational model was developed. It was intended to be suited to the free form need of the business professional as well as the needs of the data processing professional.

Ad hoc query. Converting data to DB2 provides the capability of ad hoc query. Users can formulate questions and put them directly to the database. The simplicity of the relational concept makes this possible. Tools such the Query Manager of OS/2 or Query Management Facility (QMF) of MVS provide a consistent view of the data from any platform. Data converted to DB2 provides more query opportunities with very little programming effort.

End-user access. Many of the requests for application extensions are for additional queries and reports against existing data. Relational database simplifies the user's understanding of the data. Conversion of applications to DB2 will open opportunities to end users. They will be able to define their own reports and change them at will. Reports will be more valuable and users more satisfied.

Applications extension. Most existing applications have a backlog of changes and additions waiting for implementation. By converting the application to DB2, the addition of new application and function is made much simpler. The cost of individual changes will be reduced and previously marginal changes may now be cost justified. As the additions can be made more rapidly with less impact on existing programs, it will be possible to satisfy more requests. All of this will contribute to the value of data processing to the enterprise.

Decision support. The flexibility of relational database makes it highly suitable for decision support. Data converted to DB2 becomes available for manipulation by products such as QMF or Application System (AS) to provide decision support functions. Graphics interfaces do charting to support the analyst.

CONVERSION CONSIDERATIONS

The objectives of a conversion from another DBMS to DB2 are to maximize relational capabilities while minimizing conversion costs. The techniques involved are a limited, but intelligent, conversion of the data and an analytic conversion of the application programs.

While there will be an attempt to directly translate DBMS files/tables to DB2 tables, the source data may require additional normalization to improve the relational design and reduce redundancy as much as possible. Relational features should be used to optimize the capabilities of the system. Database administrators will quickly become familiar with the conditions that will require structural changes between the two systems. This requires that those doing the conversion be familiar with the meaning of the data.

In converting the programs, it should be possible to remove some code required by the source DBMS. Some navigation routines may be eliminated. Some programmed search loops may be eliminated. Developers doing the conversion will quickly become aware of patterns of program statements that imply redundancy in the relational system.

SOURCE DBMS INVENTORY

In order to prepare accurate estimates of workloads, costs and schedules, it is necessary to thoroughly inventory each application to be converted. The conversion team should conduct an inventory of DBMS applications, analyzing the results of the inventory and ranking each application in order of conversion difficulty. The data that will be collected and the criteria that applies to that data will help make the final ranking and selection as objective as possible.

Adabas Considerations

If your are a PREDICT user, PREDICT reports can be used for some of this inventory. It should be noted that if PREDICT data is current and complete, it can be a useful tool during the database design and data conversion phases of the conversion. The conversion team should consider bringing PREDICT data up-to-date. The two primary advantages of doing so are the capability to obtain quick answers to the what-uses-what type of question and the assurance that all data entities are available for inventory. However, the time and cost of bringing the data dictionary up-to-date will still have to be weighed by the team.

DATACOM Consideration

Reports from the DATADICTIONARY can be used for some of this inventory. The best source of information for the application inventory and resulting analysis may be a DATACOM database administrator who is knowledgeable in the DATACOM database system and applications.

IDMS Consideration

The IDMS Integrated Data Dictionary (IDD) will be of considerable assistance in this effort. IDD reports can be used for a great deal of this inventory. Further, it can be a major tool for the database design and conversion phases of the application conversion. The data may be used from reports or, with some programming or interactive data manipulation, the Punch output of the dictionary may be directly manipulated to become amenable to loading into the inventory.

Basic information to be gathered and its use in the selection of an initial application for conversion are as follows:

- Application names that will be used for identification and tracking of the application.

- A brief business description of the application and its function that will enable both application analysts and systems personnel to recognize it. If a corporate data model exists, the entities of the model should be identified to allow identification of overlapping function with other applications.

- The number of records used by the application is an important determinant in relative complexity of applications. Typically, the more records used, the more complex the conversion. In addition, the number of sets identified with the records used is an indicator of complexity.

- Isolation is a major factor in degree of complexity of an application and therefore its desirability as a conversion candidate. The greater degree of sharing of data between applications complicates the conversion. If applications that do not force data to be shared between the source DBMS and DB2 can be identified, less effort will be required.

- The number of programs for the application must be identified and recorded by language. This information will determine the conversion effort for each program.

- As the application will be "locked" against changes for the duration of the conversion, the number and criticality of any outstanding change requests becomes important. Users with a large number of changes outstanding will tend to be intolerant of a major effort being applied to their application without improved function. They will not understand that changes impede the conversion. (On the other hand, if the changes are impeded by restrictions of the DBMS, such an application may be a desirable initial conversion.)

- Business timing of the conversion may be a factor and the cyclical nature of an application should be recorded. For instance, an application used primarily at year end should not be completed in January where the results of the effort will not be available for nearly a year.

With this limited information gathered, it is possible to make a determination as to the candidates for conversion with the highest priority and the lowest risk. While it is desirable to have a small, limited application for the initial phase to develop staff experience and confidence, business priorities may not permit this.

WORKLOAD ANALYSIS

The objective of workload analysis is to size the database and program conversion effort. The results are used to formulate conversion cost estimates and produce the project schedule for the implementation phases.

Note that there may be operational requirements that require workload estimates in order to produce a complete assessment for scheduling purposes. Examples are the development of testing aids, data control language to implement the security plan, and the JCL to execute various utilities such as backup and recovery. These are not addressed in this section.

The guidelines that are provided here are rules of thumb for the first conversion project. More precise estimating methods may be developed for subsequent projects based on results of the initial application.

Database Design Workload

A major and time-consuming task of database design is translating source DBMS table or file formats to DB2 tables. The number, composition, and complexity of the source may complicate data base design, particularly where they include fields with multiple occurrences.

Primary and foreign key analysis. The determination of DB2 primary and foreign keys is a substantial part of the database design. A determination must be made as to whether foreign keys will be identified during conversion or added gradually after the conversion. Programs can be simplified, but only at the cost of the effort of simplification. At the same time, new programs may be written more quickly if foreign keys (and referential integrity) are implemented. Further, end user use of the system is enhanced by the implementation of referential integrity.

There are no foreign key equivalents in Adabas, DATACOM, or VSAM, and the implementation of foreign keys during conversion may result in problems in program conversion.

Field to column analysis. The number of fields per table is an important indicator. A high number may signal unnormalized data that could change the ratio (say) of DATACOM tables or Adabas files to DB2 tables. If there is only one element or dataview per table, this could indicate multiple records types within the table. Multiple record types will mean multiple DB2 tables for the one DATACOM table.

Repeating fields. The use of OCCURS and OCCURS DEPENDING is a field mapping situation that should be highlighted because of the potential complexity added to the DB2 database design. Use of these options will require close evaluation and generally will require new DB2 tables or columns.

Coexistence issues. It may be necessary for some period of time to have data existing both in the source DBMS and DB2 tables. The impact that coexistence issues would have on the DB2 database design is normally minimal.

Special Programs and Procedures

Data conversion. The data conversion plan will require some special-purpose programs and procedures. Each aspect of the data conversion should be evaluated to provide direction for estimating the effort involved. In some cases a similar program exists that can be converted. These programs and procedures comprise a set of software needed to more the data from the source DBMS to the DB2 tables. New programs identified should be estimated according to installation standards for new application development.

Coexistence programs. Coexistence programs are programs required for passing queries and transactions between the source DBMS and DB2 in a coexistence environment. Bridge programs are another form of coexistence programs that allow access from a source DBMS application to a DB2 table and vice versa.

DATABASE DESIGN

Conversion may be done in different degrees. Conversion may be of a "compatibility" or "transparency" nature where source DBMS records are mapped directly to DB2 tables. If the data has been designed and maintained as normalized data, this approach will be appropriate. In those cases where data is not normalized, this is unlikely to provide optimum performance characteristics and the resultant system loses the productivity advantages of the relational model. Thus, while the migration is simplified, it is quite possible that the end result will be unsatisfactory for either current performance or future additions.

As a next level, it is possible to do a simple conversion with minimal analysis of the data. This provides essentially a relational result from the source data but may still not optimize performance or application design. The best—but most expensive—conversion is an intelligent analysis of the data, its logical structure, business rules, and usages in existing and planned applications. While such a complete analysis is the most expensive, it should be understood that the cost of this conversion will usually be less than the cost of a new database design. Most of the required data fields have been defined and the data exists in a processible form. Further, it should be remembered that in terms of the overall cost of the conversion, the database conversion is typically a small part.

One major difference exists between the resources required for doing a compatibility-type conversion and those required for a true redesign. In the case of a true database redesign, the availability of one or more persons fully familiar with the data and its usages is required. This knowledge need not be provided full time to the conversion team, but must be available on a demand basis. Documentation rarely provides all the information necessary to do an intelligent conversion.

Objectives of Database Design

The primary objective is to optimize both the performance and the application design. The approach is to do a limited redesign of the database and reprogram the parts of the applications that are product sensitive. Again, note that no attempt is made to change the application data requirements. The assumption is that the application will continue to need and use the data that is currently stored. It is understandable that there should be no application changes or extensions during the conversion except as may be mandatory to tolerate the change in database management systems. There will be cases where the designer recognizes that better ways exist to store the data or that some other change should be made to improve the format or structure of the stored data. Despite the temptation to make the changes that appear minor, the designer must recognize that making such changes can seriously impact application conversion and testing procedures. Assuming that the objective is to minimize the time to make the conversion, such changes should be delayed until the application enters the maintenance cycle. Such opportunities for improvements and enhancements should be noted in a journal of future potential enhancements. This ensures that the knowledge of potential improvements is not lost and the changes can be incorporated when appropriate.

Relationships

A relational database permits the direct association and retrieval of data from multiple tables (relational joins) based on any data values present in the tables. Normally such associations are based on keys. The relational model defines two specific types of keys: the *primary key*, which identifies the individual row, and the *foreign key*, which provides a reference to a primary key of another row.

Adabas considerations. Relationships in Adabas are primarily implemented through application programming with some assistance from indexes.

CA-IDMS considerations. Relationships in a network DBMS are based on definitions to the system. These relationships are implemented by an embedded pointer structure consisting of addresses of the related records. This fixed type of structure provides direct paths along relationships but effectively prohibits free-form relationships.

DATACOM/DB considerations. DATACOM does not provide a DBMS supported technique for maintaining relationships between tables, but users do implement application supported relationships. Such relationships are maintained in DATACOM/DB through the use of key values stored in one table to relate to another table.

VSAM considerations. Relationships in VSAM are primarily implemented through application programming with some assistance from indexes and Relative Byte Addresses (RBAs).

Referential Integrity

A major capability of the relational model is *referential integrity.* This capability permits the database administrator to specify consistency rules that will be maintained between tables. It may, for instance, require that an Order may not exist without the corresponding Customer. The deletion of an Order would mandate the deletion of all associated Order Items.

There are some cases where referential integrity may be inserted without increased complexity of the conversion. Where files were converted to multiple tables, referential integrity may be defined between the resultant tables to supply the same consistency that was implicit in their being in a single record. That is, if data that is now an Order Item table was previously repeating groups in an Order file, then referential integrity rules could be implemented to ensure that no Item row is created unless the Order existed and that deletion of an Order would result in the deletion of all the Items of that Order. Such an implementation will reduce the coding necessary to support the multiple table design and will reflect the same conditions that existed in the single file.

Adabas considerations. Adabas maintains interfile data consistency through application programming. The relational implementation of referential integrity controls data consistency based on data values (primary and foreign keys) in related tables. As primary/foreign key relationships are defined, the data consistency rules may be specified that replace application programming.

CA-IDMS considerations. Network DBMSs maintain data consistency through rules implemented in the set linkage definition. The relational implementation of referential integrity controls data consistency based on data values in related tables. As the linkages are replaced by keys, the data consistency rules may be specified that map to the IDMS rules.

The integrity rules in the IDMS set definitions can be directly translated into DB2 integrity rules, with the possible exception of Conditional Erase. The use of Conditional Erase creates a condition that is not clear without application analysis. If all programs are consistent in their use of this verb for the erasure of an owner, then the RESTRICT integrity option of DB2 may be used to provide equivalent support. If the term is used only in selected programs, the application logic will have to be interrogated to determine the appropriate integrity options.

DATACOM/DB considerations. DATACOM maintains interfile data consistency through application programming. It may not be appropriate to implement DBMS controlled referential integrity during conversion. Replacement of such code may unnecessarily complicate the conversion for no additional benefit. Further, program implementations may not exactly map to relational rules. The one situation in which referential integrity should be implemented is wherever a single DATACOM/DB file is split into multiple tables. These tables should be defined with referential rules to maintain data consistency equivalent to that existing when they were a single table.

VSAM considerations. VSAM maintains interfile data consistency through application programming. The relational implementation of referential integrity controls data consistency based on data values (primary and foreign keys) in related tables. As primary/foreign key relationships are defined, data consistency rules that replace application programming may be specified.

Since such rules between files are maintained by programming, in making the conversion there is a choice as to whether referential integrity should be implemented to replace the existing programming. In general, this is probably not a good choice. Replacing existing programming will complicate the reprogramming and the testing functions, thus slowing the conversion. Further, it may well be found that the rules implemented do not exactly map with any of those available using DB2 referential integrity. This will mean that results from the new system will be inconsistent with results from the old system at least to some degree. It would be better to withhold the redesign of these programs until after the conversion.

In addition, there may be inconsistent implementation of the rules in the VSAM system due to different programmers or different conditions at the time of the implementation of a given program. These situations must be resolved on an individual basis.

Record and File Ordering

Adabas considerations. Inverted files imply ordering by the search descriptors. This may usually be relied on by the application program. Where ordering is relied upon in Adabas, the relational request must explicitly call for it in converted applications. Typically, this is done using an ORDER BY clause in the SQL query.

CA-IDMS considerations. Network DBMSs permit the concept of record ordering within the set of the database. This is foreign to the relational concept. Where ordering is implemented in the network model, there must be a substitute capability provided in the relational implementation. Ordering defined on some data element in the record can be readily implemented but the problem may become complex in the cases where the order is chronological or programmer controlled rather than through a data item.

DATACOM considerations. In DATACOM, the indexes imply ordering by the key IDs. This ordering sequence may be relied upon by the application program. Where ordering is relied upon in DATACOM applications, the relational request must explicitly call for it in converted applications.

VSAM considerations. VSAM files imply ordering through prime and alternate indexes. This may be relied on by the application program. This is foreign to the relational concept. Where ordering is relied on in VSAM, the relational request must explicitly call for it with an ORDER BY clause.

File/Table Format

A relational table must preserve the capability of a user to search based on any column value. This restricts the format of the table to ensure that the search column can be identified by the database manager without ambiguity. This causes the prohibition in a relational table of the REDEFINES clause that can be used in other DBMSs.

Adabas considerations. Inverted file formats are less restricted than relational table formats. For the same reason and also to enforce normalization to the degree possible, repeating fields and groups (MUs and PEs) are prohibited. In general, the inverted file will tolerate unstructured record content except for descriptor fields. Where the structure violates the rules of DB2, a redesign or circumvention must be developed.

CA-IDMS considerations. Network record formats are less restricted than relational table formats. To enforce normalization to the required degree, repeating fields and groups are prohibited. In general, the network model will tolerate unstructured record content except for CALC and ordering fields. Where the structure violates the rules of DB2, a redesign or circumvention must be developed.

DATACOM considerations. DATACOM tables are less restricted than DB2 tables. To enforce normalization to the required degree, repeating fields and group fields are prohibited. In general, DATACOM will tolerate unstructured record content except for key fields. Where the structure violates the rules of DB2, a redesign or circumvention must be developed.

VSAM considerations. VSAM file formats are less restricted than relational table formats. To enforce normalization to the required degree, repeating fields and groups are prohibited. As with DATACOM, VSAM will tolerate unstructured record content except for indexed fields. Where the structure violates the rules of DB2, a redesign or circumvention must be developed.

Record-at-a-Time Processing

Adabas and VSAM considerations. Adabas and VSAM operate record-at-a-time as opposed to the set processing capabilities of the relational model. In some cases, such as data scrolling, the application depends on this single record mode. In cases where single record mode is required, it may be necessary to add data into the database to support specific application requirements.

DATACOM considerations. The DATACOM database, using native database calls, allows for record-at-a-time in addition to the set-at-a-time processing. In some cases, such as data scrolling, the application depends upon this single record mode. In cases where single record mode is required, it may be necessary to add data into the database to support specific application requirements. This situation will require a unique identifier to maintain the sequence of the table occurrences.

CA-IDMS considerations. Networks operate record-at-a-time[2], as opposed to the set processing capabilities of the relational model.

Undefined Fields

Adabas, CA-IDMS, and DATACOM considerations. Many Adabas users have documented all of their data in PREDICT; most CA-IDMS users have documented all of their data in the Integrated Data Dictionary (IDD); DATACOM user have used DATADICTIONARY. There are, however, some users who have documented only the fields required for the database manager. In other cases, the data documented may reflect only a default case and other fields or subfields may be redefined within the program. It is necessary to have a team member or have access to someone who can verify that the defined fields constitute all of the fields used by all of the applications.

VSAM considerations. Some VSAM users have documented all of their data in a data dictionary, but there are many others who have no dictionary or have documented only portions of the necessary data. It may be necessary to have a team member or have access to someone who can verify that the defined fields constitute all of the fields used by all of the applications.

Normalization

Older files may have a number of design compromises that have been made to accommodate the addition of new applications or for performance reasons.

---

[2]An exception exists if the Logical Record Facility (LRF) has been used to build a defined set for the application program.

For instance, common data may appear in multiple files to avoid the addition of complex retrieval logic.

Normalization will uncover the compromises for examination. The relational model is based on normalization. Therefore, to achieve the benefits, it is best to attempt to normalize the data so far as practical. A simple conversion may be done without normalization, but the result will not be as effective as when normalization is done. The limitations of unnormalized data will result in reduced flexibility, especially for the ad hoc end users.

CA-IDMS considerations. While appropriate for network databases, such compromises as we have noted may be counterproductive for relational databases.

Structural navigation usually results in parts of key values being maintained in the IDMS set owner rather than the member record itself. For instance, where records exist for Customers, Orders, and Order Items, the relational key to Order Item would probably be Customer Number, Order Number, and Item Number. However, only the Item Number would be present in the Item record; the other values would be implied by the path to the data. Application logic acquires the partial keys as the path is being navigated to the target record. As the data is redesigned for relational use, the full key must be included in the table.

VSAM considerations. Some VSAM file designs collect all data associated with an entity into a single file; this results in records unsuitable to the relational model. Such compromises, while appropriate for VSAM files, may be counterproductive for relational tables.

Repeating Groups or Fields

Repeating groups or repeating fields of a record discovered in data definitions may be handled in multiple ways. The purest way is to normalize the data and generate multiple tables. This will probably be the preferred method for repeating groups. In most cases, this will result in an additional table as some attributes will occur outside the repeating group area and require their own table and unique key. Multiple tables will complicate the conversion of the application programs and will increase the volume of data. Where the data is a variable number of repeating groups, this may be the only reasonable solution.

Note that the multiple table solution will provide the capability of framing a single argument request that searches all occurrences. Previously, programs had to provide logic to scan them.

Adabas considerations. Repeating groups (PE) or repeating fields (MU) of a record discovered in data definitions may be handled in multiple ways. As mentioned previously, the purest way is to normalize the data and generate multiple tables. This will probably be the preferred method for data defined to Adabas as PE. In most cases this will result in an additional table, as some attributes will occur outside the PE area. PE defined areas will require separate tables in order to provide a new unique key. This will complicate the conversion of the application programs and will increase the volume of data. Where the data is a variable number of repeating fields, this may be the only possible solution.

Note that this solution will preserve the capability of framing a single argument request that will search all occurrences. The Adabas capability of defining a descriptor over multiple occurrences of a field does not have a direct corollary in DB2, where multiple occurrences may not be defined.

In the case of fields defined to Adabas as MU, the creation of an independent table may be too inefficient. Where the data is a fixed number of repeating fields, then the fields can be translated to columns with unique names and the program logic adjusted accordingly. DB2 does not have the capability of searching these with a single argument.

Overlapping Fields

Inspection of record definitions may uncover overlapping or COBOL REDEFINES types of fields. Typically this condition is the result of "subtypes" of records. It is a common condition for there to be multiple types of an entity. For instance, an application may address multiple types of products that a company sells: manufactured at this location, manufactured elsewhere (plant name and shipping information required), and purchased (vendor and price required). A single record may well redefine the content for the three subtypes. In cases of redefined record content it will be necessary to analyze the data and determine whether multiple tables should be defined or whether all types of fields properly belong in the same table. It will be necessary to understand how the programmer determines which of the fields exist in the Adabas file. Decisions on how the programs are to be modified to address two tables instead of the single file will determine whether an identifier is carried into the new table.

This will require normalization of the data to determine the correct association. It will also require the assistance of someone familiar with the application and its associated data. The first test that can be applied is to determine if part of the prime key has been redefined. If so, the data is not normalized and should be divided into multiple tables with unique primary keys. In some cases data may be unnormalized but still have a single prime key.

Redundant Data

For performance, data may have been defined in multiple files. These cases may be difficult to identify due to the lack of common names. If a dictionary exists, it may contain information identifying where this occurs. Without a dictionary, it will require someone with extensive knowledge of the application to identify all of the cases.

When a decision is made to maintain redundant data, every attempt should be made to keep the data-type definitions of the redundant columns identical. This can have a positive impact on performance, particularly where the data is used as the basis of a Join.

Another concern will arise in consolidating these fields into a single version. It is almost axiomatic that there will be some inconsistencies between copies. It is necessary to have an agreed-on technique for handling these conditions. This may be as simple as ignoring all but one copy or as complex as analysis by a committee of users.

Table Combinations

Normalization of the data may bring to light instances where data in two or more files should be combined into a single table. For instance, an accounts receivable file and an order entry file may each have as one of their resultant tables, a table of customer information. While not necessarily redundant, these tables may properly be normalized to a single table. Most programs can be protected from the change through the use of views. Programs responsible for the addition or deletion of rows will be made more complicated.

Primary Key Determination

The relational model requires the existence of a primary key to ensure entity integrity—that is, the ability to uniquely identify any row. DB2, however, does not enforce this requirement except where referential constraints are defined. If it has been decided that no referential constraints will be defined during conversion, then primary keys are not required but will probably be desirable. Therefore, as the primary key does not imply referential integrity, it may be wise to assign a primary key wherever possible to allow for ready addition of referential integrity in the future.

Adabas and DATACOM considerations. Neither of these DBMSs has an object corresponding to the primary key of the relational model.

CA-IDMS considerations. As CA-IDMS has CALC and index fields that roughly correspond to the primary key of the relational model, these fields become good candidates for primary keys.

VSAM considerations. Generally, the prime key of a KSDS is a good candidate for a primary key. For an RRDS, the relative record number (RRN) may be a good candidate. Note that an additional column will have to be added to the table to hold the relative record number.

For an ESDS the RBA, though an obvious possibility, should probably be avoided. Since DB2 tables have nothing equivalent to an RBA, conversion of maintenance programs is complicated by the need to simulate new RBAs for new records. In addition, a column must be added to each table to simulate this RBA. Where practical, other fields should be selected as candidate keys for the new DB2 table. If there are not practical choices currently in the record, consider the addition of a new field, such as timestamp or an artificial identifier.

Foreign Key Determination

Even if it has been decided that referential integrity is not to be implemented to replace application code providing interfile consistency, referential integrity should still be used to provide integrity for data that has been split into multiple tables from a single file. Conversion effort can be reduced by using referential integrity in the DBMS to provide the same kind of implied rules as a single file solution. In such a case, determination of foreign keys is usually simple.

VSAM considerations. In breaking up a file into multiple tables, there will normally be a natural parent-dependent relationship. The unique (not repeating, not redefined) part of the file will become the parent table, the nonunique part will become the dependent table. If the newly created dependent table has a primary key defined, it will probably be an extension of the primary key of the parent table. Therefore the foreign key that references the parent is a subset of the primary key of the dependent table. The rule for such a relationship should be specified as Cascade to simulate the original file condition.

DBMS COEXISTENCE STRATEGIES

During the conversion process there will be data and programs that need to span the source DBMS and DB2. In some instances, coexistence will merely be a stepping-stone to full migration, but in other cases coexistence may be a way of life for a longer period of time. Therefore a plan for dealing with database coexistence issues is outlined in this section.

There are a number of different approaches or strategies that can be defined as coexistence. The levels of complexity and applicability of these strategies vary depending on the installation's requirements.

This section will cover various flavors of coexistence, beginning with the simpler ones and moving to the complex. Most installations will find that as they move through the conversion cycle, they will be implementing several variations of coexistence, depending on business situations, application types, and use of the data.

Coexistence Scenarios

In most situations, applications will be converted gradually over a period of time, requiring an installation to support two database management systems. This will result in some duplicate data definitions in the DBMSs and sometimes duplicate data itself. This section deals with the management and maintenance of data that is spread between two DBMSs.

An initial activity to any form of coexistence is the mapping of source DBMS structures into DB2 tables. After data mapping has been decided, the remaining tasks for managing coexistence can be automated to some degree, depending on the tools and aids in the installation.

Extract data for query, decision support systems. The simplest case, *extract*, is not truly a conversion condition but is worth mentioning. If the initial benefit of conversion to DB2 is to obtain the capability of using the relational model in support of end-user capabilities such as query and decision support, extract is an appropriate approach. In the case of an extract it will still be necessary to go through the database redesign effort. In fact this becomes more critical, since the support of end-user query and decision support requires stricter adherence to the relational model than production applications. Compromises in design are less acceptable.

The easiest approach is to extract data from existing source DBMS databases and load it into DB2 tables. The tables can then be accessed by a number of tools for query and decision support applications. This approach might be a requirement for data that is maintained in programs that are not to be converted immediately, yet the ability to get to the data with end user tools is a requirement.

Update of one DBMS with read of the other. These applications (often called *bridge applications*) contain database calls and logic for both DB2 and the source DBMS. This scenario may be the most widespread during the conversion effort because of the interrelationship of data and the length of the conversion effort. However, the conversion effort will be most cost-effective if the need for these applications can be kept to a minimum, because they will require at least some rework when all data has been moved to DB2. Considerations should be given to locking algorithms, commit strategies, and recovery methods when mixing the two database technologies within the same program.

Updates to both databases. Updates to both databases occur when data is replicated in the source DBMS and DB2. The approach is dependent on the timings of the updates. The first determination that must be made is whether the updates must be real-time or synchronous, or a time lag can be tolerated.

- *Time delayed updates.* Time delayed updates of DB2 data can be handled in one of three ways. All methods require a DB2 update program to be written.

    - The first method requires that the source DBMS program be altered and a transaction file be written that reflects the updates. This transaction file would then be the input to a DB2 batch or on-line updating program. Such a program might be initiated by JCL, time initiated, or be a long running program waiting for data to appear in a queue. (There is some data integrity exposure here because Adabas does not use the two phase commit protocol of CICS, and there is a slight possibility that the transaction file would not be completed or rolled back properly.)

    - If a more real-time update is needed, an asynchronous update could be accomplished by having the source DBMS program spawn an on-line DB2 transaction that will immediately schedule a DB2 updating transaction to cause the corresponding update at transaction commit.

- If longer time delays can be tolerated, then the DB2 updates can be handled using source DBMS log information. This would require an additional program to read the log, find appropriate update afterimages (except in the case of deletes where there is no afterimage), and either directly update the DB2 data or write an update file to be passed to another DB2 updating program.

- *Synchronous updates.* The most complex situations would be transactions that update both the source DBMS and DB2 synchronously with full integrity. Coordinated database updates from the source DBMS and DB2 require a level of effort. This approach may be a requirement if related production data resides in both the source DBMS and DB2 and a single transaction must update both.

  (In Version 5, Adabas offers a two-phase commit concept that is transparently handled by the system. The two phase commit allows the Adabas system to coordinate the transaction processing and restart. *It does not provide a coordinated commit between Adabas and DB2.* If this approach is used, all integrity is dependent on the Adabas system. The safest approach is to provide a near equivalent to the two-phase commit through imbedding the Adabas END TRANSACTION logic in the Task Related User Exit [TRUE] of the CICS Resource Manager Interface.)

  (Adabas [and DATACOM] use a single commit protocol and do not use the CICS Resource Manager Interface [RMI] as DB2 does. Therefore it is possible to have an in-doubt situation if either system fails after the issuing of the source DBMS commit but before the response returns to CICS so that CICS could coordinate the DB2 commit or rollback. Failures are not likely to occur and the shorter the path length between the two COMMIT statements, the less the risk. However, consideration needs to be given to this if concurrent update is a requirement in the installation.)

CA-IDMS Considerations

While every attempt should be made to avoid a conversion where only some of the records of a set are to be converted to DB2, there will be cases where it is unavoidable. This will considerably complicate both the database design effort and the application programming effort.

If it is necessary to break a set in converting data from IDMS to DB2, two basic conditions must be addressed:

- *The converted data is a member record.* If the converted record is a member of a set, the relationship to the owner must be maintained and integrity rules enforced. This will require that the member contain adequate information to address the specific owner record occurrence. Navigation will require owner information whenever a program requires access to the DB2 owner from the former member. Integrity rules will require owner information to verify the validity of inserts. This is the equivalent of a relational foreign key and may be implemented in the same manner providing the key contains all of the information necessary to navigate to the owner. In some, but not all cases, this will be a subset of the primary key of the table.

  A more complex consideration are those programs that cause ownership changes or deletions (explicit or implicit) and are not converted. This group of programs must be changed or new programs supplied. IDMS sets with the rule of MANDATORY will require careful analysis. If these programs remain in the IDMS system with the same functions, it may be necessary to change the IDMS database to incorporate a key for access to the converted data. In many cases, this key may be derived from the keys and ordering fields of the IDMS records on the path.

  An additional considerations may be whether or not it is appropriate to replicate some of the data in both systems. For performance, system isolation or integrity reasons, it may be appropriate to store some or all of the data under both systems. Data consistency will then be the issue.

- *Conversion of owner records only.* Where only the owner of a set is converted and the members are not, it will probably be advisable to leave a dummy record as the owner. In this case, it will be necessary for the DB2 table to contain key information that permits access to the dummy. The dummy record may contain not just a key, but also static information to reduce cross system access for some programs. All inserts and deletes done in the DB2 table must have corollary inserts and deletes of dummy owners.

  An alternative approach is to increase the member record with the key of the owner and store the member in an indexed set using the owner key.

SPECIAL FEATURES AND CONSIDERATIONS

Special Adabas Considerations

Adabas groups (PE). Adabas provides the user with the ability to specify groups of fields as a unit. DB2 does not provide an equivalent capability. Application programs referencing groups must be altered to specify the component columns. The inventory information will supply the mapping of columns to groups. No functional change is required in the application.

Hyper descriptors. Hyper descriptors in Adabas permit up to 20 fields or subfields to be used in an inverted list. DB2 limits an index to 16 columns and up to 254 bytes of data. In the event that a descriptor exceeds one of these limits, a compromise will have to be made. As DB2 does not require an index for all accesses, it may be possible to reduce the number of columns in the index without affecting the program logic. The impact of the reduced index on performance will have to be analyzed and the indexing columns carefully chosen.

The use of hyper descriptors in an Adabas application will require analysis. If the use is restricted to the identification of fields that are to be used as a common qualifier, the descriptor may be ignored for the purposes of data base design. If, however, the hyper descriptor is used to define search criteria that are not part of the record, additional design will be required. The data that are added to the descriptor and are not part of the record must be identified as additional columns for the DB2 table. This data may be supplied through the application program or through an EDITPROC. The additional columns must be reflected in the inventory of columns for conversion.

Long descriptors (Adabas). DB2 supports indexing values up to 254 bytes in length. In the event that an Adabas descriptor is longer than 254 bytes, a compromise will have to be made. If the index consists of multiple columns, the low order columns may be eliminated. If one (or the only) remaining column is in excess of 254 bytes, it will be necessary to reduce the length of the column. This may be done in two ways:

- *Additional column.* An additional column may be defined to contain a copy of the first "n" bytes of the desired indexing value. This may be hidden from the program logic to the extent that an EDITPROC exit may be defined for the table that will maintain the contents of the column. It will not be hidden to the extent that requests that are candidates for the index must name the new column as one of the search columns. Both the new column and the LONG VARCHAR columns will have to be named to retain identical function.

- *Split the existing column.* As the data is alphabetic, it is possible to define the one column as two with the first less than 255 bytes without loss of meaning. By moving to a structure internal to the program, program transparency is maintained. Again, SQL references must recognize that there are two columns involved in the search.

Coupled lists. Adabas *coupled lists* are not required for the equivalent function in DB2. The equivalent function is performed by a join or a subselect in the SQL language. An index may be used in assisting the performance of the join, but analysis will have to be done on the requests made to determine whether an additional index will be helpful.

Handling of nulls. The definitions of *nulls* are different between Adabas and DB2. Adabas defines blank alphabetic fields and zero numeric fields as "null." DB2 has a special meaning for null that is not zero or blank; it is *unknown.* To achieve consistency with existing application programs, the DB2 column definitions should be established as NOT NULL WITH DEFAULT. This will result in all columns not provided in an Insert being set to zeroes for numeric columns and blanks for alphabetic ones. These are the Adabas program's expectations for a null value.

This solution does not, however, solve the potential indexing problem. Where a descriptor is defined as NULL SUPPRESSED and is not valued, the records with null values for that descriptor are not indexed and cannot be retrieved by descriptor even though a record does exist. In the case of DB2, they will be indexed and the same request will retrieve them. It will be necessary for the application program conversion to take this into account, probably through additional qualifications of the SQL search arguments to exclude the Adabas null condition. This is the reason that it is necessary to record the fact that a field is defined as NULL SUPPRESSED to ensure that it is recognized during application program conversion and may be dealt with.

Subdescriptors. Where subdescriptors (partial fields) have been used in Adabas, analysis will have to be done to determine the appropriate way to replace this function. Several different reasons for the subdescriptor may exist; two are discussed here:

- *Reduced index size.* A subdescriptor may be used in place of a full field to reduce index size. Thus a City field in a file may be indexed only on the first eight characters as a reasonable compromise of result filtering and index size. The DB2 implementation of such an index will require the full field to be indexed. In the event that this is an extreme problem two compromises are available:

- Establish an additional column that is the equivalent of the sub-descriptor and is generated through the use of an edit procedure associated with the table. This approach will allow the program to be insensitive to the existence of the additional column with the exception of direct SQL usage.

- Alternatively, the first "n" characters of the field may be defined as an independent field for identifiers that contain intelligence. Such a case is really the same as a group item with the requirement that the field be defined as a set of columns.

Phonetic descriptors. If the application uses phonetic descriptors, it will be necessary to replace this capability with an equivalent capability in DB2. The simplest approach to providing this is to define an additional column in the row to contain a phonetic version of the data. An EDITPROC can be used to convert data stored in the row to the phonetic version. This EDITPROC must be defined prior to the load of the table to perform the initial propagation. There will be an impact on programming and the new column must be recorded as associated with the phonetic descriptor to ensure that program conversion personnel are aware of it.

DATACOM Considerations

Sparse indexes. DATACOM/DB permits the definition of indexes on keys that do not contain "null" values. These indexes are specified through the use of the INCLUDE-NIL-KEY=NO parameter as keys are defined. If this function has been used, the corresponding DB2 column should permit nulls.

While this facility may have been used only to reduce index size, it will be necessary for program conversion personnel to check each program that may potentially use the feature. If programs use the index to retrieve specific values, there is no impact. If, however, the program uses the index for sequencing of data, the replacing SQL statement must be written to exclude null values in order to achieve the same result. It will be necessary for the data designers to inform the program personnel of each key defined to exclude nulls so that this may be taken into account. A properly kept inventory will reflect this condition.

Shared key processing. DATACOM supports the use of shared key IDs that are used to access one or more tables by logically relating key definitions. When the application program requests data through record-at-a-time processing for a shared key, all table records are returned (one at a time) that match the key selection criteria.

Typically, this is used to simulate, through the use of application program logic, referential relationships between two tables. An example would be an Order table and an Order-Lines table, whereby an instance of an Order and all corresponding Order-Lines for that order can be returned iteratively through one DATACOM call type. DB2 provides equivalent support for this DATACOM feature through referential integrity rules and joined views.

Another use of shared keys is to request data for logically related fields on a single table, often called *merged keys*. This is implemented using common key IDs in the DATADICTIONARY that are comprised of different physical key definitions on a single table. DATACOM application program logic must determine whether redundant table instances are returned during the iterations.

DATACOM tables with merged keys may require multiple DB2 tables after normalization of the data has been done. Frequently, the merged key tables are actually multiple instance (row) types within one table. The equivalent application logic could be achieved through SQL Boolean operands and/or joins.

Table joins. DATACOM does not support the relational joining of tables. Application efficiencies may be realized by incorporating DB2 relational join capability in the table design.

Intersection tables. DATACOM database intersection tables maintain many-to-many relationships. The DB2 equivalent of this feature is a table that contains two foreign keys that together make up a primary key. Additional data may or may not be present.

Special CA-IDMS Considerations

Records using VIA. Some records are stored VIA a set owner record. In such cases, the primary key will normally be the concatenation of keys. The first portion of the concatenated key will the primary key of either the CALC record or a record stored in an indexed set. The second portion will be any ordering keys of sorted or user-defined indexed sets of all owner records on the access path. Exceptions such as the following may exist:

- *Ordering key is not part of primary key.* These are cases where the records are maintained in order (such as date) that is not part of the primary key. These can be determined through normalization or through application knowledge.

- *Records are not stored by primary key.* The purpose of storing VIA is to place records near their most commonly accessed path. Some applications are of the nature that better performance is provided by storing the data on a path other than the primary key (e.g., Order-Item VIA Product rather than Order). Such conditions can usually be identified quickly by a data administrator and may be verified through normalization.

- *Independent key.* For performance reasons, a record may be stored VIA another record despite having a unique key of its own. For instance, Order may have a unique Order Number but be stored VIA the Customer record. Data administration should be able to identify those cases where the VIA set owner key is not required. Note that inclusion of the owner key will not cause an invalid primary key, but an unnecessarily long one and one that may not be consistent with foreign keys.

- *Unordered sets or sets allowing duplicates.* Typically this will be the lowest level network set; that is, it will not be a set where the members are also owners of other sets. Such records are often not ordered as there is no application requirement for ordering and performance is improved by not requiring ordering. NEXT ordering is the usual specification for such records and will result in insertions being made at the beginning of the set unless the program intervenes. If the record is an owner, it will be necessary to assign some form of primary key. If the record is not an owner, while true relational design calls for a primary key, and if one is not apparent, a primary key may not be required. A primary key may exist but not be defined as an ordering key to either preserve an order, such as chronological, or to avoid the performance cost of sequencing. A data administrator should be able to recognize fields that can be used to create a primary key in combination with the VIA set owner key. If a primary key is required and does not exist within the record, one must be defined. Several options are possible and the practicality is dependent on the application's use of the data. Much of this can be determined by the definition of the insert logic of the set as found in the IDD.

Records using DIRECT. Such a record may or may not participate in a set. Where it does not participate in a set, it probably exists as an independent table. Such a record may or may not require a primary key. If retrieval has been by DBKEY in the past, it will require a primary key to replace the DBKEY. Such a key may be as arbitrary and as simple as using the existing DBKEY value as the primary key.

DIRECT records may also be members of a one-of-a-kind (OOAK) set with sequence maintained by the set. In such a case the discussions under ordered and unordered sets apply. Where the DIRECT stored record is a member of one or more sets, the primary key will have to be determined by analysis.

Multimember sets. There are a number of potential conditions for IDMS sets containing multiple record types. Each requires a somewhat different technique to handle. In every case it is necessary to define the different record types as independent DB2 tables. Analysis of the application must then be done to determine which condition applies.

- *Independent.* Unrelated records may be placed together in a set for the simple expediency of reducing the number of sets. If there are a number of different but rare records associated with the same owner, it may be simpler to maintain a single miscellaneous set of all types. Similarly, records that are mutually exclusive may be placed in the same set.

- *Chronologically dependent.* Unrelated records may occur within a set. For instance, transactions on an account may be of various types and may need to be kept chronologically. Such conditions can sometimes be identified by sets ordered FIRST or LAST without an ordering key. This implies chronological ordering. Sets ordered NEXT or PRIOR may also be of this type as may sets with ordering keys. In general, if there is not a readily apparent dependency, it will be necessary for someone with application knowledge to determine whether or not one exists. Such information may be revealed when determining the primary key and the set order.

  When it is necessary that multiple tables be maintained with a chronological dependency for purposes such as printing an account activity journal, then an additional time stamp key or arbitrary sequence number key may have to be added in order to permit the tables to be merged. The application may become more complex as the network application code to retrieve the records in order is replaced with code to retrieve from multiple tables and perform a programmed merge.

In some cases, there is another option. If the data formats of the multiple record types are essentially compatible, it may be expedient to design a single table definition that will embrace both designs with a record type indicator. This is not a recommended design approach, but it will minimize application logic changes.

- *Logically dependent.* It may be that the application assumes the occurrence of record type *A* is always followed in the set by record type *B.* For instance, there may be a set of Order and Item member records owned by Customer. The application assumes that after every Order record there will be one or more Item records pertaining to that Order. Following the last Item for an Order, there is either another Order or the end of the set. When Orders and Items are placed in separate tables, program logic must be changed to reflect that fact.

  Where the set consists of a few record types, processing may be simplified by always retrieving the data as a join of the parent and dependent set members.

Group level items. IDMS supports the concept of fields that are made up of a number of subfields. Date is a classic case with the subfields of month, day and year. DB2 does not support subfields, although there are two fundamental ways to simulate them. The most common will be define the subfields as columns to DB2. This approach is the most general and permits searching each of the subfields independently and allows the use of the subfields in different or overlapping foreign keys. Where it is necessary to address the group level item as well as the subfields, after the FETCH of the data, the individual columns may be moved to a structure where they can be treated as an entity.

Alternatively, it is possible to define the group level field as a column to DB2. After the data is FETCHed from the table, the data can be moved to a structured work area where it can be perceived as subfields. This will, however, prohibit the use of the subfields directly by DB2.

Junction records. IDMS database designers use the term *junction record* to refer to those records that are used to maintain a many-to-many relationship. The term used with relational data is an *intersection table.* An intersection table consists of a primary key made up of two foreign keys. Junction records are members of two sets and thus provide linkage between their owners. The

DB2 table with foreign keys referencing two types of parents is the equivalent condition.

One difference exists between the two systems in the implementation. For recursive relationships, IDMS requires the junction record for a one-to-many relationship. DB2 does not. If such uses of junction records are discovered, they may be discarded.

Junction records may contain redundant data from their owners. This data will have been put there to eliminate the need to retrieve the data from the owner when processing the set from another owner. As the applications are already cognizant of this condition, leaving the data in a translated junction record will minimize application impact. Performance impact will have to be evaluated to determine if there is value in the relational implementation of removing the duplicate data.

Logical record facility. The Logical Record Facility (LRF) of IDMS permits the database administrator to define a view of the data that may cross many records and provide a modified view of the contents. In the cases where this facility has been used, it will be necessary to carefully analyze the logic of the LRF view in order to translate it to DB2. In the majority of cases, it will be possible to replace the LRF view with a DB2 view of the data. There are two significant exceptions.

- *Programs that update LRF views that are composites of IDMS records.* The view for this capability would include a join that is not updatable in DB2. This will require a view for reading and a separate view on the base table(s) only for update. Communications with the program conversion personnel is required. Summaries of records are a variation of the same condition, though it is unlikely that a program would update a summary of multiple records.

- *LRF procedures may combine a number of records into a single set record with repeating groups.* An example would be a year's transactions may be provided in a record with 12 monthly sets of subtotals. Such types of LRF procedures are best replaced with a module to simulate the procedure within the program.

Subschema replacement. An IDMS subschema defines a subset of the database and the type of access allowed, in effect providing a window through which the database can be manipulated. It can determine which data can be accessed and how that access is performed, as well as runtime considerations such as the run unit structure and storage requirements.

The extent to which these capabilities have been used to define subschemas will affect the scope of the conversion effort. The subschemas encountered may range from small subschemas defined for specific program requirements to large general-purpose subschemas that comprise a full subset of the database schema. To document the conversion requirements, each subschema must be analyzed for the data access functions provided. In turn, each end user or program reference to the subschema must be analyzed for the data access functions actually required.

In general, the function provided by an IDMS subschema will translate into DB2 views and applications plans. Some general guidelines for translating subschemas to DB2 views are the following:

- As a general rule, always use DB2 views rather than base tables for database access.
- Define one view for every DB2 base table that is a full subset of that table.
- For small specialized subschemas, create one DB2 view to replace the subschema.
- For large general-purpose subschemas, use the full subset views of the corresponding DB2 tables for database access rather than creating a new set of views specifically for the subschema. Exceptions may be identified where a specialized DB2 view would be more suitable.

Data access can be defined with DB2 views to limit access or to simplify the coding requirements. An IDMS subschema *view-id* will convert directly to a DB2 view. LRF access can, in most cases, be replaced with one DB2 view. A notable exception is the case where the update of more than one DB2 table is required.

The use of DB2 views to control access is beneficial depending on the requirements of each use. In some cases an IDMS subschema view-id may be implemented more efficiently by specifying a subset of columns in the SQL statement rather than by defining a separate DB2 view. Also, the benefit of defining a view as a means of granting access privileges on a restricted subset of data may be diminished if the view is used only in a program that binds static SQL.

IDMS subschemas may use LRF to control database navigation by defining access paths. Much of this logic may not require conversion because the DB2 optimizer determines the database access paths used.

Special VSAM Considerations

Physical constraints. The physical limit on VSAM record size is extremely large due to its ability to span control intervals (CIs). DB2 row size is limited to approximately 32K, with a maximum of 300 columns. Extremely large VSAM records (in excess of 32K or 300 fields) may have to be split among multiple tables to accommodate their size.

Sequential processing. VSAM programs often require that data be processed in a particular order to support program logic or create output in a given sequence. Where a VSAM index, either primary or alternate, was used to order the data, SQL can create the same sequence by including an ORDER BY clause on the columns that correspond to the VSAM key fields. Skip sequential processing can be accomplished in basically he same way, with the addition of a WHERE clause in the SQL statement to begin processing from a given value in those columns.

Entry sequence processing of an ESDS may require the addition of a new column to the DB2 table. SQL guarantees no sequence unless an ORDER BY clause is specified, and in the case of an ESDS often there is no field in the VSAM record that can provide the proper ordering. In these cases a new column such as a timestamp must be added to the table and the appropriate programs modified to add this data to the new rows.

DB2/VSAM transparency. Using DB2/VSAM Transparency lets you take advantage of all DB2 usability improvements, without reprogramming, recompiling, or relinking most VSAM programs. When VSAM programs run under DB2/VSAM Transparency, VSAM input/output requests are automatically redirected to access DB2 data tables. This allows programs not yet converted to access data that has already been converted to DB2. In fact, a program can access any mixture of converted VSAM data through DB2/VSAM Transparency, unconverted VSAM data through native VSAM DML, and DB2 tables through native SQL. This flexibility greatly reduces the need for replicated data and, consequently, the number of coexistence situations that must be addressed. Where coexistence issues may be a problem, DB2/VSAM Transparency should be strongly considered as a migration aid.

LIST OF REFERENCES

1. *DBMS Conversion Guide: VSAM to DB2.* IBM Application Enabling Marketing Center, GH20-7566, December 1989.

2. *DBMS Conversion Guide: Adabas to DB2.* IBM Application Enabling Marketing Center, GH20-7563, April 1989.

3. *DBMS Conversion Guide: DATACOM/DB to DB2.* IBM Application Enabling Marketing Center, GH20-7564, June 1989.

4. *DBMS Conversion Guide: IDMS to DB2.* IBM Application Enabling Marketing Center, GH20-7562, December 1989.

Chapter 8
Migrating DB2 Systems to Production

In this final chapter, we explore the different alternatives available in both configuring the DB2 environment and migrating various DB2 elements. We will concentrate on the most common migration task: Test to Production.

TEST TO PRODUCTION

Most DP shops that install DB2 create at least two separate DB2 subsystems: one for Test, one for Production. Many shops create a third DB2 subsystem that lies between Test and Production, and is used for testing applications prior to moving completely to the Production environment. This third environment, called variously Production/Test, Quality Assurance, Education, or Stress Test, is usually used to insulate a newly developed suite of applications from both the development and production environments.

These subsystems are totally independent in that, although they may share DASD devices, they have their own Catalog Tables, Bootstrap Datasets, Logs, and Buffer Pools. Migration from Test to Production, therefore, is really a special case of a more general one: migrating from one DB2 subsystem to another. A middle environment allows systems administrators and database analysts to monitor testing and gather pertinent statistics without having to factor out external influences.

External Influences

The production environment. One external influence is the production environment. Testing an application sometimes unearths problems (invalid or incorrect program logic, bad data, abends, infinite loops, resource deadlocks, and so on). These problems may manifest themselves either in the programs themselves, the test data, or the application design. These occurrences should not be allowed to disrupt current production systems.

A separate environment can insulate production resources (and production users!) from these problems. One other possibility is that it provides a means whereby potential users can be trained in new system or application procedures. Newly developed programs can be provided to users that act on test databases. In this way, problems that occur do not affect production data, yet users get a chance to do concurrency and acceptance testing.

The development environment. Another external influence is the development environment. Here, developers continue to analyze, design, code, and sometimes unit test applications. Sometimes this involves on-line CASE tools, program editors, and interactive debuggers. This load on system resources may tend to overshadow that of new production applications. Much testing immediately prior to a move to production involves *string testing* (program-to-program data and parameter transfer), *concurrency testing* (whether programs can affect other programs running at the same time), and *stress testing* (whether the system can support a particular load or mix of transactions). It is difficult to test in this fashion in the development environment, because resource usage measurements are skewed by development efforts.

THE MIGRATION EFFORT

What things are to be migrated to the new environment? In the following section we specify the things one must migrate, along with some comments on available alternatives.

DB2 Catalog Information

Usually the first step in the migration effort, the target environment must contain the correct definitions of the required DB2 objects. This involves not only object creation but also the appropriate granting of authorities to access these objects. In some shops this may involve quite a lot of tedious work, as many users, terminals, and transactions may have specific authorities or privileges. Some installations have gone to great lengths using DB2 security mechanisms to control access to data. For example, it is possible to control specific types of access (i.e., Read Only or Update) to specific table columns for specific users. This facility gives a DB2 security administrator a great deal of flexibility in managing a company's data. Some companies, however, have taken this to extremes. I am reminded of one site where the database administrator had four assistants who spent all of their time entering GRANT and REVOKE commands on-line at the DBA's direction. Clearly, one can have too much security.

At the other extreme are those installations that have taken the approach that DB2 security is much too cumbersome and time-consuming. The customary answer in these cases is for the database administrator to grant authority to use DB2 objects to PUBLIC, and to use some other security method to control access, such as IMS Signons, CICS Signons, or an application-specific security routine.

To have the appropriate DB2 object definitions executed in the target environment requires no more than executing the appropriate CREATE and ALTER commands. This can be done quite easily using either the DB2 Interactive facility called SQL Processing Using File Input (SPUFI), or the Query Management Facility (QMF). Some care must be taken, as these commands update the DB2 catalog and may contribute to contention for these resources. Most shops prohibit such Data Definition Language (DDL) during peak periods.

As an alternative to SPUFI or QMF, the DB2 Migration Aid Utility (DBMAUI) may be used. (This utility is covered in a later section of this chapter.) These alternatives are acceptable ones if the DDL for object definition is readily available. This is not always the case, for some of the following reasons:

- *Errors made in the original object definitions.* Sometimes an error is made in the definition of an object, either due to miscommunication or human error. In these cases the database administrator must modify the object definitions.

- *Errors made in data modeling.* Regrettably, analysts and designers cannot always develop data models that satisfy all business conditions. Additional information gleaned during application coding may require a developer to rethink the data design, sometimes leading to a reconfiguration of the entities involved. This then translates into new or modified DB2 tables and relationships, including the following:

    - New columns, altered column attributes, different column positioning.

    - Addition or removal of primary or foreign keys.

    - Changed or additional performance options, including segmented and partitioned tablespaces, clustering indexes, alteration of free space allocation, and the like.

- *Data definition requiring multiple statements.* Although uncommon, some types of object relationships require more than one DDL statement to create. One example is a table that contains a foreign key column that references a primary key column in the same table. Since the rules for foreign key definition require that the referenced primary key already exist, this relationship must be defined using a CREATE statement for the base table and primary key, followed by an ALTER statement that adds the foreign key definition.

These changes require the database administrator to keep track of current and past object definitions. This is sometimes accomplished by accumulating the DDL in the members of a partitioned dataset.

Some changes to objects can be effected using the ALTER statement. This statement has many limitations, but does allow for certain types of changes to object definitions. These changes may then be kept in the appropriate partitioned dataset member.

If an object has already been created its definition may be changed using DROP and CREATE to destroy and recreate the object. The disadvantage to this method is that dropping a table, for example, automatically causes DB2 to drop any indexes on that table, as well as any synonyms or views defined for that table! In addition, all authorities for that table are revoked, and all plans that refer to the table are marked "invalid." Recreation of the table does nothing to alleviate these problems, as DB2 stores object definitions using internal identifiers assigned at creation time. Creation of a table causes DB2 to assign a new object-ID to that table that may not be the same as the previous one. The database administrator must now proceed to create the appropriate views and indexes, rebind plans, and reGRANT authorities. Users must also recreate synonyms they had defined for the table.

Rather than face this problem, most installations purchase an object management tool having an "extended alter" feature. Such features allow the DBA much more latitude in altering objects without the restrictions of the ALTER statement. In addition, they will handle most of the problems associated with dropping an object, including recreating indexes and issuing GRANTS.

Probably the best alternative for doing object definitions in the target environment is to use a tool specifically designed for migrating DDL. Many of these tools have an option that allows them to generate the appropriate DDL directly from the object definitions stored in the DB2 catalog tables. This feature permits the DBA to execute the tool in the source subsystem, generate the appropriate DDL for a set or sets of objects, and store that DDL in a file or dataset. This dataset may then be used in the target subsystem to create DB2 objects.

Program Source Code

Source code containing embedded SQL statements is no different from other source code. These should be migrated to the new environment using the shop's standard change control system. There are few situations, however, that may require some code changes during the move.

SQL libraries. Occasionally a shop will have stored all SQL statements in a library, pulling them into programs using either an SQL INCLUDE or the appropriate command to the source code management software. In such cases, the library members must be migrated as well. Possible disadvantages of this method include the following:

- *Duplicate library members.* Similar library members may already exist in the SQL library. These may be overlaid or changed.

- *Data design changes.* Changes to the data model underlying the DB2 table design may require several table or view changes. These changes may have a ripple effect on SQL statements that reference these tables or views.

- *Performance tuning difficulties.* Changes in table statistics (as gathered by RUNSTATS) may require restating queries to allow the Optimizer to make better access path decisions. The interfaces of some source code managers make it laborious work finding, say, all queries accessing two particular tables with a Join.

Use of synonyms. SQL queries embedded in programs require table names in FROM clauses. If the tables names themselves are placed in the query, then the names of the tables in the target environment must be identical. If not, the queries must be modified to reflect the target environment names. Although this may be done using the global change facility of a source code editor, a more common approach is to use Synonyms.

Each user in the development environment creates a set of DB2 Synonyms, one for each table they will be referencing in SQL queries. Programs are then coded using the Synonym names in place of table names. During the Precompile and Bind processes, the DB2 Optimizer translates these Synonyms to the corresponding table names in order to choose the correct access paths. When migrating programs from the source subsystem to the target subsystem, all that is required is to create a single set of Synonyms for the production tables. In this way, source code changes will not be required.

Program Load Modules

Load modules of programs containing SQL queries may be moved directly to the production load libraries. In general, recompile and relink are not necessary. For situations where they are required, system administration staff must also rebind applications, due to DB2's timestamping of load modules and application plans. In general, the timestamp of the plan must be chronologically equal to the timestamp of the load module, or DB2 will refuse to use the plan during execution, issuing a -818 SQLCODE.

Database Request Modules

Database Request Modules produced in the source subsystem can be moved to the target subsystem without modification as long as no source program modifications have been made. Any conventional copying method may be used, including IEBGENER, IDCAMS, or their equivalents.

If source changes have been made, it will be necessary to redo the precompile, compile, link, and bind process. This will mean recreating DBRMs in the target environment.

Application Plans

DB2 application plans are produced by the DB2 Optimizer during the bind process. Here, the Optimizer accesses the DB2 Catalog to do authorization checking, identify objects and their relationships, and choose efficient access paths. Since the object identifiers of the DB2 objects (tablespaces, tables, views, and so forth) in the target environment are different from those in the source environment, plans cannot be moved directly.

Database Request Modules migrated to the target environment must be rebound to create the appropriate application plans. This process should be done after the appropriate object definitions, data migration, reorganization, and statistics creation, so that the Optimizer has enough valid information to determine efficient access paths.

Note that if the target environment is on the same DB2 subsystem, the plan names must be different from those in the source environment.

DB2 Data and Indexes

This phase is probably the most resource-intensive of the migration process. It also involves the greatest number of alternatives, each with its own advantages and disadvantages.

Migrating DB2 table data. There are several ways to move data in one DB2 table to another in another subsystem. Most of these methods involve extracting the data into some form that is then used as input to the DB2 LOAD utility. This utility loads tables and builds the appropriate indexes for those tables. The following are some common techniques for extracting DB2 table data.

- *Using the query management facility.* Probably the simplest way to migrate DB2 table data from one subsystem to another is to use the QMF EXPORT and IMPORT commands. This method has a few minor disadvantages.

    - It is relatively expensive in terms of CPU utilization, memory usage, and elapsed time.
    - It is executed in QMF, which runs under TSO. Hence, all work is done in the TSO address space.
    - It does not support VARCHAR columns.

    The general procedure for the QMF method is as follows:

    - Enter QMF in the source DB2 subsystem. Begin at the QMF command line.
    - Access or display a table to be migrated.
    - Use the QMF EXPORT command to export rows from the table that is currently being accessed or displayed to an output sequential dataset.
    - QMF will dynamically allocate the sequential dataset. This dataset will be in a format that can be used either by the LOAD utility as the input dataset or by the QMF IMPORT command. Note that the default allocation is usually 1 track. This may not be enough.
    - Enter QMF in the target DB2 subsystem. Begin at the QMF command line.
    - Using the QMF IMPORT command the output sequential dataset can be brought into the QMF environment and then saved in a table.

The QMF EXPORT/IMPORT technique allows users to create an output dataset that can be moved physically to a different installation. The QMF EXPORT output file contains a series of header records followed by the actual data records. The header records should be removed before passing the file on to the LOAD utility. LOAD utility control cards are not automatically generated by this procedure.

- *An application program.* If the source and target DB2 tables reside in the same DB2 subsystem an application program can migrate data using multiple INSERTs with subselects that select the appropriate rows from the source tables. If this method is chosen, the program should contain some COMMIT logic that releases resources between units of work.

  If the source and target tables reside in different DB2 subsystems, a program may be written that extracts data from the source tables and writes that data to a sequential dataset. That data may then be used either by another application program or by the LOAD utility to load the data into the target tables.

- *Using the Data Extract Utility (DXT).* This utility is extremely difficult to use, as the input control statements are sometimes obscure and unwieldy, and the manuals are far from helpful. DXT copies data to a sequential dataset and creates the appropriate LOAD utility control cards. The dataset and the control cards may then be used with the LOAD utility in the target subsystem.

  The great advantage of this utility is that it has the ability to read many different forms of data as input, including the following:

  - DB2 tables
  - IMS databases
  - Computer Associates' CA-IDMS databases
  - Oracle Corporation's ORACLE databases
  - Relational Technology Inc.'s INGRES databases
  - Digital Equipment Corporations Rdb databases
  - VMS resource management sources (RMS) files
  - VSAM files
  - Other IBM and non-IBM sources through a user-written exit routine

  This capability makes DXT a potential alternative for migrating from one database management system to another.

DXT provides four ways to prepare and run the extract requests you want:

- Write your own extract request using an editor
- Using the Online DXT commands (MVS only)
- Using the End User Dialogs
- Using the Administrative Dialogs

DXT is a separate IBM program offering (#5668-788). It contains a Relational Extract Manager (REM) that reads requests, reads the DB2 catalog, and dumps requested data into a sequential data set. Use the LOAD utility to load the extracted data.

- *Using the Database Migration Aid Utility (DBMAUI).* Like DXT, this utility copies tables to a sequential dataset and creates LOAD utility control cards. The dataset and the control cards may then be used with the LOAD utility in the target subsystem.

  DBMAUI is a separate IBM product offering (#5798-DTQ), so must be purchased separately. It has additional facilities to migrate DDL statements and SQL control statements. DBMAUI control statements give one the capability to migrate any DB2 components by object name, by owner, or by subsystem name. In the case of migration by owner or subsystem, DBMAUI finds all of the related objects that must be moved and controls their migration as well. Unlike DXT, DBMAUI can only access DB2 tables as input.

- *DSNTIAUL.* This utility, which is included with DB2, works similarly to DBMAUI. It copies tables to a sequential dataset and creates LOAD utility control cards. The dataset and the control cards may then be used with the load utility in the target subsystem.

  DSNTIAUL uses dynamic SQL, and can process up to 100 tables in a single execution. It is provided by IBM as part of DB2 purchase. It reads tables and produces multiple sequential output files on SYSREC0x, with LOAD control cards on SYSPUNCH.

- *The DSN1COPY Service Aid.* This IBM program product may be used to both extract and load DB2 data. It is faster than LOAD utility. DSN1COPY has a feature that is simultaneously an advantage and a disadvantage: *DB2 is unaware that this utility is running.* This means that you can run the utility when DB2 is unavailable, perhaps extracting required data during a period when the system is not in use. Other

DB2 utilities do not have this feature, and require that DB2 be up before they can execute.

On the other hand, if you run DSN1COPY when DB2 is up, the utility may cause fatal errors in DB2 processing. In this situation it is always best to first make sure that any tables that are being affected by DSN1COPY are first made unavailable to DB2 applications. This may be accomplished with combinations of the -START DATABASE and -STOP DATABASE DB2 operator commands.

DSN1COPY is similar to the IDCAMS REPRO command, in that it directly copies VSAM datasets. When using it to load target tables it may use as input either a dataset previously created during DSN1COPY extract or a file created by DB2 IMAGE COPY.

To extract data, run DSN1COPY with PARM=FULLCOPY. This will read a tablespace and create Full Image Copy dataset. This dataset is then input to DSN1COPY to load the target tablespace. Note that the major disadvantage of using this utility is that it must be informed of the internal DB2 identifiers in the source and target subsystems that are being affected. This allows the utility to edit the extracted data and change the embedded identifiers to those in the target subsystem. This utility assumes that you know what you are doing. It does not verify that the target identifiers actually exist on the target system, so is somewhat dangerous in this respect.

Migrating indexes. DB2 indexes are usually rebuilt rather than migrated. After table migration, use the RECOVER INDEX command. If the LOAD utility was used to load target tables, it may automatically rebuild all of a table's indexes. DSN1COPY can be used to migrate individual index datasets, but it must translate internal identifiers. This requires the database administrator to be aware of the values of all of these identifiers.

SUMMARY: MIGRATING FROM SOURCE TO TARGET SUBSYSTEM

1. Source programs, load libraries and DBRM data sets may be copied using conventional copying means.

2. No precompile, compile, and linkedit is needed in the target system unless source code changes were made or parameters are different.

3. DDL and Control statement source can be copied using conventional means. Alternatively, a tool may be used to generate the DDL from the source subsystem DB2 Catalog.

4. DDL and Control must now be executed in the target subsystem to create the appropriate objects. Sometimes the order of creation is important. For example, tables containing primary keys must be created before creating a table with a foreign key column that references the primary key.

5. Migrate table data using the appropriate means.

6. Rebuild or recreate indexes (if not done already with the LOAD utility).

7. Create Synonyms.

8. Execute RUNSTATS (if necessary) for tables and indexes in the target subsystem.

9. Bind plans in the target subsystem.

Appendix

Partial List of Third-Party Tools

This appendix summarizes the features of some of the more common third-party tools used in the DB2 environment. Each entry is accompanied by a description of the tool gleaned from the vendor's marketing literature. Sometimes vendor literature is incomplete or does not accurately reflect the features or benefits of products. Readers should remember this fact, and gather more information before making any decisions based on the material found here.

This list is by no means complete. If any relevant tools have been omitted, please contact the author so that they may be included in the next edition. Every attempt has been made to confirm the information in the tool descriptions; however, *the reader assumes any liability for use of this information, and should hold the publisher and the author harmless.*

The tools in this chapter have been separated into the following categories. In cases where a tool belongs in more than one category it was placed in the category deemed most fitting. Some categories need a bit of explaining, and this explanation is included in a short preface to the section.

- Audit Reporting
- Catalog Information
- Database Editor
- Data Compression
- Data Reporting
- Migration Aids
- Performance Monitor
- Plan Analyzer
- Security Manager

AUDIT REPORTING

DB/AUDITOR for DB2 (Systems Center)

DB/AUDITOR for DB2 is a complete audit reporting system for DB2. DB/AUDITOR enables security administrators, auditors, and data base administrators to distill large volumes of SMF, log, and catalog data into meaningful DB2 audit information. The DB/AUDITOR Log Processing Facility provides information about the transactions captured by the DB2 log. This information is presented in an easy-to-read report that details all the activity performed within your DB2 tables.

DB/AUDITOR includes 19 pregenerated reports that provide information on access attempts and a variety of DB2 activities. The product also produces plan management reports using data from the DB2 catalogs. DB/AUDITOR allows you to customize its pregenerated reports and create your own reports using its SQL-like report language.

With the information provided by DB/AUDITOR, you can easily and efficiently get a comprehensive view of your DB2 system and its resources. DB/AUDITOR also helps you protect critical DB2 applications and ensures you have the information needed to satisfy internal and external auditing requirements.

Extracting SMF data. The standard DB2 SMF audit records do not contain object names, only numeric object IDs (OBIDs). These OBIDs are assigned by DB2 and change whenever an object is dropped and recreated, making it difficult for auditors or security analysts to determine the identity of an object. DB/AUDITOR alleviates this problem by matching OBIDs with the corresponding object name from the DB2 catalog to provide easy-to-use, meaningful audit reports. You run the standard DB/AUDITOR reports simply by selecting one of the options on the online screens. The product automatically generates the necessary job control language (JCL) and optionally submits your job on request.

With DB/AUDITOR you can produce comprehensive audit reports without a lot of time or technical expertise. Because DB/AUDITOR makes extracting audit data from SMF files fast, easy, and accurate, it reduces the time you must spend creating audit reports and helps protect the integrity of your DB2 data.

Reports on data changes in tables. The DB/AUDITOR Log Processing Facility allows you to identify all changes made to a specified table during a given date range or unit of recovery. Because the Log Processing Facility does not require traces to be turned on or real-time monitoring to be performed, it in no way impacts DB2 performance.

The report produced by the Log Processing Facility identifies the columns in a specified table that have been updated, deleted, or inserted. Updated data is displayed both before and after the update. Inserted and deleted rows are shown in their entirety and are identified as new or old data.

The DB/AUDITOR Log Processing Facility enables you to answer important questions such as the following:

- Who is updating a certain table?
- What data is being updated?
- How was the data changed?
- When was the data last updated?

Having answers to these types of questions provides you with better control of your DB2 resources and better protection for your DB2 data. With DB/AUDITOR, you always know when and how your data is being updated and who is updating it.

Report tailoring. DB/AUDITOR produces 19 pregenerated audit and plan management reports. These reports provide information on a variety of DB2 activities, including the following:

- Unauthorized access attempts
- Authorization change activity
- Create, alter, and drop activity
- Attempted read/writes
- Utility access
- Plan privilege assignment
- Table access and update activity

DB/AUDITOR provides an SQL-like report language that allows you to create your own reports or tailor the pregenerated reports. Using familiar SQL syntax such as SELECT, WHERE, and ORDER BY, you can easily control report content, format, and sequence.

Using DB/AUDITOR, not only can you report on important auditing and plan management information, you can also customize the information and generate reports when you need them and in the format most helpful to you. The easy-to-use DB/AUDITOR report language makes it easy for you to customize and create a wide variety of reports without having to use the complicated coding and syntax common to so many of today's report generators.

Comprehensive audit trail. As you place more and more DB2 applications into production, you also put more of your DB2 data at risk. DB/AUDITOR can help protect your data even though user access to it is increasing. Using DB/AUDITOR, you can easily identify authorization ID changes, monitor unacceptable privileges, flag unauthorized access attempts, and determine who is granting and being granted Plan privileges. For extra control over sensitive applications, DB/AUDITOR can report on every read/write access attempt, providing you with a comprehensive audit trail.

Satisfying audit requirements. An important part of any audit is producing detail and summary information for long periods of time. The DB/AUDITOR History File Facility makes it easy for you to generate summary or detail reports that cover a specified time period. Because DB/AUDITOR lets you generate historical reports, it helps you satisfy company, government, and external auditing requirements and identify areas where potential problems exist. This capability also reduces the time and effort needed to extract and summarize DB2 audit records from the SMF log files.

CATALOG INFORMATION

Overview of the Problem

The DB2 system catalog is composed of a set of relational tables that function as a central repository for all the objects and access privileges defined in the DB2 system. By retrieving and analyzing the information in the system catalog, you can monitor and maintain the DB2 system.

IBM does not provide a facility within DB2 for querying the system catalog. You must design and create your own SQL SELECT statements to query the numerous catalog tables. Many of these tables must be combined (JOINed) to obtain all the information for a particular DB2 object. The results from these SELECT statements then need to be formatted into clear and readable reports.

Some users, out of necessity, have used IBM's QMF product or SPUFI to build programmatic solutions for retrieving information from the system catalog. This involved designing, creating, and testing all the SQL statements, QMF FORMs, and PROCs required to produce the desired reports. Documentation and support became a burden for the DB2 technical administrators as these PROCs were distributed and changed by other users and new releases of DB2 became available. Moreover, the QMF/SPUFI solution is not conducive to rapid problem resolution.

Using QMF and SPUFI to retrieve and report DB2 catalog information is not an effective solution.

Restrictive selection criteria. First, you must create the SQL to generate the report. If you want to change selection criteria to view different objects, you must exit the report and adjust the SQL to reflect the new selection criteria. You cannot dynamically modify the selection criteria while viewing the report results.

User authorization. In order for users to retrieve catalog information, they must be granted SELECT authority on the catalog tables. Many users must be granted these authorities, or someone must create views for each user needing to retrieve information from the system catalog.

Isolated reports. There is no mechanism provided to allow the user to jump easily from one report to another (that is, to view a related object). Each report exists in isolation.

DB2 releases. New releases of DB2 mean modifications to reports. DB2 technical administrators must alter reporting procedures to integrate new features for each DB2 release, and they may have to support multiple DB2 versions.

One SQL statement limit. Multiple SQL statements are not allowed. The complexity of information retrieved is restricted by the one SQL statement limit imposed by QMF.

System administration overload. As SQL queries and procedures are distributed to and changed by the user base, documentation and support become an increasingly costly burden for the DB2 technical administrator.

Dynamic SQL. Even for reports that are generated regularly, the SQL is bound at execution time. Each time a query is requested, a plan must be generated using newly created SQL. THis process consumes time and resources.

Development problems. Developers must create their own queries and forms to access DB2 system catalog information necessary to create and modify plans and to monitor and maintain the DB2 system. Detail information about objects cannot be displayed on a single screen because of the restrictions of a columnar form. Developers must scroll through multiple pages to find all the information they need.

Because no split-screen mode is available within QMF, developers must constantly alternate between creating queries and forms in QMF and adjusting code to reflect changes necessary due to new information. They also cannot query multiple DB2 subsystems.

Platinum Database Analyzer (Platinum Technology)

A major problem confronting the DBA is *managing physical DB2 objects.* To maintain an efficient DB2 system, you must tune object definitions, monitor DASD space usage and growth, verify object integrity, and schedule DB2 utilities.

DB2 does not provide the facilities to perform effective object management. DB2 does NOT provide sufficient space statistics or space usage history, update activity and free-space usage information, or a mechanism for verifying the integrity of DB2 objects and easily correcting problems when they occur. DB2 provides statistics for optimizing SQL SELECT statements, but it leaves the critical task of managing DB2 objects to you.

Platinum's Database Analyzer (PDA) is a DB2 DASD and database monitoring, analysis, verification, and tuning tool. It supplies all the necessary tools to manage your physical DB2 objects. Major components include the following:

- *Collection System.* Collects DB2 object statistics online or in batch mode. The "Auto Build" feature automatically includes new objects as they are added. All statistics are maintained in DB2 tables and generations of statistics are maintained for historical growth and trend analysis.

- *PDA Audit Facility.* Verifies DB2 objects during statistics collection and produces comprehensive reports detailing any problems.

- *Statistical Action Director.* Directs PDA to take specific actions when predefined thresholds are reached. For example, PDA can automatically generate and optionally submit image copies when update activity occurs and/or perform reorganizations when free-space depletion occurs.

- *Reporting/Query Facility.* Reports all PDA statistics in a variety of comprehensive on-line and batch reports. Each report can be customized, and PDA provides an interface to Platinum's Report Facility for generating sophisticated ad hoc reports.

- *Page Display Facility.* On-line display of DB2 object pages for viewing and optionally updating. All internal DB2 page types are supported and you may access an object's pages even if DB2 is not active. You can make changes to correct errors and perform an online audit to verify the changes *before* they are applied.

ProAlter/Plus (On-Line Software)

ProAlter/Plus is a fully integrated solution for DB2 object management. ProAlter/Plus provides you with ISPF-like panels that enable you to easily:

- Analyze DB2 catalog data
- Analyze DB2 access paths and plans
- Alter DB2 objects and propagate changes to dependent objects
- Migrate DB2 objects
- Download DB2 data
- Clone or revoke DB2 security
- Invoke DB2 utilities
- Interface with ProEdit, the leading DB2 application testing tool.

Without writing a single line of SQL you can do all this and gain insight into object dependencies and relationships—at a glance.

- Display lists of DB2 objects in an easy-to-understand hierarchical format; also display object definitions, statistics, and security. Print out any of this information for easy reference.

- With a Show or Print command, you can get more detail on any object or set of objects. For example, you can zoom in to see all the referential constraint dependencies for a table.

- You save valuable time because you no longer have to repeatedly query the DB2 catalog with cumbersome SQL.

Improve application quality and efficiency

- All the information you need to analyze an application plan is placed at your fingertips:

    - BIND parameters
    - SQL source from the program
    - Access paths available for each table
    - Definition and statistics on the particular object
    - DB2's access path choice

- Reports showing all SQL access to a DB2 table enable you to see and understand how DB2 is accessing a particular table or set of tables—

so you can optimize access to the table. This information is summarized by the following:

- SQL statement (SELECT, INSERT, UPDATE, DELETE)
- Access paths being used by DB2
- Application plans

Alter database design

- You simply specify the change you want to make to a DB2 object—without writing SQL. ProAlter/Plus automatically
  - Locates all dependent objects
  - Analyzes the change specification
  - Generates and executes the necessary SQL
  - Restores object and dependent-object authorizations
  - Optionally recreates the data, application plans, views, and security authorizations
- Work with familiar ISPF commands to make changes to your database. When you need to alter an object definition, ProAlter/Plus splits the screen; the old definition is shown on the top half, and you simply type over these values on the bottom half.
- ProAlter/Plus features full support for referential integrity, displaying relationships among tables and providing a means to rebuild foreign key relationships when you alter a primary key column. It also allows you to partition or repartition tablespaces and indexes.
- On-line real-time options include SQL ALTER Immediate, DROP Immediate, REBIND Immediate, and FREE Immediate.

Smooth migration

- Use a panel-driven approach to move DB2 systems from test to production faster.
- Easily migrate an object or set of objects from within the same DB2 subsystem or from one subsystem to another.

- Migrate data, views, and security authorizations as well.

- ProAlter/Plus can apply user-defined naming conventions to ensure migrated objects will automatically have the desired names.

Automatically invoke DB2 utilities

- Submit standard DB2 utilities on a DB2 object and any or all of its dependents:

  - MODIFY
  - REORG
  - RUNSTATS
  - CHECK
  - STOSPACE
  - IMAGE COPY (Full, Incremental, Merge)

- This facility allows you to run utilities against multiple objects one at a time.

- ProAlter/Plus automatically generates utility control statements, JCL; even calculates space requirements for utility work and output datasets.

Personnel management

This product allows you to easily manage employee hires, terminations, and changes in job responsibilities.

- Now you no longer have to spend long hours creating SQL statements when you need to adjust DB2 security authorizations.

- ProAlter/Plus automatically creates and executes the SQL GRANT and REVOKE statements you need to set, duplicate, or revoke any user's security.

- You can also display and print out all object security and security propagation.

Download DB2 data

- Extract data described by any valid SQL SELECT statement and download it into a physical sequential data set. ProAlter/Plus can also generate DB2 LOAD utility control statements.
- ProAlter/Plus is the only product that lets you describe what you want unloaded with an SQL SELECT statement. The statement can even include UNIONs or JOINs.

DATABASE EDITING

Overview of the Problem

DB2 is the relational database management system of choice, but to fully utilize the power of DB2, you need to create and maintain DB2 objects, test and debug SQl, copy data between DB2 tables, and browse/edit DB2 data. Your ability to perform these critical functions with ease greatly enhances the benefits of DB2.

DB2 provides a powerful DBMS but is missing the tools necessary to perform certain functions.

Object management facilities

DB2 provides the DDL portion of SQL to create, alter, and drop DB2 objects. However, DB2 does not provide the following:

- A menu-driven facility that reduces the amount of keying needed to create and maintain DB2 objects. You must hand-code the DDL into a dataset and execute it through SPUFI.
- A DB2 Space Calculator for calculating the DASD space requirements for DB2 objects. Inappropriate DASD specifications directly affect system performance and increase how often you must perform tablespace and index maintenance.
- A facility for understanding the often baffling relationships among column types, row size, and DB2 page usage. Inappropriate design choices can cause inefficient DB2 space utilization.

- A comprehensive object change management system. The DB2 ALTER command can change only the most basic object attributes. For example, you cannot change a column's name, data type, position, or length without a complicated and lengthy rebuilding of structures and dependencies.

DB2 data editor. DB2 does not provide an on-line editor for browsing and editing data in DB2 tables. DB2 does provide the SQL INSERT, DELETE, and UPDATE statements to be used by application programs but not for interactively entering and maintaining DB2 data.

DATA copier. DB2 does not provide an interactive facility for easily copying data between DB2 tables with appropriate column mapping and data conversions.

Embedded SQL support. DB2 does not provide an interactive facility for constructing and testing SQL as it is being developed in a program. The application programmer must precompile the program to find any syntax errors and then execute the program to discover if the SQL statements perform the desired operations. This is a very time-consuming, costly, and tedious process.

Batch processor. DB2 does not provide a true batch processor for executing SQL statements, dynamically allocating files, executing DB2 utilities (REBINDs, LOADs), dynamically switching between DB2 subsystems, and performing authorization ID switching.

DB2 provides SPUFI for executing SQL in "batch" mode. However, SPUFI actually runs as a batch job under TSO, which uses considerable resources. SPUFI can execute only standard SQL statements. It does not contain the facilities mentioned in the preceding paragraph, which are necessary for sophisticated DB2 object management functions.

ProEdit for DB2 (On-Line Software)

Building a DB2 test environment

- Create and template DB2 tables and indexes using a fill-in-the-blanks approach.

- TEMPLATE command enables you to duplicate existing tables and their referential integrity definitions.

- INTEGRITY command lets you define primary and foreign keys.
- COMPLEX command helps you create indexes with special attributes such as subpages, buffer pools, etc.
- SQLID command enables you to conveniently change SQL authorization IDs across development environments.
- QSAVE command saves the SQL ProEdit generates in a dataset.

Manipulating DB2 test data

- Edit Data Panel lets you use familiar ISPF commands to manipulate data in DB2 tables.
- Query Parameters facility lets you include or exclude columns, order by any columns, and use WHERE clauses.
- Line commands let you insert, delete, and replicate blocks of rows.
- CHANGE command lets you change multiple rows at once.
- FIND command lets you quickly locate a specific value in a column.
- ZOOM command places column value of interest into an ISPF EDIT session and handles all character data types.
- FORMAT command lets you edit one row at a time.
- COPY command lets you quickly load data from a new table into an existing one.
- UNLOAD command unloads DB2 tables to a sequential file.
- LOAD command loads data back into DB2 tables to refresh your test table.

Testing SQL application code

- Logical Compare facility automatically compares before and after images of data after you run a program test.

- Embedded SQL Testing facility lets you test all SQL from within the ISPF editor. ProEdit automatically prompts you for values of any host variable and provides EXPLAIN information on DB2 access.

- SPUFI Emulator gives you everything on SPUFI, *plus the ability to edit any resultant tables;* there's actually no need to use SPUFI ever again.

Platinum RC/UPDATE (Platinum Technology)

RC/UPDATE is a DB2 object and data management tool that provides *all* the necessary functionality to manage and maintain DB2 objects and data effectively and to support the application development area. Major components are the following:

- *RC/OBJECT.* Online screens are provided for creating, altering, and dropping DB2 objects. You can use the TEMPLATE option to create objects based on existing objects. All DB2 options are supported, including referential integrity and secondary IDs. The generated DDL may be executed on-line or in batch mode.

- *RC/ALTER.* The RC/ALTER component is automatically invoked whenever an object alteration not supported by DB2 is requested. RC/ALTER will create the job to unload all the necessary data, drop the object, recreate the object with the new definition, and then recreate all dependent objects, authorization chains, and reload data without any user intervention.

- *RC/EDIT.* RC/EDIT is a complete ISPF-style editor for editing or browsing data in DB2 tables. All DB2 data types are supported and the data can be viewed in column or form mode.

- *RC/COPY.* RC/COPY copies data between DB2 tables. You can select the data to copy and can also request that the target table be created automatically during the copy process. All necessary data conversions are automatically handled.

- *RC/SQL.* RC/SQL is a facility for executing SQL statements contained within a dataset. You are prompted for any host variables and you can execute the extracted SQL statements in batch or on-line mode.

An "Interactive SQL" facility is also available for entering and executing any SQL statement.

- *Platinum Batch Processor.* The Batch Processor executes SQL statements, DB2 Utilities, IDCAMS requests, DB2 commands, and application programs in batch mode (not TSO batch) or interactively. A full audit trail is produced and the user may also perform authorization ID switching for creating objects for other users.

DATA COMPRESSION

Overview of the Problem

DB2's method of allowing compression of data is via the EDITPROC clause of the CREATE TABLE statement. The EDITPROC clause specifies the name of a program that is to be invoked by DB2 every time a row in the table is retrieved or stored. The program receives a buffer containing the row and a flag indicating if the row is being retrieved or stored. If the row is being stored, the program compresses the row in the buffer. If the row is being retrieved, the buffer contains a compressed row that needs to be decompressed.

To implement a compression routine for an existing table, you first have to unload and drop the table. Then you recreate the table, specifying the compression routine in the EDITPROC clause of the CREATE TABLE statement. Finally, the data is loaded back into the table. The table, of course, is unavailable while the compression routine is being implemented. For new tables, the compression routine can be specified when the table is created.

Evaluating the use of a compression routine requires you to determine the amount of DASD space that could be saved, along with the time required to perform the compression/decompression.

One method of determining the measurements is actually compressing the data. In this way, you can easily measure the amount of DASD space saved. Without the proper tools, it's more difficult for you to measure the amount of time a compression routine takes to perform its work.

A compression that saves 50 percent of the current DASD space would be great, but not if it adds an additional 5 CPU seconds for retrieving one row. If you find that the compression routine doesn't save very much DASD space and takes too much time to perform the compression, you have to remove the routine from the table definition. This is a lot of work just to see if a compression routine is worth using.

DB2 REDUCE (Boole & Babbage)

DB2 REDUCE substantially reduces the space needed for medium to large DB2 tables by using the proven Huffman algorithm to efficiently compress the data.

- Compresses DB2 large table spaces by over 50 percent.
- Compresses I/O operations by squeezing more data into the same pages.
- Speeds QMF batch processing.
- Compresses load elapsed time and log volume.
- Improves SQL statement response time.
- Frees DB2 application developers from building tablespace optimization into designs.
- Does not modify code or control blocks of DB2.
- Application receives data in uncompressed form.
- Compression is "transparent" to DB2 applications.
- Uses only approximately 0.5 CPU seconds to process 1MB of original data which is partially offset by other savings.
- Uses standard EDITPROC interface.

PLATINUM Data Compressor (Platinum Technology)

The PLATINUM Data Compressor utility provides excellent compression routines and enables you to perform comprehensive analysis of any compression routine's effectiveness and accuracy *before* implementing it.

- PLATINUM Compression Routines help save valuable DASD space while conserving CPU time. You can choose from several routines, each adapted to a particular data mixture. The Compression Routines understand DB2 data—so they consider factors such as NULLS, DATE, TIMESTAMP, and VARCHAR during compression. The routines store all information necessary to compress/decompress the data in the actual row. This eliminates the need for a key to decompress the data. The routines do not need to access external key tables, so their performance is faster and more reliable than other compression routines.

- *Routine evaluation.* You can evaluate *any* compression routine to determine which compression routines are right for which tables.

- *Space usage analysis.* Complete space usage analysis is given for each compression evaluation. Space usage analysis information includes the following:

    - CPU time used to compress the rows
    - Maximum, average, and minimum record lengths before and after compression
    - Byte usage before and after compression
    - Number of pages required for REORG before and after compression
    - Estimated savings in tracks and 3380 packs

    Analysis can be performed on-line or in batch mode.

- *Best and worst compression.* For each compression analysis, you can view the five best-compressed and five worst-compressed rows.

- *Compression verification.* This is provided for both the compression and decompression portions of your compression routine to verify its accuracy.

DATA REPORTING

Overview of the Problem

One of the purported benefits of DB2 is easier end user access to data without costly reliance on traditional data processing personnel and methods. These past methods were a major cause of cost overruns, delays, and backlogs in information services departments, resulting in user frustration and, in many cases, significant monetary losses.

When using DB2, end users (1) use a special language called Structured Query Language (SQL) to access DB2 stored data; (2) view all data stored in DB2 as two-dimensional tables, an easy concept to grasp; and (3) request data without concern for specifying or understanding the access paths required to retrieve the data. SQL brings end users closer to the actual data without worrying about the technical details so prevalent in the previous generation of data base management systems.

However, there are some problems involved with using SQL to retrieve information.

Difficulty of use. SQL can be a difficult and time-consuming language to master unless you are performing the simplest of requests. To take full advantage of SQL, the user must not only know the names of any referenced tables and columns, but also understand JOINs, subqueries, correlation variables, and other complex functions.

The difficult concepts and syntax of SQL can negate the positive impact of the new DB2 relational technology.

Teleprocessing environments. For DB2 and SQL to be successful, tools must be provided that enable users to enter and execute SQL statements from multiple teleprocessing environments (for example, TSO and CICS). DB2 provides tools (QMF and SPUFI) that execute only under TSO, which was not designed for cost-effective end-user transaction processing.

Performance. A poorly written SQL statement can require significant amounts of CPU time and storage, returning or scanning millions of rows when only a few were really wanted. For example, when JOIN conditions are not specified or are specified incorrectly on queries that reference multiple tables, all rows from all tables are taken as a product of one another. This causes a severe memory and performance impact.

SQL and DB2 do not give the user adequate warning that an SQL request is poorly written or that it will not return the intended results.

Reporting. SQL is not a report language but a data retrieval language. An SQL statement returns results; it does not produce reports. All results returned from an SQL statement are in a basic list (columnar) format.

You cannot format the listing to include breaks (with corresponding calculations), headers, footers, or other report-related information. You cannot specify edit codes or masks to format the data in the columns, nor can you create other report types such as label, block, or freeform.

Administration. SQL and DB2 do not provide the necessary facilities for managing queries and reports and effectively sharing them among users. Users need to obtain lists of available queries/reports easily in order to select, create, copy, delete, and submit them for execution.

Clearly, SQL and DB2 do not provide the necessary tools to manage and generate queries and reports based on DB2 data effectively. What is needed to solve these problems is a report writer designed specifically for DB2 and the end-user community.

DB/REPORTER (Systems Center)

DB/REPORTER (formerly VMSQL/REPORT) is a sophisticated report writer for IBM's SQL/DS and DB2. Designed for relational database management systems, DB/REPORTER lets database programmers use a combination of procedural and nonprocedural instructions to build reports quickly and easily.

DB/REPORTER's powerful interpretive language allows you to execute SQL statements that access report data and generate sophisticated reports without having to write line after line of COBOL or PL/I code. With DB/REPORTER's precise formatting instructions, you can control exactly how and where you want information to appear on the page. Complex data manipulation is possible using DB/REPORTER's procedural control statements and arithmetic, logical, and string-handling expressions.

Tabular-style reports, single- and multipage reports, form letters, invoices, telephone directory listings, and mailing labels are just some of the many types of reports you can create with DB/REPORTER.

DB/REPORTER makes it easy to produce complex reports that meet your site's exact requirements. By nesting SQL SELECT statements, you can process data in multiple tables or even simulate an outer join between two tables. This capability makes building complex reports such as invoices, packing slips, pick lists, disjoint query, and outer join-style reports much easier.

DB/REPORTER is an alternative to single query report writers that require you to redefine your query until the data fits the report.

Platinum Report Facility (Platinum Technology)

The PLATINUM Report Facility (PRF) is a DB2 end user reporting tool that executes under multiple teleprocessing environments. PRF delivers on DB2's promise of easy data access and provides needed relief to the data processing department without forfeiting the necessary control. PRF's major capabilities are described in the following paragraphs.

Build query facility. A menu-driven Build Query Facility automatically generates SQL statements based on a user's selections and displays the SQL in a window at the bottom of the screen. An SQL parser immediately flags missing JOIN conditions and other problems to prevent incorrect or long running SQL statements. Very complex queries can be created with only one invocation of the Build Query screen. Extensive field-sensitive on-line help adds to the product's ease of use.

Build form facility. A menu-driven Build Form Facility is provided for interactively generating reports based on the results of a query. A sample report line is always displayed to aid the user in creating and formatting the report. Like the Build Query Facility, the Build Form Facility is designed to require a minimum of keystrokes and screens to construct a report. PRF supports six report types—Column, Label, Letter, Block, Extract, and Freeform—each with its own interface.

Multiple environments. PRF executes under CICS, TSO, and "native-mode" batch. All queries and forms may be shared among teleprocessing environments. PRF executes as a standard CICS transaction and therefore can operate in MRO and ISC environments. Under CICS, an Activity Monitor tracks each PRF user's resource consumption.

On-line report display. PRF enables the user to view the full page layout of an executed query or report, including all headers, footers, break text, and subpages. The Preview function uses simulated data to enable you to verify report layout without accessing DB2.

Performance optimization. The system administrator can dynamically control resource consumption by user and by environment. An exit is provided before an SQL statement is executed for further control.

Administration. Library Facilities are provided for selecting and managing all stored queries and forms. A User Profile Facility controls individual or group access to PRF and performance options. Using these facilities simplifies administration of complex sets of queries.

COBOL generation. A COBOL program can be generated to produce the query or form (report) as a batch COBOL program. The generated COBOL code can then be compiled and executed as a static DB2 program. The user can modify the COBOL program to produce more complex reports or batch update programs.

MIGRATION AIDS

Overview of the Problem

DB2 was designed to provide the user with an efficient means of retrieving and storing data. Tables, views, synonyms, and indexes can be created at any time based on user demands. Security is granted to each user on each object.

Referential integrity rules define "logical" relationships between tables, even if those tables appear in different tablespaces or databases.

The very nature of DB2 promotes a large number of objects with an increasingly large dependency tree. As the system grows, the relationships among objects, security, and users become complex and difficult to manage and visualize. Migration and alteration of DB2 strictures becomes exponentially more complicated, time-consuming, and costly.

Migrations. When it comes to migration, DB2 does not provide a means of moving DB2 objects and/or data between different DB2 subsystems or within the same subsystem. There are several situations that call for migrating DB2 objects:

- *Subsystem to subsystem.* There are many reasons why you want to migrate objects and/or data between DB2 subsystems: (1) moving objects from testing to production, (2) moving objects and data (subsets) from production to testing, and (3) creating new testing environments for developers by duplicating a master testing structure.

  While performing these types of migrations, you may want to migrate specific objects without migrating the whole structure or any of the test data. You may also want to make global changes to the objects for creator IDs and storage allocation.

- *User to user.* New users need access to specific DB2 objects. If their access and security needs match those of a current user, you want to migrate the DB2 authorities from current to new users.

- *Plan migration.* When a DB2 plan is ready to be moved into production, you want to migrate all objects that the plan is dependent on. You also want to make global changes to the objects for production IDs and storage allocations.

Alterations. DB2 also lacks the necessary tools for object alteration. It permits only the alteration of an object's basic attributes. DB2 doesn't allow you to perform simple alterations like column name, length, and data type changes without dropping the object and recreating all the dependencies.

There are many reasons why you need to automate the alteration of DB2 objects. Some of them are listed here:

- *Table changes.* You want to change the name of a column or its data type in a table. Column changes also need to be propagated to dependent objects.

- *Tablespace changes.* You may want to move the table to a partitioned tablespace or convert a tablespace that contains multiple tables into a segmented tablespace.

- *Global changes.* Storage allocation changes (VCAT or Storage Group), buffer pool changes, and creator and name changes can cause hundreds of changes to dependent objects.

Needed also is a system that will allow multiple changes to be made by multiple users in one execution. In large systems these changes need to be accumulated over time and consolidated.

Due to the increasing complexity of DB2 and the constant need to migrate and alter objects, DB2 object migration and alteration presents the most perilous challenge facing any DB2 site. You need an easy, efficient, and accurate facility for performing DB2 object migration and alteration.

PLATINUM Pipeline (Platinum Technology)

Converting systems to run under DB2 is an issue that is getting a lot of attention lately, as seen by the number of sessions on this topic at the 1990 International DB2 Users Group (IDUG) conference. Questions are being raised about how to convert data and what type of performance overhead data conversion programs will incur, and of course they include the biggies: How long will it take and how much will it cost? Also to be considered is the fact that the old system cannot be turned off and the new one turned on overnight. There is an inevitable overlap of maintaining and operating two systems.

Once you have made the decision to take on a conversion, one of the first questions you should ask is this: Should the DB2 structures just replicate the existing structures, or should the new database be remodeled to take full advantage of DB2? Considering how much time it will take to write just straight conversion programs, you may not want to undertake the task of restructuring the database. But if you had a method to significantly decrease the amount of time it would take to write the conversion programs, you would be more likely to evaluate the new database structure.

Defining requirements. Let's assume for a moment that you have decided to create a new structure. Once you have decided how you will group the existing data into the new structure, you will decide how it should be stored. This is where the requirements for the conversion programs begin to grow.

After you have defined all the requirements for the new database, you want quick results. But coding and testing conversions programs is typically a lengthy task, requiring many resources. As an alternative, Platinum technology has introduced PLATINUM Pipeline for DB2 to provide the quick results you are looking for. PLATINUM Pipeline allows you to begin using the new DB2 system with minimal start-up time and cost.

PLATINUM Pipeline provides methods for defining the existing structures from which data will be extracted, defining the DB2 tables to be loaded, and maintaining the old environment and the new environment simultaneously. You define the source and target environments to Pipeline through its on-line, menu-driven Data Dictionary. To execute the extract and load process, you simply submit jobs from Pipeline's Utility Menu. Depending on the complexity of the source and target environments, you can have your DB2 table created and loaded within a few hours. This allows you to show quick results without a heavy investment of time or money.

Product architecture. So how does PLATINUM Pipeline work? Pipeline's Data Dictionary requires you to define the source structures. Valid source structures are VSAM datasets, physical sequential datasets, and IMS databases. You simply define the copy member libraries used for these files and the DBD library used for IMS. Pipeline allows you to use multiple record formats. The format functions are used to indicate what formats exist and what fields will indicate to Pipeline the format in effect.

Once you have defined the source structures, you define the target tables and which records/segments will be used to load them. Before we discuss how this occurs, it is important to note that if your DB2 table does not yet exist in the DB2 catalog, you can request that Pipeline generate the CREATE TABLE DDL from table definition stored in Pipeline's Data Dictionary. The DDL can be executed on-line or in batch mode through the PLATINUM Batch Processor. The DDL can also be saved in a dataset for future use.

To define your target table to Pipeline, you start by indicating the table name. (If the table exists, Pipeline uses the DB2 catalog definition.) Now you must tie the source records/segments to the table. Pipeline allows up to 15 source records/segments per table. You then choose which fields from the identified records/segments will make up each column of your table.

You can indicate which column(s) will serve as the key and also each column's size, data type, and nullable attribute. Pipeline's Data Translation feature allows you to indicate that data conversion should take place before storing the data in the column. With this feature, you can indicate date and time conversions, choose an occurrence of a subscripted field, summarize field values, count segment occurrences, or store the previous value of another column. If your needs exceed these translations, a user exit is provided for more specific conversions.

Subset conversion. In many applications, or quite probably in a pilot project, you may want to convert only a selected set of data. You can achieve this by using Pipeline's selection criteria features. Criteria can be identified in many fashions. Some of the methods for identifying selection criteria are as a range of values, a relative value, a LIKE value, and, of course, absolute values.

At this point, your conversion routines have been effectively written. You need only submit the utilities that will validate your source and target relationships, extract the data, and load the tables.

This is all well and good if you need to load the tables only on a periodic basis. But what if your source system continues to operate? You would have to extract and reload on a nightly basis (or perhaps even more frequently). If the tables are small, this might not be a problem. But if they are not, extracting and reloading nightly may not be an option. Pipeline's Capture/Update Service relieves this problem in an IMS environment by intercepting the transactions and updating the appropriate tables.

The source and target definition process described previously is the first step in describing a "capture" environment. The second step consists of executing a set of utilities that set up the Capture Service. Pipeline's DL/I interface simply interrogates the IMS request and determines if the transaction affects a table defined to Pipeline. If it does, Pipeline writes the transaction to its own Capture Log Database. You have control over when the transactions will be reflected in the DB2 tables. Another set of utilities is available to extract the updates from the Capture Log Database, prepare them for the updating, and then update the tables.

Other points of note. Several points should be noted here. IMS applications must either relink using Pipeline's DL/I interface replacement or recompile to call Pipeline's DL/I interface. Pipeline supports IMS Batch applications, as well as Message Processing and Batch Message Processing programs, and no changes to IMS or DB2 are required. Also, Pipeline does not use the IMS log; rather it uses its own log, which can be a HDAM or DEDB IMS database. Both full-function IMS and Fast Path functions are supported.

PLATINUM RC/MIGRATOR (Platinum Technology)

RC/MIGRATOR completely automates the DB2 object, data, and security migration and alteration requirements that arise in the daily use of DB2. It permits you to shape the migration or alteration to fit your particular requirements. You decide what is included and when the migration or alteration should actually be performed. It's easy, fast, and accurate.

RC/MIGRATOR gives you these facilities:

- *Strategy Services.* Strategy Services is a comprehensive facility for creating, deleting, copying, updating, and analyzing RC/MIGRATOR strategies. An RC/MIGRATOR defines the DB2 migration or alteration. There are many different types of strategies, but they are *all* created and managed from the Strategy Services Facility.

- *DB2 object migrations.* There are three RC/MIGRATOR strategy types for DB2 migrations: *Object*, *Plan*, and *Security*. All three strategy types support migrations within the same DB2 subsystem or to a different DB2 subsystem. The target DB2 subsystem can be on a different CPU.

- *DB2 object alterations.* The alteration strategy permits you to change any number of DB2 objects with all changes automatically propagated to dependent objects, including views and indexes. Any number of users can alter any number of objects, including the same object, and all changes are consolidated and processed in one execution.

- *Analysis Facility.* The Analysis Facility produces executable output to perform the requested migration or alteration. The analysis function can be executed in on-line or batch mode, and many options are available for controlling the generated output. Comprehensive messages detailing any potential warnings are displayed as part of the analysis execution.

- *Execution Facility.* The Execution Facility executes the output produced by the Analysis Facility in either on-line or batch mode. A JCL job can be generated to execute the analysis output at a later time (off hours). All RC/MIGRATOR executions are fully restartable. A complete audit trail is produced as part of the execution, and all DDL is logged to the PLATINUM log tables.

- *Execution Monitor.* The Execution Monitor tracks the execution of analysis and execution runs. Synchpoints and messages are displayed showing the progress of the batch execution. From one display, you can view the progress of executions running on *multiple* DB2 subsystems.

RC/MIGRATOR gives you these benefits:

- *Increases productivity.* Migration and DB2 object alteration are performed regularly in any DB2 environment. RC/MIGRATOR automates the whole process. Any number of users can update the same migration or alteration definition. Once all changes and specifications are made, you simply execute the analysis function, review the analysis output for warnings, and execute the migration or alteration. You can execute the migration or alteration immediately or write the job to a dataset for later execution by a job scheduling system.

The simplicity and completeness of RC/MIGRATOR provides immediate productivity gains in any DB2 environment.

- *Maintains DB2 system integrity.* RC/MIGRATOR automatically maintains the integrity of the DB2 structure(s) as part of a migration or alteration. Any necessary SET CURRENT SQLID or Authorization ID switching is performed to correctly set the CREATOR and CREATEDBY fields. Synchronization points are taken after every logical execution step for restartability.

  All objects are created in a specific order to ensure correct object definitions. For example, before a view is created, any tables, views, or synonyms the view refers to are created, and any changes made to those objects are propagated to the dependent view.

- *Performs impact analysis.* You can request an impact analysis as part of any alteration or migration. A summary that shows the effect of the DB2 object alteration or migration is provided. You may also request data statistics that detail the volume of data to be unloaded/loaded as part of the migration of alteration.

- *Provides DDL backup.* RC/MIGRATOR provides a "DDL Only" option that generates the necessary DDL statements to recreate a DB2 structure. The generated DDL recreates the DB2 structure, including any referential integrity rules or security. The DDL can be saved in a dataset and used as backup to recover from accidental drops or object alterations.

- *Facilitates global changes.* The Global Change Facility permits you to specify global changes as part of any migration. Global changes are automatically propagated to dependent objects and are consolidated with any specific object edits. You can make a substantial number of changes to DB2 objects with minimal effort.

- *Preserves referential integrity.* Referential integrity can be preserved without having to know all the relationships between the parent and child tables. The GLOBAL RI option automatically includes any tables contained within the referential integrity structure. You can be assured that your referential structures will remain intact during alterations and migrations. For example, if you change the definition of a foreign key column, the changed column is automatically changed in any related tables.

PERFORMANCE MONITORING

Overview of the Problem

DB2 does not contain any facility to monitor resource consumption or contention in real time.

DB2 MANAGER (Boole & Babbage)

DB2 MANAGER solves DB2 performance management problems with a unique combination of capabilities:

- DB2 MANAGER operates on-line, in real-time, with a comprehensive set of monitoring and analysis features. Identification and resolution of problems is immediate.

- From a single vantage point, you can monitor all DB2 accesses, through TSO, IMS, and CICS. In fact, you can monitor multiple DB2 systems on multiple CPUs that are geographically dispersed, key to future distributed database strategies.

- Most important, DB2 MANAGER is integrated into an existing, proven, multisystem architecture with effective links to other Boole & Babbage performance management products for complete system control.

- Data Center Management can offer the advantages of DB2 to end-users and still meet service level objectives in a cost-effective manner. DB2 MANAGER is easy to use, so less-experienced personnel can handle DB2 problems. Management can maximize the productivity of personnel and the efficiency of system resource usage.

- Operations productivity is increased. DB2 MANAGER alerts operations staff to exception conditions to eliminate constant monitoring of messages and to assure fast response to problems. Productivity is further increased because operations can monitor multiple DB2 systems, including remote sites, from a single point. And with the additional information provided by DB2 MANAGER, they can effectively support an increased number of DB2 users.

- Technical support staff will appreciate the fact that DB2 MANAGER operates on-line and allows multiple system control. DB2 MANAGER alerts the technical support staff to DB2-related problems in real time by displaying critical exception messages, and it provides meaningful screens for problem analysis. The staff can react before degradation or outages result, maximizing system availability. By tracking usage patterns over time, technical support can effectively manage resource utilization. And DB2 MANAGER helps train and support operations personnel.

- Applications development staff can determine the resource consumption of new DB2-related applications before migrating them to production. DB2 MANAGER takes the guesswork out of implementing new applications.

- *Analyzer services.* DB2 MANAGER analyzer services show the status, activity, and utilization of key DB2 resources. Because information is available on-line in real time, you can react to problems immediately; automatic exception analysis saves valuable time.

  Comprehensive information, presented in concise and meaningful displays, facilitates problem identification. DB2 MANAGER automatically cycles displays so you can continuously monitor multiple DB2 and other subsystems.

- *Monitor services.* On-line, time-driven monitor services track key indicators of DB2 resource utilization and compare performance to user-specified thresholds. When acceptable limits are exceeded, DB2 MANAGER issues warnings so you can intervene early, preventing costly system outages. Auto-operator products can also intercept these warnings to automate the process.

Insight for DB2 (Goal Systems)

Use of DB2, IBM's premier relational database management system, is becoming increasingly widespread within the MVS user community. Many users are discovering the importance of using a DB2 performance monitor, such as Goal Systems' Insight for DB2, in all stages of DB2 migration and development. Insight for DB2 is being used to fine-tune DB2 by DBAs, systems programmers, application developers, and auditors.

OMEGAMON for DB2 (!Candle)

OMEGAMON for DB2 is a performance management software product that provides a real-time window into the operation of DB2. It helps you improve system availability and transaction response time by monitoring and analyzing critical information within DB2, in addition to factors that may affect DB2 such as MVS, IMS, and CICS performance. Results are displayed on any 3270-family terminal.

In either a production or development environment, OMEGAMON for DB2 highlights potential performance problems, displays suggested solutions, and helps you manage resource overhead. It does this by checking the critical areas within the DB2 system every few seconds and automatically issuing warnings with color or highlighted display fields. This Exception Analysis is performed against threshold values that may be dynamically changed to meet your specific requirements.

Comprehensive performance analysis. The Exception Analysis function of OMEGAMON for DB2 generates messages to warn data center staff of impending problems. For example, there are messages that warn of locking conflicts, SQL calls causing too great an impact on other DB2 workloads, or a buffer pool reaching or exceeding a normal level of utilization.

The Locking Conflicts display lets you determine which thread owns the locks and which threads are waiting on a particular lock. There are also screens for locks causing a thread to wait and locks owned by a thread.

The All Threads display shows all of the currently active threads and users, arranged from top to bottom by the thread that was active the longest in the DB2 system. The highlighted areas identify potential problems.

The DB2 Address Space Virtual Storage Map is valuable in analyzing real-time storage. For ESA, XA, and non-XA storage, you can see immediately how much space is allocated in user and system areas, whether or not storage in these areas is fragmented, and how much is available.

The System Console and Message Traffic screen lets you route commands to DB2, MVS, CICS, or IMS.

Historical reporting. OMEGAMON for DB2 contains a reporting feature that lets you view, manipulate, and print historical data about your DB2 system by extracting DB2 statistical and accounting data from SMF and loading this data into DB2 tables. You can use this data along with the queries in OMEGAMON's sample library to generate historical GDDM Graphs and QMF reports. The following are just a few of these reports:

- Subsystem Service Statistics
- Buffer Pool Statistics
- EDM Pool Statistics
- Log Manager Statistics
- Locking Statistics
- SQL Statistics
- Bind Statistics
- Thread Summary
- Time Summary
- Buffer Manager Activity
- Resource Limit Facility Activity
- Accounting Detail

Application Trace Facility. The Application Trace Facility lets you selectively trace applications that are executing under DB2 and view all of the collected application information interactively. The information presented assists in the analysis of application flow and resource consumption. The types of performance information that are available include the following:

- SQL trace information
- Sort activity information
- Pageset access and scan information
- Locking information
- Application In-DB2 time and In-DB2 CPU time

The Application Trace Facility is available only to OMEGAMON users who are monitoring DB2 Version 2 Release 1 or above.

Resource manager information. OMEGAMON provides information about various DB2 resource managers including the DB2 buffer manager, DB2 log manager, log datasets, and EDM pool. It also provides DB2 bind statistics. This information gives you the ability to analyze the performance and use of these critical components.

Installation parameter information – DSNZPARM. OMEGAMON provides easy access to information about the parameters in the DSNZPARM Installation Module. A series of screens presents the values contained in the

DSNZPARM module that are currently in use by DB2. These screens group the parameters into logical areas such as DB2 thread-related parameters, DB2 logging parameters, and DB2 dataset and database parameters. Using this feature, you can review these important values that control the performance of DB2—while DB2 is running.

Automated exception logging. OMEGAMON provides an easy way to log exception information to a dataset for later viewing or printing via options on the Set Exception Analysis screen. The Exception Logging Option allows you to view exception data and related problem solving data at a later time, even if you are not at your terminal when the exception occurs.

PLAN ANALYSIS

PLATINUM Plan Analyzer (Platinum Technology)

The focal point of the product is the Plan Analyzer Main Menu, with entries for Plan EXPLAIN Services, Plan Reporting Services, Plan Management Services, and Miscellaneous Functions.

EXPLAIN Services is the cornerstone of the Plan Analyzer. Most of you are familiar with the nightmare of dealing with EXPLAIN output. Many hours have been wasted looking at row after row and column after column of confusing PLAN_TABLE data. EXPLAIN Services wakes you from this nightmare by giving you EXPLAIN output in simple, easy-to-read reports. Gone are the days of having to look through the cryptic and encoded PLAN_TABLE output that the DB2 EXPLAIN process creates. Don't waste any more time learning to speak DB2's language. EXPLAIN Services speaks *your* language.

EXPLAIN Services. EXPLAIN Services gives you the ability to do the following:

- Obtain analysis of access paths in clear, concise English paragraphs. This analysis includes not only the access path chosen, but also the factors that led to the choice of this access path. These factors include DB2 catalog statistics and physical object configurations.

- Run your SQL through the PLATINUM rule-based SQL Expert System. This system applies the wealth of knowledge contained in a rule base holding years of experience gathered by the industry's foremost DB2 experts. Hundreds of rules are used in monitoring your

SQL and the underlying physical objects to notify you of potential problems that may arise. You will even receive recommendations on how to rewrite your SQL or rearrange your physical objects to achieve better performance.

- EXPLAIN at different levels of granularity. Instead of just being able to obtain EXPLAIN output at the plan level, PPA allows you to EXPLAIN whole DB2 systems, specific plans, specific DBRMs, specific types of SQL statements, or even all of the SQL statements that perform certain functions or access certain tables.

- Group logically related plans, DBRMs, and statements into EXPLAIN strategies. For example, you can group all of the plans in your Payroll system into a strategy, and then you can perform EXPLAIN analysis on the strategy without having to remember the names of the various plans that make up the Payroll system.

- Obtain versions of EXPLAIN output every time you perform EXPLAIN analysis against a strategy. Each version of output will be saved in the EXPLAIN Services historical database, giving you the ability to perform subsequent queries and historical analysis against this data using a simple menu-driven interface.

- Compare versions of EXPLAIN output to discover what has changed in your application over a period of time. The comparison will show you what SQL has been changed, added, and deleted as well as what changes have occurred in the related access paths. This gives you an easy way to track both SQL and access path changes over any period of time.

- Customize the SQL Expert System's rule database with an online system that allows you to create custom sets of rules for DB2 subsystem and even per application. This rule base contains a variety of thresholds that can be customized to allow subsystem-specific tuning of your DB2 applications. For instance, the number of rows allowed in a table where a tablespace scan is being performed is a customizable threshold value. Of course, default threshold values are supplied and only need to be changed to meet your requirements. You can create as many custom sets of rules as you wish and have separate threshold values for each set. This allows you to apply exactly the desired set of rules and thresholds when EXPLAINing an application.

- Obtain a variety of reports about your SQL and its performance. For instance, for any group of SQL, you can view a cost analysis report that will show you what is the most expensive in terms of I/O and CPU consumption. You can view predicate analysis reports that will show all involved predicates and whether they are indexable and/or sargable (Stage 1). These are just two of the many reports that EXPLAIN analysis can produce for you.

- Perform EXPLAIN on your production DB2 subsystem for a plan that resides on your test subsystem. This gives you a method for tuning applications on your testing subsystem without having to guess how they will perform when bound to your production subsystem.

Reporting Services. Reporting Services provides four basic reporting options that can be navigated on-line to produce a variety of reports detailing the plan information from your DB2 system catalog. Plans, DBRMs, statements, authorities, dependencies, and the relationships among these items may be viewed.

Plan Reporting offers nine separate reports that offer invaluable assistance in exploring your catalog. All reports support Distributed Data Facility (DDF) Locations, and by allowing you to change the Location and the DB2 SSID on any report screen, they provide an incredibly versatile method for navigating your way through many DB2 subsystems. Locations and DB2 SSIDs can even be selected from lists by entering a question mark in either of these two input fields. All reports can be produced in on-line or batch mode. You can also extend the WHERE clause on any of the SQL by using PLATINUM's Extended Query Facility.

DBRM Reporting gives you facilities similar to Plan Reporting, but from a DBRM point of view—for instance, if you want to see a list of all plans that include a specific DBRM. Object Reporting provides you with a very powerful way at looking into SQL dependency. Using this feature you can view all plans, DBRMs and the SQL that are dependent on a given database, tablespace, table, index, view, synonym, alias, or even column. With this power you can enter such queries as Show me all of the SQL in my system that updates the SALARY column of table DEPT103_PAYROLL.

Statement Reporting is the only syntax-driven SQL query tool in the industry. You can use this option to report on all of the SQL within your subsystem or plans that meet certain syntax configurations. This flexibility gives you a powerful method of monitoring and enforcing SQL standards within your shop. There is no other method available to you for doing such things as finding all SQL with only Stage 1 predicates or finding all SQL containing correlated subqueries.

Plan Management Services contains an Identify Problem Plans facility and SQL options that give you an easy way to look for exception conditions. For example, you can easily find all plans that are inoperative, or you can find all SQL that causes tablespace scans. This gives the busy DBA an easy way to focus attention on problem areas. The Create User PLAN_TABLE(s) facility gives you a sophisticated menu-driven system to easily create EXPLAIN output tables for one or more users without needing to remember the table format.

SECURITY MANAGEMENT

Overview of the Problem

To perform any function in a DB2 system, a user must have authority to do so. Any privilege not specifically granted to a user is, by default, denied.

There are over 40 distinct DB2 privileges, ranging from complete access to the system to update access on a specific table column. Many DB2 privileges are associated with users' access to objects. As an organization's use of DB2 grows, the numbers of objects and users grows—and so does the job of managing security. Security administration for a DB2 system can easily become a full-time job of coding and executing statements to grant and revoke privileges. Moreover, many problems are associated with administration of DB2 security. The following are some of them.

No security administrator. DB2 combines related authorities into groups called *administrative authorities,* which can be granted with a single statement. However, DB2 does not provide a *security administrator* authority. No single authority lets a user grant privileges without first having the privileges. A central security administrator must have SYSADM authority, which conveys authority to do anything in the DB2 system (for instance, viewing sensitive personnel data). Many organizations feel uneasy about giving anyone SYSADM authority.

No user or privilege groups. Within DB2, each user and object privilege is treated separately. There is no way to group DB2 object privileges and/or users into logical domains according to applications. You're forced to execute several GRANT statements for each new user or object. (All you can do is create a Partitioned Data Set [PDS] with the commands to grant or revoke authorities for a job function to certain users.) Because revoking privileges for one of a user's functions may take away privileges needed for an entirely separate function, security administrators must painstakingly research security concerns for each object and user before revoking privileges.

Secondary IDs. Using secondary IDs can cause severe performance penalties because DB2 must search both primary and secondary IDs when accessing DB2 resources. In addition, it's not an easy task to query the DB2 catalog to view all of a user's authorities because many authorities are under the user's secondary IDs. If you use RACF group names for secondary IDs, a portion of DB2 security is managed outside DB2.

No templating privileges. DB2 doesn't give you an easy way to grant one user the same authorities as another, so you have to write and execute GRANT statements for each new user. When users leave a department, there is no quick way to revoke their privileges.

No reporting facility. If you need to find out all the privileges a user holds or which users have access to a specific object, you have to write and execute SQL to retrieve the information from the DB2 catalog tables, considering both primary and secondary IDs.

DB2 security hierarchy. The hierarchy of DB2 authority grows more complex each time a user is granted a privilege with the option of granting it to others. If a privilege at any level in the hierarchy is revoked, so are all of the privileges dependent to it.

No audit trail. DB2 Version 2 provides only the TRACE facility, which logs executed and attempted grants and revokes in hard-to-access SMF or GTF datasets.

DB/SECURE for DB2 (Systems Center)

DB/SECURE for DB2 is a security administration system for simplifying and enhancing DB2 security. It provides an easy-to-use, comprehensive means of controlling access to DB2 systems, resources, and data. DB/SECURE also maintains a complete audit trail of all generated SQL statements and reports on DB2 users, objects, and activities.

DB/SECURE simplifies DB2 security administration functions. Its easy-to-use ISPF screens let you group DB2 privileges and users as your site requires. You can easily enroll new users and grant or change privileges by assigning one or more Security Classes to a particular User Group—DB/SECURE automatically generates the necessary SQL GRANT and REVOKE statements.

DB/SECURE is a safer, simpler alternative to existing DB2 security administration products. The Resource Access Control Facility (RACF) and other MVS-level security products do not provide sufficient control within the DB2 subsystem. DB/SECURE provides a centralized, up-to-the-minute source for all DB2 security information and maintains a complete audit trail of all generated SQL statements. It also provides comprehensive SQL reports on DB2 objects and activities.

DB/SECURE provides database administrators and security analysis with a powerful tool for managing DB2 security efficiently and cost-effectively. It pays for itself may times over by reducing personnel costs and preventing security breaches. Since its initial release in 1986, DB/SECURE has beocme the standard security administration system in over 175 DB2 installations.

Full-screen menus. DB/SECURE uses ISPF full-screen menus to make managing DB2 security simple, fast, and accurate. These menus allow security and database administrators to manage DB2 security without being DB2 experts. The menus prompt you with authorization IDs, resource names, and privilege commands—eliminating the need to remember this information.

SQL generation. Enrolling users is often a complex, time-consuming process in DB2. DB/SECURE simplifies user enrollment by allowing you to easily group users into User Groups and automatically generate the necessary SQL GRANT and REVOKE statements as users are added and removed from a User Group. DB/SECURE simplifies security privilege assignment by allowing you to define Security Classes of DB2 privileges needed by a particular User Group.

Allows decentralized security administration. Since each DB2 site has unique security requirements, DB/SECURE provides the flexibility to implement security in two ways: centralized and decentralized. In a centralized DB/SECURE system, you assign the control of security to one DB/SECURE Administrator. The Administrator controls security by creating and maintaining User Groups and Security Classes.

In a decentralized DB/SECURE system, you assign overall DB2 security management to the DB/SECURE Administrator, who then assigns departmental security control to Department Administrators. Department Administrators maintain the security for their departments by creating DB/SECURE User Groups and Security Classes and assigning managerial control for these groups and classes to Department Managers.

Decentralized security administration allows you to distribute the DB2 administrative workload more evenly without compromising the security and control of your database. It also allows you to provide each department with its own DB/SECURE "environment."

RC/SECURE (Platinum Technology)

RC/SECURE's Security Request Services (SRS) simplifies maintenance of DB2 security through user and application domains that you define for your organization. Simply set up a user domain for each group of users performing similar functions. Then, to create an application domain, specify the DB2 object privileges needed for a particular application.

When you define relationships between user and application domains, RC/SECURE's Security Request Services (SRS) handles the required processing to grant and/or revoke the necessary authorities. Both primary and secondary authorization IDs are supported.

SRS separates ownership of objects from the ability to administer security on the objects so that an administrator can grant privileges he or she does not possess. Security administration can be central or departmental.

To assign a user access to a set of DB2 objects, place the user in a user domain, then relate the user domain to one or more application domains. When you add users to the user domain, they are automatically granted the authorities in all related application domains. Adding a DB2 object privilege to an application domain grants the privilege to all users in related user domains. When you remove a user from a user domain or delete a DB2 object privilege from an application domain, associated privileges are revoked unless they are required by another domain relationship.

Standard Grant/Revoke Services (GRS) provides a fast and easy online method of granting and revoking DB2 privileges without creating user and application domains. The user requesting the grants and revokes must hold the necessary DB2 authorities, so GRS can't be used to bypass SRS or DB2's own security system.

Easy Online Grant/Revoke Screens let you grant and revoke privileges without having to hand-code the necessary commands. Choose the objects, authorities, and users from a single screen, and all the grants or revokes are automatically generated and executed.

Revoke Impact Analysis enables you to assess all the effects a revoke will have on other users before you issue the revoke statement.

Bibliography and References

DB2-RELATED BOOKS

This section contains an annotated list of popular books available on DB2 and related topics. When the book has been reviewed in a technical journal, the periodical and date are noted parenthetically. A key to the periodical abbreviations appears on page 226.

The Programmer's Guide to DB2, by Paul H. Byall. John Wiley & Sons, 1991, ISBN 0-471-52155-8, 236 pages, $44.95. An introduction to basic SQL and DB2 topics. Basic DB2 objects, SQL, Cursors, DCLGEN, EXPLAIN (V2R2), Load, RUNSTATS. No IMS environment considerations, no additional utilities or service aids, few internals. Short, basic, costly.

The Relational Model for Database Management, Version 2, by Dr. E.F. Codd. Addison-Wesley, 1990, ISBN 0-201-14192-2, 504 pages. Dr. Codd's long-awaited treatise. Although not precisely aimed at IBM's DB2, this book will probably be *the* seminal work on the relational model for a long time to come. Contains coverage of Codd's position on missing data and nulls, and a bundle (333) of new rules/features of RM/V2. Not light reading. (Reviewed in DBPD, Sept 1990.)

A Guide to DB2, Third Edition, by C.J. Date and Colin White. Addison-Wesley, 1989, ISBN 0-201-50113-9, 535 pages. Probably the best-known of the various DB2-related books. The only good review of the IBM Relational Productivity Family. Includes Cross System Product (CSP), Host Data Base View (HDBV) and Enhanced Connectivity Facilities (ECF). (Second Edition reviewed in DBPD, Aug 1988.)

Relational Database Writings: 1985-1989, by C. J. Date with Andrew Warden. Addison-Wesley, 1990, ISBN 0-201-50851-8, 519 pages. A collection of Date's recent papers and articles on relational database topics. Excellent coverage of referential integrity, three-valued logic, and critical looks at the problems (and promises) of SQL.

Working With DB2, SQL/DS, SQL, and QMF, by Tony Fabbri and A. Robert Schwab, Jr. Tab Books, 1990, ISBN 0-8306-9508-7, $32.95. An overview of common DB2 topics. Not much detail. Covers basic SQL, but little intermediate or advanced information. No IMS or CICS considerations. No internals, not much on the optimizer.

SQL Programmer's Guide, by Umang Gupta and William Geitz. Que, 1989, ISBN 0-88022-390-1, 294 pages, $29.95. A book on generic ANSI SQL. Adequate coverage of most topics, few DB2 specifics.

DB2 Version 2: Database Design and Administration, by Robert Heydt and Diane Heydt. John Wiley & Sons, 1989, ISBN 0-471-62051-3, 242 pages, $33.95. A fair, although academic, treatment of DB2. No IMS- or CICS-related issues. Similar to IBM manuals. (Reviewed in DBPD, Dec 1989—but that review seems much more positive than the book warrants.)

DB2: Maximizing Performance of Online Production Systems, by W.H. Inmon. QED, 1988, ISBN 0-89435-256-3, $44.50. Intermediate-level overview of DB2 topics. Difficult to reference, as the index is a bit sparse. (Reviewed in DBPD, May 1989.)

The Database Expert's Guide to DB2, by Bruce L. Larson. Intertext/McGraw-Hill, 1988, ISBN 0-07-036488-5, 365 pages, $37.50. Introductory SQL, DB2, including utilities. Excellent graphics. Small table of contents and small index make it difficult to find anything. Some typographical errors. (Reviewed in DBPD, Mar 1989.)

DB2 For Application Programmers, by Pacifico A. Lim. Prentice-Hall, 1990. ISBN 0-13-199795-5, 220 pages, $40.00. Some technical and typographical errors. Minimal coverage of DB2, and it's not obvious whether this book is current with V2R2. Somewhat small and relatively expensive. (Reviewed in DBPD, Dec 1990.)

The Database Expert's Guide to SQL, by Frank Lusardi. Intertext/McGraw-Hill, 1988, ISBN 0-07-039002-9, 151 pages, $24.95. Some copyediting and typographical errors. Program examples are in C, book is aimed at ANSI

SQL, not DB2 (no Synonyms, Utilities, Commit, EXPLAIN, etc.). Good glossary. (Reviewed in DBPD, Mar 1989.)

DB2: Concepts, Design, and Programming, by James Martin, with Kathleen Chapman and Joe Leben. Prentice Hall, 1989, ISBN 0-13-198581-7, 315 pages, $48.00. Basic SQL and a detailed table of contents. No IMS- or CICS-specific issues. Although relatively expensive and short, this book covers all the basics.

DB2/SQL: A Professional Programmer's Guide, by Tim Martyn and Tim Hartley. Intertext/McGraw-Hill, 1989, ISBN 0-07-040666-9, $39.95. Basic SQL, no IMS- or CICS-related issues. No dynamic SQL, no EXPLAIN.

SQL and Relational Basics, by Fabian Pascal. M & T Publishing, 1990, ISBN 1-55851-063-X, 324 pages, $28.95. An average book covering ANSI SQL and relational databases, mostly on PCs. Some discussion of Codd's rules for relational databases.

A Guide to SQL, by Philip J. Pratt. Boyd and Fraser, 1990, ISBN 0-87835-336-4, 194 pages, $18.95. Simple introductory SQL, no glossary. ANSI SQL, not DB2. (Reviewed in DBPD, Sep 1989.)

Embedded SQL for DB2: Application Design and Programming, by Jonathan S. Sayles. QED, 1990, ISBN 0-89435-308-X, 345 pages. General overview of DB2 application coding considerations.

DB2: The Complete Guide to Implementation and Use, second edition, by Jeff D. Vowell, Jr. QED, 1988, ISBN 0-89435-230-X, 359 pages, $49.95. A few scattered technical and typographical errors. Most topics are overview, rather than detail. Relatively expensive. (First edition reviewed in DBPD, Nov 1989.)

DB2 Design and Development Guide, by Gabrielle Wiorkowski and David Kull. Addison-Wesley, 1988, ISBN 0-201-16949-5, 322 pages, $36.75. The best (and perhaps only?) guide to the DB2 Optimizer and DB2 access path selection. No IMS- or CICS- specific issues. Very small index. (Reviewed in DBPD Nov, 1988.)

Guide to DB2 & SQL/DS, by Fritz Wipper. McGraw-Hill, 1989, ISBN 0-07-055170-7. 273 pages, $29.95. Basic SQL for DB2 and SWL/DS, with few advanced topics. Coverage of date and time arithmetic. (Reviewed in DBPD Oct 1990.)

SUGGESTED READING—ARTICLES

This section contains a representative list of DB2-related articles that have appeared in technical journals within the last two years. These articles were chosen for their technical content and usability as references and teaching aids. Abbreviations for the periodicals cited are as follows:

CW	*ComputerWorld,* Framingham, MA.
DBPD	*Database Programming and Design,* Miller Freeman Publications, San Francisco, CA.
IW	*Information Week,* CMP Publications Inc., Manhasset, NY.
ESJ	*Enterprise Systems Journal* (formerly *Mainframe Journal*), Thomas Publications, Dallas, TX.
RJ	*Relational Journal,* Codd & Date, CA.
SW	*Software Magazine,* Sentry Publishing Co., Inc., Westborough, MA.

Recent DB2-Related Articles

Alur, Nagraj, "A Look at Version 2.2's Performance Enhancements," RJ, Nov 1989, 1,10-11. Technical review of DB2 2.2 performance.

Backs, William, "How the Headlong Rush to DB2 Spawns Poor Designs and Worse Performance," RJ, Apr/May 1990, pp. 2-4. General overview of design issues. Design problems and scenarios. Comparison with IMS design. Relational system design.

Bochenski, Barbara, "Coercing DBMSs to Cooperate," SW, Nov 1989, pp. 70-82. Customer anecdotes and opinions.

———, "Planned or Inherited, the Mess in DP is Real," SW, Aug 1989, pp. 49-60. A quick introduction of the IMS versus files versus DB2 problem. Description of IDES, PDES, CALS, and DoD.

———, "Links, Ties, Maps, Twists Can Get You There From Here," SW, Jun 1990, pp. 56-67. Cooperative processing, heterogeneous database access. Networks, transport protocols, client/server connectivity.

Braasch, Bill, "Early Adopters Report Architecture Has Pluses," SW, Apr 1990, pp. 63-69. Client/server stuff, tool list.

Bursch, Steve, "Dynamic Remote Applications for DB2," DBPD, May 1990. Technical overview of DDB and LU6.2.

Caballero, Carlos, "Migrating to DB2," MFJ, May 1990, pp. 40-47. Management overview. Change control and configuration control are indispensible prerequisites for migration.

———, "DB2 Change and Configuration Management," MFJ, Jun 1990, pp. 78-80, 89. General technical overview. Dependencies between various DB2 objects. Some simple migration considerations.

Celko, Joe, "The Zen of SQL," DBPD, Dec 1989. The effects of nulls and unknowns on SQL logic are explored.

Chouinard, Paul, "Supertypes, Subtypes, and DB2," DBPD, Oct 1989. A comprehensive overview of different implementation strategies for supertype and subtype entities within DB2.

Codd, E. F., "DB2's Insufficient Support For Referential Integrity," RJ, Nov 1989, pp. 1-5. The industry's guru explains with excruciating detail the various (many) weaknesses of RI in DB2.

Coleman, George J., "When Will IMS Go Away?," DBPD, Nov 1989, pp. 26-32. Technical overview. DB2 was supposed to sweep away its older relative, but the slow pace of change shows that the users still question its superiority.

Courtney, Philip, "To Use or Not to Use A Tool is the DB2 Security Question," SW, Aug 1990, pp. 52-60. General technical overview. DB2 security facilities, many claim, have proven overly flexible and unrepresentative of the security procedures found in most organizations.

Dale, Richard, "Database Migration: Keeping a Steady Course," DBPD, Apr 1990, pp. 31-38. A few migration ideas and considerations.

Date, C. J., "Beware of SQL EXISTS!," DBPD, Sep 1989. SQL flaws involving the EXISTS function.

———, "Why Is It So Difficult to Provide a Relational Interface to IMS?," InfoIMS 4, no. 4 (4th quarter 1984). A list of the difficulties to providing a relational interface to IMS/VS.

Edelstein, Herb, "Breaking Down the Production Barrier," SW, Sep 1989, pp. 73-81. Vendor anecdotes, tool user success stories, list of tools.

———, "Casual DB2 Discourse Still an Elusive Quest," SW, Feb 1990, pp. 59-64. Overview of Query Languages.

———, "Tools to Database: Hey, Can We Talk?," SW, Jul 1989, pp. 67-73. Overview of CASE tools, tool list. Some tool descriptions, tool user quotes.

———, "Look for Relational to be 1990s Data Model," SW, Jan 1990. Addresses the trauma that many firms undergo, while examining their committment to a relational DBMS.

Fosdick, Howard, "Moving to TSO/ISPF Programming," DBPD May 1990, pp. 46-50. Excellent overview comparison of TSO/ISPF versus IMS versus CICS. Advantages and disadvantages.

———, "DB2 on the Desktop," DBPD, Dec 1989. Discussion of the role of the OS/2 Database Manager in the desktop product scenario. The similar and disparate features of the Database Manager and DB2 are discussed.

———, "Programming SQL With Cursors," DBPD, Jun 1989. Detailed technical overview of cursor processing. Program examples in C.

Francett, Barbara, "From IBM or non-IBM, The Move Is On To DB2," SW, Sep 1989, pp. 50-61. Quotable quotes, opinions, and some vendor comments.

Galat, Andrew, "Just Browsing," DBPD, Jun 1989. Short review of browsing DB2 data.

Gawn, Jim, "The Dubious Advice to Denormalize: Misconceptions Yield False Economies," RJ, Oct 1989, pp. 12-15. A detailed technical review of some misconceptions about denormalization, along with an attack on William Inmon.

Gibson, Stanley, "They Came To Praise DB2," CW, Aug 21, 1989. An overview of the International DB2 User Group's recent meeting in Chicago.

Goldring, Rob, "Application Design for Distributed DB2," DBPD, Sept 1990. SAA distributed DBMS levels and DB2.

Goldstein, Joel S., "Should DB2 Be Your DBMS of Choice?," MFJ, May 1989, pp. 52-54. Opinion and overview.

———, "Large DB2 Buffer Pools May Hurt On-Line Transaction Performance," ESJ, Mar 1989. Short review of DB2 buffer pool considerations.

———, "DB2 Prefetch and Sort Considerations," ESJ, Apr 1990. Short technical review of DB2 V2.1 and V2.2 sequential prefetch.

Gowland, Russell H., III, "Tackling DB2 Index Design," DBPD, Dec 1990. Some basics for designing indexes for table access.

Hackenberg, Steven, "Software Queuing Considerations Accessing DB2 From CICS," ESJ, Jan 1989. Considerations for implementing DB2 applications in a CICS environment with emphasis on queuing.

Harms, Steven L., "Updating Catalog Statistics to Simulate Production Data," RJ, Dec 1989, pp. 11-13. Technical review. Catalog table columns. A simulation methodology.

Hayward, Mark, "DB2 in FOCUS," DBPD, Mar 1989, pp. 42-46. Brief description of the FOCUS-DB2 interface. Some technical considerations.

Heydt, Robert, "DB2 Lock Relationships," ESJ, Jan and Feb 1990. A technical discussion of how page and tablespace locks relate.

———, "DB2 Precision, Scale, Overflow and Date Arithmetic," ESJ, Dec 1990. Introduction to the way DB2 handles time and date calculations.

Hoffmann, Robert, "Keep on Moving," DBPD, May 1990, pp. 19-24. Technical overview of data migration management facility (DMMF). Allows programs to call a routine that does the data update.

Huntley, Alton F., "Getting From Here to There," DBPD, Mar 1989, pp. 26-35. Honeywell COBOL to Informix conversion. Uses special tables and programs as a data dictionary.

Inmon, William H., "Alternate Data Organization in DB2 and Oracle," ESJ, Sep 1990. Brief comparison of some physical design concerns using DB2 and Oracle.

Kneiling, John, "DB2 and CICS: What You Need to Know To Manage the Delicate Relationship," RJ Aug/Sep 1989, pp. 16-19. Technical overview. Threads, the Attach Facility, transactions and pseudo-conversations, RCT entries, dynamic plan selection.

———, "Beyond the Plan That Ate Chicago: Flexible Plan Management Techniques," RJ, Nov 1989, pp. 6-9, 11. Technical overview of CICS plan management.

Korzeniowski, Paul, "A Consumer's Guide to Essential Tools," SW, Nov 1989(s), pp. 21-31. General tool overview, along with some quotes from vendors. Mention of Terry Mason's (Bank of Montreal) IDUG speech.

Kull, David, "Juggling DBMS's," IW, Dec 4, 1989. Some of the immediate strategies for coexistence of DB2 with at least one other DBMS are addressed.

Larsen, Sheryl, "You Can Look, But You Better Not Touch," DBPD, Jul 1990. Detailed overview of browsing and scrolling through DB2 tables.

Lewis, Barry, "DB2 Storage Groups: A Viable Production Alternative," MFJ, Aug 1989, pp. 38-39. Minimal technical overview.

Lichtig, Bernard, with M. Schoenberg and D. Young, "I/O I/O It's Off to DB2 I Go," ESJ, Mar 1990. Detailed benchmark of IMS/DB2 applications by Amdahl.

Lyon, Lockwood, "IMS/VS and DB2: Working Together," DBPD, Jun 1988. Technical review of implementing DB2 applications in an IMS environment.

Markham, Stephanie, "Change Management In The DB2 Environment," ESJ, Sep 1989. When DB2 is used as a production, transaction-driven DBMS, change management can become complicated. This article explores several solutions to change management problems inherent in DB2 application development.

Martyn, Tim, and Tim Hartley, "Semantics & Logical Errors Using SQL," DBPD, Jun 1990. SQL statements and misstatements, including syntax and logic errors.

McLellan, Vin, "The Coming Battle Over DB2 Security," IW, Oct 9, 1989. Maintaining MVS and DB2 security systems is both expensive and intrinsically difficult. IBM (RACF) and CA (ACF2 and Top Secret), are racing to provide internal security control, which currently resides in the DB2 database subsystem.

McMillan, Helen, "Welcome to the Big Leagues," DBPD, Feb 1990. Discussion of TRW's support of a DB2 database consisting of over 400 million rows.

Melton, Jim, "SQL The Sequel: An Emerging Standard," DBPD, Nov 1990. Description of SQL2 features.

Moran, Robert, "IBM Retunes DB2 Upgrade," CW, Oct 9, 1989. This article discusses the possible impacts of DB2 V2.2 transaction and query performance improvements. Many of the performance boosts come from changes in the optimizer and its indexing techniques. Given the complexity and variety of DB2 queries, various effects will be felt.

Mull, John R., "DB2 Call Attach Facility," ESJ, Sep 1990. Nice overview of CAF, with some details.

Mullen, Nancy K., "How Do You Get to DB2?," DBPD, Apr 1990, pp. 70-75. Technical issues and approaches to DB2 migration and conversion.

Mullins, Craig S., "DB2 v. 2.2: A Few More Bells & Whistles," DBPD, Jun 1990, pp. 59-61. Short technical overview.

———, "Effective DB2 Object Monitoring Using the DB2 Catalog," MFJ, May 1990, pp. 12-18,106. Technical overview with SQL examples.

Myers, Michael W., "Understand DB2 Access Methods," ESJ, July 1990. Brief overview of DB2 V2.1 join methods.

Olson, Jack E., "DB2 In An IMS World," MFJ, Apr 1989, pp. 82-84. General commentary. The author suggests strategy stages that IS shops go through as they realize DB2 must coexist with IMS.

Pace, Philip, "Setting the Table for DB2," DBPD, Jan 1989, pp. 50-55. Management framework for DB2 implementation. General ideas.

———, "Choosing the Right Course for DB2," DBPD, Feb 1989, pp. 34-38. General overview, quick tool overview, quick training curriculum.

———, "DB2 Behind the Scenes," DBPD, Aug 1990, pp. 41-50. Technical overview. General DB2 under-the-covers stuff. The Relational Data System, the Data Manager, etc.

———, "DB2 Dataset Internals," DBPD, Aug 1989. Technical review of some DB2 internals.

———, "Tuning Lethargic Queries," DBPD, Dec 1989. Short review of basic query tuning.

Pasley, Robin, "Physical Design for Difficult Data Structures," DBPD, May 1989, pp. 46-59. Some general logical models of business problems are presented, along with various IDMS and DB2 implementation alternatives.

Rettig, Marc, "Recipes for the DB2 Catalog," DBPD, Feb 1989. Simple DB2 catalog queries.

Rodgers, Ulka, "Care to Denormalize?," DBPD, Dec 1989. Data management and denormalization.

Sayles, Jonathan, "Formatting a Kinder, Gentler SQL," DBPD, Oct 1990. Standardized formatting of SQL statements.

Schmieder, Tom, "What's Behind the DB2 Bind?," ESJ, Nov 1990. Basic introduction to BIND processing.

Shaw, Thomas, "Taking Test to Production," DBPD, Jan 1990, pp. 19-20. Some opinions on DB2 conversions, some technical points. Article addresses some of the pitfalls that may arise when large complex DB2 applications are moved into production.

Snyder, Michael, "DB2 Retrieval Efficiency," ESJ, Nov 1989. An in-depth technical discourse on performance trade-offs in using the query optimizer. Also discussed is writing SQL queries to utilize the optimizer most effectively.

Stacey, Douglas J., "Buffer Pools: Daring to Be Different," DBPD, Oct 1990. Alternatives to BP0.

Stevens, Lawrence, "Referential Integrity In DB2," ESJ, Dec 1989. With many companies installing DB2 V2.2, the implementation of rules and procedures in referential integrity bring IS and the business areas closer together. This article discusses some possible pitfalls to be avoided.

Tatro, Paul A., "STOGROUPs vs. User-Managed VSAM: How Do You Decide?," DBPD, Mar 1990, pp. 72-79. Technical overview.

Werman, Aaron, "Automating the Mundane," DBPD, Dec 1989, pp. 34-44. Abbreviated product review.

———, "DB2 Support Tools," DBPD, Dec 1989. An overview of support tools which mechanize many of the thoughtless repetitive activities of the DB2 DBA.

———, "Mostly DB2: Design Reviews," ESJ, Sep 1990. Brief overview of design reviews in a DB2 application environment.

Young, Casey, "Performance Basics," DBPD, Dec 1990. Basics on EXPLAIN, additional anecdotes on performance.

Recent IMS-Related Articles

Coleman, George, "When Will IMS Go Away?," DBPD, Nov 1989. A good technical overview. DB2 was supposed to sweep away its older relative, but the slow pace of change shows that user still question its superiority.

Cover, Jeffrey, and Carol Chrisman, "IMS Automated Change Control," ESJ, Oct 1990. A case study of a change control system handling IMS application program and control block changes.

Fair, John, "IMS/ESA – An Overview," ESJ, Jan 1990. Short overview of ESA features.

Gandolfo, Paul, "IMS Batch Tuning: A Cookbook," DBPD, Jul 1989. IMS and VSAM system tuning for I/O performance.

Lyon, Lockwood, "IMS/VS and DB2: Working Together," DBPD, Jun 1988. Technical review of implementing DB2 applications in an IMS environment.

———, "Distributed? Relational? IMS?," DBPD, Jan 1990. Distributed database in an IMS environment.

———, "VSAM Performance Tips for IMS/VS Databases," ESJ, Mar 1990. Technical overview of VSAM dataset tuning in an IMS environment.

———, with James Strauss, "Coming of Age in a Relational World," DBPD, Feb 1989. The story of George Programmer's introduction to relational database.

Olson, Jack, "DB2 In An IMS World," ESJ, Apr 1989. Short review of IMS-to-DB2 conversions or installations.

Rygmyr, Gary, "IMS Fast Path Data Entry Database Tuning," ESJ, Jun 1989. Technical review of DEDB tuning.

Smars, Mary, "A Global Recovery Plan With IMS," ESJ, Nov 1990. Basics of disaster recovery planning for IMS systems.

Recent CICS-Related Articles

Bookman, Harvey, "From Batch to CICS: VSAM Differences," ESJ, Apr 1990. Using VSAM in a CICS environment.

Donofrio, Phyllis, "CICS Exploitation of ESA," ESJ, Feb 1990. Short overview of CICS LSR pools in ESA.

———, "CICS Dump Processing With DFHPDX," ESJ, Aug 1989. Technical review of CICS dump formatting.

———, "CICS/ESA 3.1: It's Been Announced!," ESJ, Oct 1989. CICS/ESA features.

———, "VSAM Exclusive Control Conflict Enhancements," ESJ, Oct 1990. A discussion of VSAM file control and deadlock in new CICS versions.

———, "CICS/ESA 3.2 and Other Related Announcements," ESJ, Nov 1990. Review of new releases of CICS/ESA 3.2, CICS/VSE 2.1, DB2 2.3, QMF 3.1, VS COBOL II 3.2, and IMS/ESA TM 3.2.

Goldstein Wayne S., "Dynamic Plan Allocation in CICS/DB2," ESJ, Oct 1990. Brief description of dynamic plan allocation.

Hackenberg, Steven, "Software Queuing Considerations Accessing DB2 From CICS," ESJ, Jan 1989. Considerations for implementing DB2 applications in a CICS environment with an emphasis on using queuing theory to assist with estimates.

Henken, Paul, "Streamlining CICS Input Editing," ESJ, Oct 1990. Three components of a Minimum Data Flow Strategy are discussed: the shadow screen, the SAVE procedure, and the edit shell. These three concepts are explained in terms of BMS, with an emphasis on simplification of edit processing and fast turnaround.

Hudders, Eugene S., "VSAM Optimization and Design Performance Improvements Under CICS/VS," ESJ, Mar 1989. Optimizing VSAM performance in CICS.

———, "VSAM Considerations – CICS/VS," ESJ, Oct 1990. Basic VSAM parms for CICS usage. Continued in more detail in succeeding article (ESJ Nov 1990).

———, "VSAM Optimization: CICS/VS Considerations," ESJ, Nov 1990. More innards of VSAM for users through CICS/VS.

Keller, Ted, "CICS Temporary Storage Performance," ESJ, Apr 1989. Tuning CICS TempStore.

———, "Local Shared Resources in CICS," ESJ, Feb, 1989. Tuning and measuring LSR pool performance.

———, "Queuing Theory: An Aid In Analyzing CICS Performance," ESJ, Nov 1989. A mathematical approach to measuring CICS on-line performance.

———, "Estimating CICS Workloads," ESJ, Mar 1990. General overview of CICS resource utilization.

Kriegel, John, "CICS Dump Tutorial," ESJ, Mar 1990. Detailed technical review of CICS dump analysis.

Lyon, Lockwood, with James Strauss, "Coming of Age in a Relational World," DBPD, Feb 1989. The story of George Programmer's introduction to relational database.

Miller, Thomas, "CICS Testing: Man vs. Machine," ESJ, Mar 1989. Short overview of testing and quality assurance.

Monks, Tony, "CICS Version 3 Looks Good," ESJ, Jun 1990. A short overview of the main components and architecture of the new CICS, including domain-based architecture, the Database Control (DBCTL) subsystem, and other new features.

Nicolette, David, "Managing Memory-Resident Data In CICS Applications," ESJ, Jul 1989. Technical overview of reducing I/O overhead by maintaining data in memory. Several options are compared.

Nikula, Richard, "CICS Shared Resources: Triumphs And Tragedies," ESJ, Apr 1989. Technical review. Buffer considerations.

Tiernan, Donald, with W. Danker, "Improving Mainframe COBOL/CICS Programmer Productivity," ESJ, Jul 1989. A short account of using PCs and related software products to develop applications.

Tracey, J., "CICS Loves Fast Engines," ESJ, May 1990. Technical review of how CPU choice affects performance.

Some Relational Modeling and RDBMS Articles

Chouinard, Paul, "Normalization: Don't Overdo It," DBPD, Feb 1989. Short review of first normal form.

Codd, E. F., "Derivability, Redundancy, and Consistency of Relations Stored in Large Data Banks," San Jose, IBM Research Report RJ599. A classic. The seminal work on the relational model.

———, "A Relational Model of Data for Large Shared Data Banks," Communications of the ACM, 13:6. Another classic.

David, Michael, "Ins & Outs of Outer Joins," DBPD, Feb 1990. An in-depth look at how outer joins work, including syntax, optimization, single-path versus multipath joins, and procedural joins.

———, "The Outer Join and Online Environments," DBPD, Dec 1990. Description of outer joins, various problems, practical examples.

Finkle, Robert, "The Semantic Alternative," DBPD, Dec 1990. Overview of the semantic data model, relationship to E-R diagrams, implementation and comparison of semantic data model DML with SQL.

Hiebert, Lindsay, with D. Stuppy, "Exploiting the Relational Model," DBPD, Apr 1990. Review of relational modeling and integrity rules.

Huntley, Alton, "Moving Data to a Relational DBMS," DBPD, Mar 1989. 4GLs and migration.

Hursch, Jack, "Joins: More Than Meets the Eye," DBPD, Dec 1989. The perils of natural joins for normalization purposes are explored and a checking algorithm for poor joins is presented.

Liberman, Daniel, "DBMS Evaluation by the Rules," DBPD, Dec 1988. Codd's 12 rules for evaluating the relationality of a DBMS.

McGoveran, David, "Better Relational Performance," DBPD, Jul 1989. General overview of relational DBMS performance.

Glossary

Abend: Abbreviation for "abnormal end." Do not use this word in speaking to a user. Also avoid such terms as *abort*, *bomb out*, and *blew up*.

Access Method Services (VSAM): A multifunction service program used to define, reorganize, back up, list, convert, and secure VSAM datasets; define and build alternate indexes; and allocate space for VSAM files and indexes.

Accounting Facility (DATACOM): Contains accounting and statistical information.

ADAM (ADABAS): ADABAS Direct Access Module. Using this, records can be retrieved directly from Data Storage, bypassing the Inverted Lists. The Data Storage block number for each record is calculated using a randomizing (hashing) algorithm based on the record's ADAM key field, which must hold unique values.

AdaSQL (ADABAS): A subset of standard SQL, which can be embedded in COBOL and PL/I programs.

Address Converter (ADABAS): Used to map the logical record address to the physical record's address. A separate Address Converter is maintained for each ADABAS file. It is created and maintained by ADABAS and cannot be directly referenced by the user.

Alternate Index (VSAM): An index on an ESDS or an additional index on a KSDS that provides direct access and sequencing by a set of fields other than entry sequence or the prime key.

Alternate Key (VSAM): The key fields upon which an alternate index is based. Unlike prime keys, the values in these fields need not be unique.

Application Plan (DB2): See **plan**.

Area (DATACOM): A physical space allocation for one or more table types.

Area (IDMS): Physical space allocation for one or more record types. Typically multiple record types.

Associator (ADABAS): Contains internal control information for the entire database: space allocations, Data Storage physical block number of each record (Address Converter), the Inverted Lists, and the Field Definition Table.

Back Out: The process of undoing changes to a database. Usually accomplished by reading the log file in reverse order. All database updates performed by an application are thereby removed.

Batch Message Program, or BMP (IMS): An online IMS program that is initiated by JCL and runs under the control of the IMS Control Region.

Bind (DB2): The process of merging several **database request modules** (DBRMs) into a single **plan**. The DB2 **optimizer** is invoked to analyze access paths for SQL statement in the DBRMs.

CALC Key (IDMS): A record with a key field that is hashed (randomized) to a DBKey for retrieval or storage.

Catalog (DB2): The active, integrated location of physical data definitions.

Catalog (VSAM): A dataset containing information that VSAM requires to locate datasets, to allocate and deallocate storage space, to verify the authorization of a program or operator to gain access to a dataset, and to accumulate usage statistics for datasets. Also includes master catalogs and user catalogs.

Change Accumulation (IMS): The process of creating a condensed version of one or more IMS/VS log datasets. This procedure is done by eliminating records not needed for recovery and by combining multiple log records that record multiple changes to a single segment.

Checkpoint (IMS): A point in the execution life cycle of an application when the program commits that the changes it has made to the database are consistent and complete. Checkpoints therefore provide points at which a program can be restarted.

Cluster (VSAM): A structure containing a related group of components, such as the prime index and data portions of a KSDS file, or just the data portion of an ESDS.

Clustering Index (DB2): A table index that will attempt to maintain the rows of the table in physical sequence the same as the key of the index. A performance option.

Column (DB2): An attribute of an entity.

Command Log (ADABAS): Contains information on all ADABAS commands entered during the ADABAS session.

Commit Point (DB2): The point in the execution life cycle of an application when the program commits that a unit of work is complete and that the data it has either modified or created is consistent and complete. A commit point occurs when a program terminates normally or when it issues a **checkpoint** or **synchpoint** call or command. *See also* **synchronization point, synchpoint**.

Compound Boolean Selection, or CBS (DATACOM): Performs run-time optimization and data access path selection to retrieve sets of data for a single table.

Connection (DB2): A set of control blocks associated with an attachment between DB2 and another subsystem. Analogous to a railroad right-of-way, the connection specifies the characteristics of the path between DB2 and, say, IMS. The so-called **thread**, corresponding to the railroad tracks, is a specific pathway. *See also* **thread**.

Control Area (VSAM): A group of control intervals used as a unit for formatting a dataset before adding records to it.

Control Interval (VSAM): A fixed length area in which VSAM stores records.

Control Region (IMS): The operating system's main storage region, in which the IMS/VS control program executes.

Conversational Processing (IMS): An IMS facility allowing an application program to amass information obtained through multiple interchanges with a terminal, even though the program terminates between interchanges. Note that this IMS/VS definition does not refer to generic conversational programs.

Cursor (DB2): A DB2 object that is used by an application program to point to a particular row that is of interest within a result table and to retrieve rows from that table, possibly making updates or deletion. Cursor processing includes open, fetch, and close.

Database (DB2): An administrative unit encompassing a set of tables.

Database (DATACOM): A logical group of related DATACOM tables sharing a common index.

Database (ADABAS): May consist of a maximum of 255 logical ADABAS files. These files are physically contained in the components Associator and Data Storage.

Database Record (IMS): An IMS database root segment along with all of its dependents, if any. The database record is the unit of locking in IMS.

Database Record Enqueuing (IMS): As database segments are updated, IMS locks the corresponding database records by using an enqueue table.

Database Repositioning (IMS): When an IMS program issues a checkpoint call, the positioning on all non-GSAM database is lost. This forces IMS programs to reestablish their current position, if required.

Database Description, or DBD (IMS): A collection of statements describing an IMS/VS database, including its hierarchical structure, IMS/VS access method, device type, segment lengths, sequence fields, and search fields.

Database Request Module, or DBRM (IMS): The collected SQL statements from an application.

Data Dictionary (DATACOM): The repository of the physical and logical definitions of the data in the DATACOM database. Program information may be recorded. Relationships among all entities are maintained.

Data Protection Log (ADABAS): Contains information on all updates performed during an ADABAS session.

Dataset Group (IMS): A dataset containing a subset of an IMS/VS database. Each dataset group contains one or more unique segment types. At least one dataset group is required for an IMS/VS database.

Data Storage (ADABAS): Contains the compressed data records for all ADABAS files. A single Data Storage physical block contains a variable number of logical records.

Dataview, or Element List (DATACOM): A list of fields that can be accessed and maintained from one and only one table.

DBKey (IDMS): The physical storage location of a record consisting of the page and record position on the page. May be accessed by a program for use in retrieval of a record. Provided by a program for DIRECT storage mode.

Deadlock: A situation where a required resource is not available because it has been allocated to another user.

Deadly Embrace: A special case of **deadlock**. In its simplest form, two users each allocate a resource and then attempt to allocate the other's resource. Whichever software product is the one managing locks (for example, the IMS Resource Lock Manager) must then recognize this situation and take appropriate action.

Debugging: The process of proving to yourself that your program has no errors. (You can never prove this to anyone else.) Note that debugging demonstrates the presence, not the absence, of bugs.

Dependent Row (DB2): A row that references another row by means of a foreign key. May be the same or different table.

Dependent Table (DB2): A table that references another table by means of a foreign key. May be the same or different table.

Descriptor (ADABAS): A field or set of fields defined to the system and for which an inverted list (index) is built.

DIRECT storage mode (IDMS): Definition for records that are to be stored using a programmer defined DBKey. It is the programmer's responsibility to provide an appropriate value.

Element (IDMS): A field in a record.

Entry-Sequenced Dataset, or ESDS (VSAM): A dataset whose records are stored in the sequence they are added to the file, without regard to their content. It does not have a prime index, but may have alternate indexes. It may also be processed sequentially or by direct address (RBA).

EXPLAIN (DB2): A facility used to analyze the access paths DB2 may choose for a query.

Field (ADABAS): The smallest logical unit of information which may be referenced.

Field (DATACOM): A field in a table.

Field (VSAM): In a record, a specified area used for a particular category of data or control information.

Field Definition Tables (ADABAS): Define the logical structure of all the files. A separate table exists for each ADABAS file. It contains the name, level number, format, length, and definition options for each field within a file. The table is created when the file is initially loaded.

File (ADABAS): Consists of a collection of identically defined records.

File Coupling (ADABAS): A means of physically coupling a pair of files so that data in one may be used as a search argument to the other. Makes use of Coupling Lists.

Foreign Key (DB2): Column containing the value of a primary key of a row in the same or another table for the purpose of identifying a relationship. DB2 uses the foreign key definition for the specification of referential integrity constraints.

Group (ADABAS): A set of contiguous fields that can be referenced as a unit by the programmer.

Group (Compound) Field (DATACOM): A field that associates together one or more fields for the purpose of referencing those fields as a unit. A group (compound) field is a logical concept and has no direct physical attributes – it inherits attributes from the fields it associates together.

Indexed Set (IDMS): Records that are maintained in a sorted sequence by a system index. Storage and retrieval are managed by the index.

Integrated Data Dictionary, or IDD (VSAM): The repository of the physical and logical definitions of the data in the IDMS database. Program information may be recorded. Integrity rules, validation tables, security, and maps are also included. Relationships among all entities are maintained.

Intersection Table (DATACOM): A table that is a concatenation of primary keys from two or more tables and exists for the purpose of relating the tables in a many-to-many relationship.

Inverted List (ADABAS): A list of the different values of a descriptor, together with the count and the ISNs of the records that contain each value.

ISN (ADABAS): Internal Sequence Number. Each logical record in every ADABAS file is assigned an ISN. The ISN is used as a logical identifier or address of the record.

Journal (IDMS): System file containing recovery information.

Junction Record (IDMS): A record that is a member of two or more sets and exists for the purpose of relating the owners in a many-to-many relationship.

Key-Sequenced Dataset, or KSDS (VSAM): A dataset whose records are loaded in ascending key sequence and controlled by a prime index.

Linear Dataset, or LDS (VSAM): A dataset that contains data but no VSAM control information.

Log (IDMS): Contains accounting and statistical information.

Logical Record Facility, or LRF (IDMS): An exit driven by IDMS to permit user-specified retrieval and formatting of a logical record. May have multiple database requests for a single user request.

Master (Parent) Table (DATACOM): A term for the primary table in a relationship.

Master Key (DATACOM): A table with a key field that is the logical primary identifier of the table.

Member (IDMS): A record in a set that is owned by another record of the set. All the members are forward linked together and optionally backward linked and linked to the owner record. Constraints specify rules for the connection requirements to the owner and for the rules to determine system action in the event of the erasure of the owner.

Merged Key (DATACOM): Logically related fields on one table, sharing a common Key-ID.

Message Processing Program, or MPP (IMS): An on-line IMS program that is initiated by an IMS transaction and (usually) communicates with a user's terminal.

Native Key (DATACOM): Table occurrences that are maintained in a sorted sequence by a system index. Upon initial load, the table will physically be in sequence; after update activity it will not necessarily retain physical sequence.

Null Value Suppression Option (ADABAS): The NU option affects storage of null values (alphameric blanks or numeric zeroes). If the option is defined for a field, a one-byte indicator is established. Null occurrences are recorded in this indicator rather than being stored. The indicator is a count of the number of consecutive fields following which are null. No inverted list entry will be generated for a null field.

Off-line Database (IMS): An IMS database not defined in the IMS Control Region JCL.

On-line Database (IMS): An IMS database that is defined in the IMS Control Region JCL.

Optimizer (DB2): The DB2 component that processes SQL statements and selects access paths.

Ordered Set (DATACOM): A set whose table occurrences are returned by the database manager in a sequence defined on a field or set of fields.

Owner (IDMS): The owner record of a set is the beginning of a chain of member records of that set.

Parent Row (DB2): A row that is referenced by a foreign key of another row. May be the same or different table.

Parent Table (DB2): A table that is referenced by a foreign key of another table. May be the same or different table.

Partition (DB2): Tables may be split into partitions for availability reasons. Each partition covers a key range. The partitioning is transparent to the program.

Path (VSAM): A name for the combination of an alternate index and the data it references, or an alias for a VSAM data set.

Periodic Group (ADABAS): A group that may repeatedly occur within a given record.

Phonetic Descriptor (ADABAS): Specified for an elementary field in order to be able to perform phonetic searches in which the phonetic value of the field will be used rather than the actual value.

Plan (DB2): The compiled set of interfaces required for the execution of a program. Includes mapping and navigation to the data.

Primary Key (DB2): The unique identifier of a row.

Prime Index (VSAM): The index component of a KSDS.

Prime Key (VSAM): In a KSDS, one or more characters which uniquely identify the record. The prime index is based on the prime key. When processed sequentially, KSDS records are retrieved in prime key sequence.

RECID (DATACOM): The physical storage location of a table occurrence. May be accessed by a program for use in retrieval of a table occurrence.

Record (VSAM): A set of data treated as a unit.

Record (IDMS): A definition of a collection of data elements that constitutes a physical database entity.

Recovery File (DATACOM): System log file containing recovery information.

Referential Integrity (DB2): The specification of business constraints to the database manager concerning the maintenance of relationships between tables. Implemented through primary and foreign keys.

Relative Byte Address, or RBA (VSAM): The displacement of a data record or control interval from the beginning of the dataset.

Relative Record Data Set, or RRDS (VSAM): A dataset whose records are loaded into fixed length slots and are accessed by the sequential slot number.

Relative Record Number, or RRN (VSAM): A number that identifies not only the slot, or dataspace, in a RRDS but also the record occupying the slot. Used as the key for keyed access to a RRDS.

Rerun: To re-execute an abended program. *See also* **restart**.

Restart: To resume execution of an abended program at a given synchpoint, usually the one immediately preceding the point of the abend. *See also* **rerun**.

Roll Back: The process wherein IMS or DB2 undoes any database or table changes made in the current unit of work.

Row (DB2): A set of attributes associated with an entity.

Schema (IDMS): The global definition of all of the related IDMS data.

Set (DATACOM): A group of table occurrences returned by a set-at-a-time request against one table type.

Set (IDMS): An IDMS set is an association between records. Generically, the association is one to many with the "one" being an owner and the "many" being a member. The relationship between owner and member is maintained with links or pointers.

Set-at-a-time (DATACOM): Relational-like access to data within a single table. Does not support table JOINs.

Shared Key (DATACOM): Key IDs which are used to access one or more tables by logically related key definitions.

Sorted Set (IDMS): A set whose members are maintained by the system in a sequence defined on a field or set of fields.

SQL (DB2): Structured Query Language. ANSI, ISO, and SAA standard language for relational data base.

Subdescriptor (ADABAS): A descriptor that is derived from a portion of an elementary field. The values are created by ADABAS and maintained in the Inverted List for the file.

Subschema (IDMS): The specification of all of the data that a program may access. Includes security constraints and access restrictions. May be one per program or may be shared by multiple programs.

Superdescriptor (ADABAS): A descriptor that is derived from a combination of several fields or portions of fields. The values are created by ADABAS and maintained in the Inverted List for the file.

Synchronization Point, or Synchpoint (IMS): A point in time in the execution life cycle of either an application or of the IMS/VS system. At this point IMS or the application can start over if a failure makes recovery necessary. There are two types of synchpoints: (1) system checkpoints done by IMS itself; (2) application program synchpoints (also known as **commit points**) done by individual programs.

Table (DATACOM): A definition of a collection of data fields that constitutes a physical database entity.

Table (DB2): A set of rows with a common definition.

Tablespace (DB2): A physical space defined to hold one or more tables, usually one.

Thread (DB2): A DB2 structure that describes an application's connection, traces its progress, provides a resource function processing capability, and delimits the application's accessibility to DB2 resources and services. Most DB2 functions execute under a thread structure. *See also* **connection.**

Two-phase Commit: A process whereby two systems such as DB2 and IMS cooperate in the commit process.

Unique Descriptor (ADABAS): This option may be used to indicate that a descriptor must contain unique values.

VIA Set (IDMS): A set where the members are stored VIA the owner.

View (DB2): The ability to define a virtual table made up of data from one or more tables. May be dynamic or static.

Work (ADABAS): Used to store data protection information, intermediate results of FIND commands and ISN lists resulting from FIND commands.

Index

access path, 105
ad hoc, 92, 123, 129, 143, 155
alternate index, 152
Attachment facility, 110, 113
attribute, 23
audit reporting, 99, 187

back-end CASE tools, 24, 33
Batch Message Program (BMP), 110-111, 114-115, 117-119
bind, 22, 81, 83, 107, 115, 179, 185
boundary value analysis, 54-55
bridge applications, 160
buffer pool, 19-20, 84, 88, 106, 175

cache controller, 17
caching, 93
CALC field, 153, 166
capacity planning test, 52
catalog information, 187
cause-effect lists, 55
checkpoint, 21, 56, 98, 111, 115, 118
CHKP, 111
Codd, Edgar F., 73-76
code generation, 24
collision field, 121
commit, 14, 21, 56, 98, 111, 161
Common User Access (CUA), 100
Computer-Assisted Software Engineering (CASE), 5, 23, 30, 33, 40-41, 55, 58-59, 69, 77-78, 81, 85, 90-91, 129, 132
concurrency, 139
concurrency testing, 52, 176
Conditional Erase, 151
connection, 110-111, 114
control region, 110
conversational program, 21
COPY utility, 80-81, 88
coupled lists, 164
cursor, 14, 26, 79, 110, 115, 120
Cursor Hold, 14

data compression, 187
Data Definition Language (DDL), 79, 177-178, 184-185
Data Extract utility (DXT), 57, 84, 182-183
Data Facility Storage Management Subsystem (DFSMS), 142
Data Manipulation Language (DML), 79

Data Propagator, 13, 84
database, 79
database editor, 99, 187
Database Request Module (DBRM), 19, 79, 89, 180, 183-184
DATADICTIONARY, 145, 154, 166
DB2 Catalog, 22, 25, 27, 80, 86-87, 99, 171, 178, 180, 184
DB2 Migration Aid Utility (DBMAUI), 177, 183
DB2 Optimizer, 25, 29, 81, 83-84, 107, 126, 141, 144, 179-180
DB2 Performance Monitor (DB2PM), 21
deadlock, 49, 51, 57, 113, 117-119, 121
deadly embrace, 113
delete rules, 23, 45, 107, 124
denormalization, 24, 30, 82
DIRECT, 168
Direct Access Storage Device (DASD), 2, 17, 21, 27, 35, 38, 48, 50, 82, 84-85, 92-94, 99, 101-103, 106, 123, 131, 175
distributed database, 91, 142
distributed processing, 91, 129
domain, 23
DSN1COPY, 183-184
DSNTIAUL, 183
dynamic SQL, 80

EDM pool, 19, 88
Enhanced Connectivity (ECF), 123
equivalence classes, 54
equivalence partitioning, 53-54
EXPLAIN, 16, 24, 80-81, 89, 125-126
extended alter, 178

Fast Path, 111, 115-116
foreign key, 16, 23, 44, 90, 125, 147, 150-151, 158
freespace, 83
front-end CASE tools, 23, 33

General Sequential Access Method (GSAM), 115-116, 118

heuristics, 2
Hierarchical Storage Manager (DFHSM), 142
Host Database View (HDBV), 123
hybrid systems, 4, 32
hyper descriptors, 163

IMS Resource Lock Manager (IRLM), 19, 30, 88, 106, 121
in-doubt, 113, 118
index, 125
Integrated Data Dictionary (IDD), 145, 154
integration test, 52
inverted file, 153
ISAM/OSAM buffer pool, 19

join, 13-15, 25-26, 28, 80, 83, 136, 143, 150, 166
joint application development (JAD), 77-78, 129
junction record, 169

lights-out operation, 49
list prefetch, 106
LOAD utility, 57, 80-81, 83, 88, 117, 182-185
locking, 139
logical data modeling, 129
logical record facility (LRF), 170-171
long descriptors, 163
lower-case tools, 33

macrotuning, 92
member record, 155, 162
merged keys, 166
Message Processing Program (MPP), 110-111, 118
message switch, 114
microtuning, 92
migration, 3, 99, 187

nonconversational program, 21
nonrecoverable database, 22
nonresponse MPP, 114
normalization, 136, 144, 154-155, 157
nulls, 140, 164

OSAM sequential buffering pool, 19-20

performance appraisal, 67
performance monitor, 99, 187
performance tuning, 105
phonetic descriptors, 165
plan, 46, 79, 87, 104, 114, 180
plan analysis, 99, 187
predicate, 125
PREDICT, 145, 154
primary key, 16, 23, 90, 147, 150-151, 157
prime index, 152
Program Control Block (PCB), 117
program isolation (PI), 121
prototyping, 77, 129

Query Management Facility (QMF), 119, 123, 177, 181-182

rapid analysis, 129
re-engineering tools, 77-78
RECOVER utility, 184
redundant data, 157
referential integrity (RI), 23, 44-46, 56, 87, 90, 124-125, 129, 138, 141, 150-152
regression test, 52
relational database management system (RDBMS), 29, 76
relational model, 73, 80, 136
relative record number (RRN), 158
reload, 131
REORG utility, 80-81, 83, 88, 131
repeating groups, 155-156
Residual Recovery Entry (RRE), 113
Resource Access Control Facility (RACF), 110
Resource Control Table (RCT), 12, 19, 117
rollback, 51
row length prefix, 124
RUNSTATS utility, 21-22, 80-81, 87, 126, 179, 185

schema, 40
Scratch Pad Area (SPA), 22
scrolling, 94
security, 89, 139
security management, 99
sequential prefetch, 106
service level agreement, 97
set owner, 155, 162
set-at-a-time processing, 25, 93
shared key processing, 166
space management, 99
sparse indexes, 165
SQL Communications Area (SQLCA), 25, 49, 56
SQL Processing Using File Input (SPUFI), 57, 125, 177
SQLCODE, 25, 46, 49, 51, 56-57, 110, 114-115, 117, 120-121, 180
SQLWARN, 25, 49, 56
standard work unit, 13-14, 98
statistics, 87
storage group, 17, 79
storyboarding, 129
STOSPACE utility, 21, 80-81, 86
stress test, 52, 176
string test, 52, 176
Structured Query Language (SQL), 10, 14-16, 24-26, 31-32, 46, 56-57, 68-69, 79-80, 86, 109-110, 114, 117, 119, 123, 125, 136-137, 139-140, 152, 179-180
subdescriptors, 164
subschema replacement, 170
synchpoint, 21, 56, 98, 111, 117
synonym, 79, 179, 185
Systems Application Architecture (SAA), 1, 12, 100, 142
Systems Development Life Cycle (SDLC), 5, 23, 33, 39-40, 82

tablespace, 79
tablespace scan, 83
third-party tools, 2-3, 57, 68, 86, 88, 90, 131
thread, 88, 110, 114
timeout, 49, 51, 57
TRANSACT macro, 114
two-phase commit, 113, 119, 160

union, 15, 137
unit of work, 49
unit of recovery (UR), 111-112
unit test, 52
upper-case tools, 33

VARCHAR, 124, 181
VCAT, 17
VIA, 166-167
view, 79, 137
virtual memory, 18
virtual storage constraints, 18, 20
Volume Table of Contents (VTOC),
 27, 88
VSAM shared resources pool, 19